Hinduism
in the context of
Manusmriti, Vedas
&
Bhagavad Gita

Hinduism
in the context of
Manusmriti, Vedas & Bhagavad Gita

R Ramachandran

Vitasta

Vitasta Publishing Pvt. Ltd.
New Delhi

Renu Kaul Verma
Vitasta Publishing Pvt Ltd
2/15, Ansari Road, Daryaganj,
New Delhi - 110 002
info@vitastapublishing.com

ISBN 978-81-89766-49-8

First Edition 2009
Fourth Reprint 2022

MRP ₹ 795

Cover Design and Layout by Vitasta Publishing Pvt. Ltd.
Printed by Vits Press, New Delhi

Dedicated

to

My Grandchildren

Rahul Iyer, Meha Iyer, and Balram Sharma

Content

PART-II
Hindu Society

Preface

This book represents the outcome of my efforts to understand Hinduism which has many facets—from the most sacred spiritual tradition to the worship of demons and animal sacrifice. It has taken me decades to understand the totality of Hinduism and then articulate the end results of my learning process. I do hope that the book will help others to understand Hinduism better.

My journey begins with early childhood when I obtained training from my family particularly from my father, who was a keen student of Linguistics, a scholar in Sanskrit, and a good critique of Hindu philosophy. As a child, I was used to Vedic rituals and the recitation of mantras. I learned the Devanagari script at the age of four. I remember my father reading to us Valmiki's *Ramayana* verse by verse and then explaining to us their meaning. I went through the processes of *upanayana* and the annual *upakarma* and learned to do my daily *sandhya vandana* rituals, although I did not then fully appreciate their meaning. Sanskrit was very much a second language at home, since all my brothers and sisters learned Sanskrit at school and recited verses from the works of Kalidasa. I did study Sanskrit for a few years in school, but did not continue the course further.

As I entered adulthood and college, I became an agnostic. I firmly believed that all religious rituals are a waste of time. I discontinued all rituals and went to temples only on rare occasions. I did all along believe in an abstract God, who I thought would not respond to my petty demands and prayers. I accepted full responsibility for all my failures and thanked God for my successes.

After college and upon entering into employment in the academic field, I became a keen student of history, sociology, and social anthropology besides geography, which was my own area of specialization. Indeed, I was interested in all social sciences that made me read widely. As a student and as a teacher in Indian and foreign universities, I had access to excellent reading material and I took full advantage of it. I read about Hindu religion, other religions, and western philosophy. Much of this had nothing to do with what I taught at the universities nor my own research and publications. This was done purely for personal satisfaction.

Still later, as I approached retirement, I made up my mind to learn Sanskrit afresh and study the Hindu scriptures. This was my way of keeping my mind and intellect occupied after retirement. As a preparation for this, I bought books on Sanskrit grammar together with an advanced dictionary. After retirement from the University of Delhi in 1996, I devoted full time to the learning of Sanskrit grammar.

Bhandarkar's two books on Sanskrit grammar was the foundation on which I obtained a grasp of the language. This was supplemented by books in Malayalam script on Sanskrit grammar. Malayalam was the medium of instruction while I was in school. Further, most Hindu scriptures in Sanskrit are available in the Malayalam script with translations and explanatory notes in many cases. My familiarity with both the Malayalam and

Devanagari scripts was of great advantage to me. The learning of Sanskrit grammar took two years, but it was time well spent; the reason is that to obtain a clear and unbiased understanding of the scriptures one has to study the original texts in Sanskrit. There is no short cut.

After two years, I was ready to read the original Sanskrit texts. My first choice was the *Bhagavad Gita* with Sankara *bhashyam* in Sanskrit prose. I got a copy of the *Bhagavad Gita* in Devanagari script with the *bhashyam*. I devoted two years to the study of the *Bhagavad Gita*. It was a difficult exercise. I greatly appreciated Adi Shankaracharya's explanations, verse by verse. It tells us the essence of the spiritual path that all of us have to follow, at least to the extent possible.

The next step logically was to look into the *Manusmriti* which focusses on the practice of religion; it has more to do with the social system, rather than the metaphysical aspects of religion. The *Manusmriti* is nearly four times larger than the *Bhagavad Gita*; however, it is much easier to read and understand, since it deals with day to day life. It is written in a simple and straight forward style. At first, I had a negative view of the *Manusmriti*; but later, I realized that I am looking at it through coloured glasses. It is about a society that is no longer extant. It did play a major role for over 2,000 years and until the beginning of the 20th Century. But we cannot understand the past without reading the *Manusmriti* and its description of Hindu dharma.

There are several texts of lesser importance which I read (in Sanskrit) more casually as and when time permitted. Among such texts of importance are the *Brahmasutra, Kathopanishad,* and

Pantanjali Sutra in translation, an anthology of important verses from the *Upanishads*, and the well-known *Yaksha Prasna*.

After completing the study of the above classics, I strongly felt that I need to go to the roots or origin of our religion and trace its evolution. For this, one must study the *Rigveda*. Fortunately, a friend gifted me a copy of the four *Vedas*—in four volumes—consisting of the mantra part alone. I was, in particular, fascinated by the *Rigveda*. Understanding and appreciating the *Rigveda* is impossible without some understanding of social anthropology, since we are dealing with a tribal society that existed about 3,500 years ago. My knowledge of social anthropology and ecology helped me greatly to understand and appreciate the *Rigveda*. I interpreted the *Rigveda* essentially as a study in human ecology of a bygone age. The *Rigveda* has no parallels in any other religion. It is not mythology. It is pure religion in verses composed by poets, who were human beings with real names and who lived a long time ago. All other *Shruti* texts are also real but they include some legends as well, while the *Puranas* represent true mythology.

Upon completion of my reading of the *Rigveda* and the other three *Vedas*, I reached a stage when it was necessary for me to put down in writing what I had learned. I did this over a long period of time - years in fact. Starting with an enquiry into the nature of Hinduism, I moved on to an article on a synoptic view of the evolution of Hinduism, before attempting articles on the substantive works. Eventually, I ended up with 21 articles divided into two parts—the religious part and the social part. These articles were suitably modified and put together in the form of the present book.

In my experience, I have found no work in the English language that gives an authentic introduction to Hinduism. I have tried to achieve two objectives in this book. The first objective is to provide a historical and social frame of reference for understanding Hinduism. The second objective is to give an authentic overview of three scriptural texts, namely, the *Rigveda*, the *Bhagavad Gita* and the *Manusmriti*. These three texts define Hinduism both in terms of its religious and social dimensions. Further, I have added a few chapters to focus on contemporary issues, such as our caste system and the impact of science and technology. Above all, this is a holistic exposition of Hinduism. It is my belief that those who have never had an opportunity to read religious texts in original will find this book very useful.

Writing a book requires inspiration and I owe this largely to my brothers and sisters, all elder to me, who have themselves read the Sanskrit texts and are conversant with all religious concepts and rituals. My contribution has been the interpretation of Hinduism in the light of my knowledge of social sciences. From the start, I circulated my papers by email, not only to my brothers and sisters, but a much larger audience of relatives and friends. I am thankful for their words of encouragement and at times criticism.

In November 2006, I gave an open lecture on the evolution of Hinduism, as part of a short series of lectures on the Historical Geography of India, in the Department of Geography, Delhi School of Economics, University of Delhi. The response to my lectures overwhelmed me and the idea of publishing this work originated at that point in time. Dr Anu Kapur, a former student and a member of the faculty, insisted that I take steps to get the book published and the present work owes much to her help in this regard. I am indeed grateful to all my friends, former colleagues and students of the University of Delhi for their enthusiastic support. I do hope that they will enjoy reading this work as much as I have enjoyed writing it.

R Ramachandran

Introduction

The origin of mankind, according to modern science, occurred in Africa about 60,000 years ago and from there people migrated to all parts of the world. The Indian Subcontinent received its first batch of migrants only about 12,000 years ago. From this date onwards, we have archaeological evidence of human habitations in some parts of the subcontinent. These early inhabitants practised agriculture and animal husbandry and they buried their dead, thereby indicating that they practised some form of religion.

Migrations of people into the Indian Subcontinent occurred from several directions—from the west along the Makran coast (modern Baluchistan and Iran), and the various mountain passes of the north-west; from the north by way of Tibet; and finally from the south by way of Burma. These migrations occurred periodically and continued up to the Middle Ages (1600 AD).

The subcontinent's oldest civilization, namely the Harappan Civilization, which dates back to 2500 BC, has made significant contributions to the present day religious belief and practices. The Harappan script has not been deciphered so far and hence the elements of the Harappan culture and religion have come to us indirectly through an oral tradition. They were later transformed into a written tradition, first by the Buddhists and Jainas in the Pali language and later by Brahmanas in the Sanskrit language.

The Rigvedic people constitute a very important migratory group who came to the subcontinent at around 1500 BC. They made an impact far greater than their numbers would warrant. The reason for this is that they memorized their religion in the form of verses and preserved not only their religion but also their language, that is, Sanskrit, for posterity. Sanskrit, however, ceased to be a spoken language around 1000 BC while its importance as a literary language continued for about 2,000 years.

What is notable here is that many other groups of people also came to India in later periods and today they constitute the majority of the population of the region west of the Ganga River.

Religion is as old as mankind. The earliest migrants as well as those who came in the later periods to the subcontinent had their religions. Many of these religions or at least some of their religious practices have continued into the present through an oral tradition. These are clearly evident in rural India even today.

Around 600 BC, two other major religions of India came into being, namely Buddhism and Jainism. They also have significantly influenced religious belief and practices in India in later time periods. Buddhism and Jainism are well documented and are traceable to historical persons. This period also witnessed the demise of the Rigvedic religion and in its place the emergence of two major schools of thought—the Poorva Mimamsa school and the Uttara Mimamsa school. The former, founded by Jaimini, the disciple of the great Rishi Veda Vyasa, is well illustrated in *Manusmriti*, while the latter represents the religion of the *Upanishads*, which is later expounded in the *Bhagavad Gita*.

From around 200 AD, we find the emergence of a new religion in the Sanskrit language. The texts describing this religion are known as *Puranas*. They also include the two great Indian epics—*Ramayana* and *Mahabharata*. This religion is known as Hinduism.

Where does the word 'Hinduism' come from and what does it mean? The term 'Hinduism' does not occur in any Sanskrit text. This word is of Persian origin and it was extensively used by the medieval rulers of India, who used Persian as their court language. The word 'Hindu' was first applied to the people of India in general and later to its religions as well.

Hinduism became the most accepted name for the religion(s) of India during the British period and today it is accepted by one and all. Nevertheless, there are a few who would like to call this religion as *dharma* or *sanatana dharma*. These two terms can be traced to the *Manusmriti*. This classic text of social laws is no longer acceptable to the majority of Indian people and as a result, the suggested terms are ignored by a large majority of Hindus.

The word Hinduism includes not only the religion(s) based on Sanskrit texts, of which we have a large number, but also the hundreds of religions of rural India which have come down to us through oral tradition and whose origin, in a number of cases, is older than the religions represented in the Sanskrit texts. The importance of Pre-Rigvedic religions to the totality of Hinduism has largely been ignored in the past. In *Manusmriti*, there are passing references to the religious practices followed by the Shudras. *Manusmriti*'s *dharma* is largely meant for the upper three *varnas*—Brahmana, Kshatriya and Vaishya—and it hardly attaches any significance to the religions or religious practices followed by the Shudras.

Hinduism is a unique religion. There never was a concept of religious conversion in Hinduism. The religious beliefs, rituals and associated social practices can vary greatly among Hindus. Yet there are certain common ideas, beliefs, and practices acceptable to all. Unlike other religions, Hinduism does not insist on conformity and a Hindu has absolute freedom of thought. There never was a controlling authority in Hinduism. The practice of Hinduism is purely voluntary.

The term 'Hinduism' will be used in this work as a collective noun; it represents several religions which are in some ways very similar to each other. Hinduism stands in stark contrast with the major religions of the Middle East. Christianity and Islam are based on a messenger of God, while Hinduism does not have a historical person as its originator, although many made significant contributions to it. Again, unlike Hinduism, both Christianity and Islam have definite religious texts—the *Bible* and the *Qur'an*—which are sacred and sacrosanct.

Another notable aspect is that the religions of the Middle East display little tolerance towards other religions. Islam preaches good Muslims to convert people to Islam. Evangelization is a common feature in Christianity. At the birth of Christianity and

Islam, there were numerous other faiths. However, majority of these have now vanished. Yet pagan beliefs and practices do exist even among Christians and Muslims in various countries even today. These are grudgingly tolerated at best.

Hindus do have several scriptural texts. We have the four *Vedas*, namely *Rigveda*, *Samaveda*, *Yajurveda* and *Atharvaveda*, the *Upanishads*, and the *Bhagavad Gita*. All these are written in Sanskrit. The fact of the matter is that few people know Sanskrit and even fewer have actually read these texts. Unlike the *Bible* and *Qur'an*, our religious texts are not published in large volumes; nor are they translated into modern Indian languages. An English translation of the *Rigveda* does exist but ironically, it is very difficult to obtain a copy of the oldest and most sacred *Rigveda*.

In India and East Asia, a wide variety of religions co-exist without acrimony. In rural India, different *jatis* in the same village follow different religious practices and worship different Gods. Many religions based on Sanskrit co-existed with a variety of other religions from pre-historical times. In the past, they had separate identities but now they share a common name. However, a common name does not mean uniformity. There was no stress on uniformity and other religions, sects and cults in Hinduism co-existed peacefully in the same region. Hinduism is very unique, positive and liberal and has hardly any rigidity associated with Middle Eastern religions. It is open ended and broad based, allowing greater flexibility and individual freedom.

In China, the question what is your religion would most likely not be answered at all. This is true of Japan as well. People follow Taoism, Confucianism, Buddhism, or Shintoism but refuse to be tagged. It is impolite and rude to ask such persons to name their religion. The situation is more or less similar in India; the Hindus do give a ready answer, however, it can have plethora of meanings. Hinduism is not a single religion but a mixture of many religions. The label 'Hindu' is really unimportant; the important ones being concepts, beliefs, and practices.

Despite these, there exist profound similarities, sharp dissimilarities and utter variance in religious beliefs and practices among all Hindus in India. But the question is how can we understand these complexities.

I have tried to simplify the situation by recognizing two admittedly artificial categories of Hinduism. The first, but not necessarily in that order, are the religions based on Sanskrit texts; and the second, hundreds of local religions which do not have a religious text but have legendary Gods of their own and age-old forms of worship. These include the Harappan culture and its successors. The worship of God Shiva and Goddess Shakti, animals, stones, trees and host of spirits have their roots in the pre-Rigvedic culture. *Bhakti* and puja, as forms of worship, were alien to the Vedic age. The forms of worship practised today may have come forth either from pre or post-Rigvedic era. However, I have focussed only on the religions that existed before the Puranic period (before 200 AD) as revealed by Sanskrit texts. The Puranic religion based on Sanskrit texts represents an integration of the earlier Sanskritic religions with a number of non-Sanskritic religions of India. This point will be elaborated upon in a subsequent chapter.

The objective of this book is to present my understanding of Rigvedic religion and its two successors, that is, the Poorva and the Uttara Mimamsa school, according to the original Sanskrit texts. The interpretation is based on my knowledge of social sciences, particularly ancient Indian history and social anthropology. It is intended to present them as they existed at the time of their origin and not in the form in which we understand or use them today. Unlike the Middle Eastern religions, Hinduism has evolved from prehistoric times to recent times through a gradual process of change.

A religion can be understood only in the context of the social conditions of the time in which it was actually in vogue. We have an excellent account of the society and religious practices around 300 BC in the *Manusmriti*. This classic and valuable historical document has been reviewed in depth in this book in order to get an insight into the society of the pre-Puranic age. In fact, *Manusmriti* should be used as a yardstick to judge religions and societies before and after its time.

Organization of Book

This book is divided into two parts; the first deals with religious issues and the second focuses on the social aspects. In the first part, the nature of Hinduism is examined, followed by a synoptic view of its evolution from Rigvedic times to its current state. Three chapters are devoted to the *Rigveda*, which represents the root of Hinduism based on Sanskrit texts. The religion that emerged in the later Vedic period is then interpreted. This religion is rather unique, as it differs from both the *Vedantic* school as well as the Poorva Mimamsa school. This is followed by a summary of the *Bhagavad Gita* in four parts—a synthesis of various schools of thought presented in the Puranic story-telling context. Nevertheless, the Vedantic school's thinking predominates over all the other schools of thought.

This religion is known as the Upanishadic religion and was interpreted by Adi Shankaracharya in 8th Century AD. This part concludes with a review of *Bhaja Govindam*, where Adi Shankaracharya renders advice to all householders. This is valid even today as it was in 800 AD.

The second part begins with the origin of the Indian Subcontinent, particularly the Indo-Gangetic Plain, and further examines the historical and pre-historical evidence of human habitations, migrations, and emergent civilizations in the subcontinent.

Three chapters are then dedicated to the *Manusmriti*, which outlines the *varna*, *ashrama*, *dharma*, *raja dharma* and finally the issue of divine punishment for violating *dharma*. These chapters stand apart from the subsequent ones, focussing on a particular time in the Indian history and informing about the society that existed then. The later chapters focus on the current day society in India, as understood in relation to the past and hence the relevance of the *Manusmriti*.

The chapter also explains the caste system in India, both in terms of its historical origins and its contemporary relevance and importance. The terms *jati*, *varna*, and *gotra* are all examined in depth and the confusion that the term 'caste' raises has also been resolved in the chapter. Like the word 'Hindu', the word 'caste' also has multiple connotations and it is necessary to fully comprehend the differences in meaning when using this term.

Births and deaths are integral to any religious discussion. In the chapter on *janma*, karma and *bhaga*, the relative importance of birth, human action through the exercise of free will, and the chance factor are analysed.

India has now emerged as a world leader. It has a rapidly growing economy based on science and technology. India has been going through a scientific industrial revolution for the past 150 years. What impact does science have on religion and in particular on Hinduism? What is the prognosis? This aspect is addressed in the chapter on society, religion, and science.

What do Hindus believe in today? This is too difficult a question. Nevertheless, one can make a few statements on what educated Hindus believe in today. However, opinions may vary as these statements may be considered true or false.

If faith is the basis for defining a religion, then it is possible to define a Hindu in terms of what he believes in. Fortunately, such a definition exists in the *Bhagavad Gita*. This is reframed in a slightly different form in a chapter on the definition of Hindu.

The concluding chapter of this book looks at the future scenario and what one can learn from the study of the past. Hinduism has many ideas to offer to the world. Nevertheless, religion is a personal matter and every individual may choose what is relevant to him or her. This study represents an exploration of religious ideas expounded in ancient Sanskrit texts and these are presented here in their original form without bias or distortion. The objective of this book is to help the reader to form his own appreciation of the Hindu religion.

PART I

Hindu Religion

One

Nature of Hinduism

Introduction

What is Hinduism? Most of us will have considerable difficulty in articulating an answer to this question. Part of the problem is, perhaps, that Hinduism is not one religion but an amalgam of several religions or religious ideas.

At the grass roots or village level, we have many religions with distinctive names for their Gods, local legends and festivals, and various colourful religious rituals and beliefs. Take for example the worship of Ayyanars in Tamil Nadu. Anyone travelling through rural Tamil Nadu would notice five or six colourful terracotta statues, standing six to eight feet tall, near the entrance to the villages. These statues represent God or demon and each one has a distinctive name. They are legendary and are sacred to the villagers who worship them. While some of them, like the ones above, are very ancient, others may be of recent origin; they are all considered to be an integral part of Hinduism, although they never find any mention in religious Sanskrit texts.

At the elite Hindu population level, both in rural and urban areas, there is a set of four religions based on Sanskrit texts—the Rigvedic religion, the Upanishadic religion, the Puranic religion, and the Humanistic religion. The last one is actually an offshoot of the Upanishadic religion, but it stands apart in conceptual terms. Besides these, there were several other schools of religious thought dealt with in Sanskrit texts. However, they are ignored here for the sake of simplicity. They will receive due attention at a later stage.

Today, the practice of Hinduism is more or less identified with the vast Puranic literature written in Sanskrit and other major languages of India. Nevertheless, strands of Upanishadic, Rigvedic, and even Humanistic religions are very much present today, even if they are less than conspicuous. The practitioners of Upanishadic religion, although few in number, are very articulate and are heard and appreciated by elite Hindus. The Puranic religion, which is based on Sanskrit texts, has imbibed many ideas and practices from local cultures, both from North and South India, representing the composite culture of India.

Rigvedic Hinduism

The Rigvedic people were nomadic pastoralists who had organized themselves into small tribal communities. They lived in the plains of Punjab and later migrated eastward to the Yamuna River and nearby areas. The *Rigveda* comprises over 10,000 verses written at various points in time from around 1500 BC to 800 BC. The first verse was written by a sage named Angiras, who is considered as the doyen of poets and priests of Rigvedic times. In the later Rigvedic period, he became a legend and was equated with *Agni*, the Fire God, and in the Puranic period, he rose to become a God himself, or at least the chief priest of the Gods. He is given the titles of Brihaspathi and Brahmanaspathi in the *Rigveda*.

The Rigvedic verses are indeed very simple and easy to understand; they are set to one of several meters with musical quality. They are superb in style, articulation, and are rich in symbolism. At times, they are mundane and at others highly exemplary. They are simplistic and enigmatic, coupled with a rare sense of humour and wit. But the question that arises is what is this Rigvedic religion all about.

Question: Who will help us get food and water, protect our lives and those of our children and warriors, protect our cattle and horses, increase our numbers and those of our cattle, and maintain our welfare?

Answer: Gods, namely, *Agni*, *Indra*, *Varuna*, *Savita*, *Mitra*, *Rudra*, *Vayu*, *Aapa*, and a few others.

Question: How can we get Gods' help?

Answer: Offer food and verses of praise to *Agni*, the Fire God. Food means meat, dairy products and an alcoholic beverage called *soma ras*. *Agni* will carry food and mantras to the God or Gods to whom the verses are addressed. *Agni* will also bring back presents from the Gods. Elaborate rituals based on the above principles were performed by the tribal community as a whole with poets and priests reciting the verses in front of the sacred fire. Rigvedic verses invariably use the pronouns 'us' and 'we', meaning the community as a whole; the pronoun 'I' is not mentioned anywhere. This is an egalitarian society united in the cause of the welfare of the community as a whole.

Upanishadic Hinduism

The Rigvedic religion came to an end with the demise of the tribal community life at around 1000 BC. The practice of Vedic rituals, namely *homa* and *yaga*, continued unabated. The prayers were now increasingly directed to find solutions for family and personal problems. The *Yajurveda*, *Samaveda*, and *Atharvaveda* came into existence at this time and they truly reflect this trend. These three *Vedas* are merely in the nature of adaptations of the Rigvedic verses to suit newer purposes and are not to be considered as independent works. The *Yajurveda* and *Samaveda* have verses that are taken from the *Upanishads*. In the light of this context, the *Upanishads* could claim Vedic authority. While most priests adapted themselves to the new situation, a few were disillusioned with the new trend; they established ashrams in less accessible locations to recreate the old tribal ambience. They contemplated on the relationship between man and God. This gave rise to the *Upanishads*, in which contemplation is recommended again and again by the teacher to his students.

The *Upanishads* gave the concept of Absolute God or *Brahman* which is perhaps the most original and valuable of the new ideas. Equally important, and far more relevant to the common man, is the concept of cycle of birth and death, and its causal mechanism, the law of karma. These concepts form the backbone of Indian religious thought even today. Nevertheless, the poet-saints were not happy with the scheme of births and deaths. They invented the concept of the self—the atman—as the mirror image of the Absolute God, the *Brahman*. Atman is at the core of the Upanishadic religion. The object of life is to attain eternal bliss by realizing atman by contemplation and getting released from the cycle of birth and death. The process of self-realization, which involves self-enquiry, is as follows:

Question: Who am "I"?
Answer: I am the pure soul or atman or I am the impure soul or *jivatman*.
Question: What is my problem?
Answer: My atman is subject to endless cycles of birth and death.
Question: What do I want?
Answer: *Moksha*, permanent release of my atman from the cycles of birth and death.
Question: What should I do?
Answer: Follow a moral code of conduct in life (*yama* and *niyama*). Follow any one of the following spiritual paths, namely, *marga* or *yoga*:

1. The path of knowledge – *jnana yoga*
2. The path of work – *karma yoga*
3. The path of devotion – *bhakti yoga*
4. The path of meditation – *dhyana yoga*

The first option is recommended only for those who are inclined to take *sanyasa* from the *brahmacharya* stage itself. Those who enter *grihastha* stage may take up the second option and continue with it until their eldest child is an adult and is in a position to take care of the family. At the fag end of the *grihastha* stage, one may take up the third path and continue with it to the next stage, that is, the stage of *vanaprastha*. After the *vanaprastha* stage, one may withdraw from family and society, that is, he may accept *vairagya* and *sanyasa*. He will also be expected to take guidance from a teacher or guru before he takes *sanyasa*. At this stage, one can practise *dhyana yoga*. The classic work *Patanjali Sutra* outlines the eight-fold path for self-realization known as *samadhi*. This is the basic guide to *dhyana yoga*. While based on the *Upanishads*, the practice of all *yogas* belongs to the Puranic period. In the modern period, the *yogas* in their pure form are practised by a select group of intellectuals.

Puranic Hinduism

The *Puranas*, 18 in all, belong to the period 200 AD to 1400 AD. Along with the *Smritis*, the *Bhagavad Gita* and other epics, they constitute Hinduism as practised in India for over 2,000 years. In the Puranic period, a feudal system with a king at the apex prevailed. The first kingdom emerged at around 600 BC. This was the kingdom of Kasi with its capital at Varanasi. Many historians have explained the process of emergence of kingdoms in the middle Ganga plains between 1000 BC and 500 BC. From 600 BC, there was a steady increase in the number of kingdoms. Around 200 AD, there were over 200 kingdoms in Northern India alone. This period also saw the emergence of Buddhism and Jainism and for a while, Hinduism had a very subdued existence. The revival of Hinduism needed new ideas.

The first major thrust came with the notion of incarnation of Gods in human form. The ten *avatars* of Vishnu gave ample scope for new legends, eventually leading to two great Indian epics, *Mahabharata* and *Ramayana*. The 10 incarnations of God start from fish, progresses towards animal forms and finally reaches man. In the final stage, all Gods appear in human form, including the Rigvedic Gods, who are now portrayed in a new light. Idol worship was the next step. Gods appear not only as humans but in some cases, notably in the epics, as kings and rulers. Gods tend to be equated with kings or vice versa. This strengthened the feudal system. Rejuvenated, Hinduism flourished and assimilated tribal cultures all over the country.

The tribal Gods were integrated into a three-fold system of Gods—Shiva, Vishnu and Brahma. The most notable example of integration of tribal Gods into mainstream Hinduism is Lord Jagannath of Puri.

The concept of cycle of birth and death and the law of karma remained the focal theme of Hinduism. These concepts are also accepted in Buddhism and Jainism. Gods multiplied in number with the integration of tribal Gods and so did the forms of worship. The family emerged as the basic unit of society. Rituals were performed by the head of the family. Individuals could also pray to God and offer food or money to solve their problems. They can ask questions or ask for special favours, which will be answered by God.

As in the case of the Upanishadic religion, the approach here is highly individualistic, with the inclusion of family and the community as a whole in certain contexts.

Question: Who can help me and my family in times of need?
Answer: Your favourite God. There are many Gods and you can choose any one. You can also select your favou-

rite place of worship. There are family Gods and their temples, local Gods, community Gods, and sectarian Gods and their temples. You can choose your own form of worship at home or at a temple. There is no controlling authority on religion. You may, however, prefer to follow your family, *jati*, or local community traditions. There is complete freedom of religion. Non-practice of religion is, for the most part, tolerated. One can also choose a teacher or guru and follow his advice. You can change a guru at will. A Hindu has the widest range of choices in terms of rituals. There is no pressure from society or any one else.

Theoretically, there are two supreme Gods or *ishwaras*—Shiva and Krishna. Parvati, known by various other names as well, is equally important. She is Shakti, the Mother Goddess, often considered to be more powerful than other Gods. The three Gods form the focus of three major sects in Hinduism—Shivaites, Vaishnavas, and Shaktas.

Question: How can I seek God's help?

Answer: Follow *varna*, *ashrama*, *dharma*. Perform puja, *homa* or *yajna* with the help of a priest or by self. Visit temples regularly. Feed the poor, or give them clothing, grains or money. Perform austerities, penance, or pilgrimages. You can seek whatever you want through direct oral prayers. You may vow to perform special pujas or offer special gifts if your wishes are fulfilled. Remember your favourite God whenever you are in distress or in need. He will help you.

Humanistic Hinduism

The notion of the Absolute God has its origins in the Upanishadic period. However, it has no relevance to common people who seek help and solace from God. Nevertheless, the concept of the Absolute God is important in itself. Even in the Middle Eastern religions, the concept of the Absolute God exists. Further, this concept offers teleological explanation to the origin of the universe, the origin of life and so on, which is still beyond our grasp. Humanistic religion is concerned with the welfare of the human race, the world and the universe. The basic question then is:

Question: Who created the universe, the sun, the earth, all living things, and above all man?

Answer: We do not know. According to some, everything in the universe owes its existence to an unknown and humanly incomprehensible entity, which may be described as the 'Absolute God'. In the *Upanishads,* the Absolute God is known as *Brahman*. The whole phenomenal world is created by the Absolute God. The human mind has created all other Gods, but the Absolute God is beyond the mental ability of man. However, man can use his brain to explore and discover facets of life on earth and origin of the earth, the sun and the universe. Our knowledge has increased manifold, but there is a lot that is yet to be known. The Absolute God is one thing that we do not know and may not know. There is an element of mystique around this concept. We can accept it just as we accept all other Gods; it is a matter of faith.

Question: Will the Absolute God help me, my family, society, state, or world?

Answer: No, not directly in any case. If you understand the ways in which the Absolute God influences life on earth and if you can modify your actions accordingly, you may get some help; you would be better off than before. You may also seek its help in dire need just to console your mind. There is no harm in doing this. Do not expect the Absolute God to solve your personal problems. Trust your reason. You may find solutions to most of your problems yourself.

Summary

The Rigvedic people also sought help from Gods as we do. However, the tribal society of Rigvedic times and the feudal society of our recent past no longer exist. We live in a free society. Nevertheless, we still need the sheer mystique of God. It gives man hope in despair, relieves his mental pain, and enables him to look to the future with optimism.

Hindus have always believed, from Rigvedic times, in several Gods. Each God highlights some aspect of the ultimate truth. All Gods, in the final analysis, are one and the same. Furthermore, the Absolute God is one and the same for all humanity and at all times. Hindus know of it as 'Brahman'. Hinduism is the only world religion that treats all Gods as equal; further, it emphasizes the notion that through the worship of any God one can get to the ultimate truth or Absolute God.

Brahman, the Absolute God, resides in the sky (*kham*), and in the sun (*Savita*). The same God resides in us and in all living things. The Sun God is next in importance to Absolute God, according to the *Vedas*. The unity of Hinduism is based on the above concepts.

Two

Evolution of Hinduism

Introduction

Hinduism can be understood only by going back to its origin and tracing the sequence of its changes till now. This chapter attempts to do that by using genetic approach. However, tracking the exact sequence of changes in a religion as old as Hinduism, spanning over 4,000 years, is indeed difficult. Further, presentation of the results of such a study would involve considerable simplification. Yet, such a synoptic view of evolution is essential for proper understanding of the basic concepts of Hinduism, whose origin is not specific to a historical person, a point of time or a geographical location.

This chapter has four sections; each examines the social systems and the religious concepts that were in vogue during an important period in the evolution of Hinduism. Religion and society are like Siamese twins and hence the dualistic approach. Further, there were many more sub-periods and developments. For the sake of simplicity, this book will focus on four primary periods. The time frame follows the normal convention and hence it is of least significance.

Rigvedic Period: 1500 BC to 1000 BC

The *Rigveda* is the ancient religious text of humanity preserved in its true form. It was the religion of several ethnic communities of the Indus-Yamuna region. There were other tribal and non tribal peasant communities living in the same region, practising different religions and speaking different languages. Often this aspect is either ignored or undervalued. A realistic picture is presented below.

Society

Thousands of tribal and peasant communities of varied ethnic and linguistic groups were scattered all over India. The Palaeo-Mediterraneans were in majority and others including Australoid, Negroid, and Mongoloid were negligible. The Rigvedic tribes from Central Asia represented the latest arrivals. They were Caucasoids of Central Europe and they spoke Sanskrit that has a great degree of affinity with several Germanic languages.

- The Rigvedic tribes lived only in the Indus Valley to begin with but they moved eastward to the Yamuna later. This region was inhabited by other tribal and peasant groups as well and they far outnumbered the Rigvedic tribes. In my own estimate, the Indo-Gangetic plains then had a population of about two million, and the Rigvedic people accounted for less than one lakh people or about five per cent.

The Rigvedic people spoke Sanskrit and practised the Rigvedic religion. It was preserved for posterity by memorizing, as the Rigvedic people did not know the art of writing. Interestingly, the verses were written and compiled into a text around 400 BC or later, several centuries after it ceased to exist as a living religion.

The Rigvedic tribes consisted of five groups (*pancha jana*), and each group had less than hundred communities with their own religious beliefs and Gods. Rigvedic people did not live in isolation but freely mingled, interacted and possibly intermarried with other groups and gradually their ethnic and cultural distinctiveness were watered-down. Hence, Rigvedic verses reflect not only their original culture but also that of other tribes. Surely, many religions coexisted with the Rigvedic religion but sadly little is known about its contemporaries in the absence of documentation. However, we have evidence of the emergence of these religions into greater prominence in the later Vedic period (after 600 BC).

The unfortunate fact is that Sanskrit survived only as a literary language of the elite. However, it influenced many commonly spoken languages, more particularly in their literary works leading to the evolution of modern Indian languages. Except for Tamil, the literary form is always highly Sanskritized in almost all the languages. The level of Sankritization is at times so high that it goes beyond layman's wisdom. Tamil is the only language of ancient India that virtually remains both a spoken and literary language. Classic Tamil is free from Sanskrit words. However, the content of the ancient Tamil literature amply showcases the influence of Buddhism and Jainism, the Sanskritic Hinduism and the religions of the Tamils.

Religion

The reader will now be fully aware that each tribal community had its own mythology, cultural practices and religion and so did the Rigvedic tribes. The religions of the Rigvedic tribes and other numerous tribal communities have been delivered to us more or less intact. We now have a mass of religious practices all over India that vary from the Vedic religion and they have been subsumed under the title of Hinduism ignoring its independence. Rigvedic religion now exists only in a literary form as its rituals hardly appealed the masses.

The mode of worship of *Agni* with *homa*, so characteristic of the Rigvedic tradition, has at best remained in theory while the age-old and undocumented religions of ancient tribal India that more or less retained their originality are still followed especially in rural areas.

The Rigvedic religion and its associated language, namely, Sanskrit have come down to us through a very select group of Brahmanas, who took great pains to memorize the Vedic verses and the rules of rituals associated with it. They also preserved the language for posterity. From 1000 BC, the Rigvedic religion, the Sanskrit language, and the practice of Vedic rituals were confined to an elite but small population. The rituals based on Rigvedic tradition never had mass appeal.

To suggest that present day religious practices are derived from the *Rigveda* is indeed wrong. Hinduism represents the composite culture of the subcontinent and the role of Rigvedic religion is minimal for it has very little in common with the later schools, a point that will become clear as we discuss the changes that took place over the centuries.

We know quite a lot about Rigvedic religion. The Rigvedic people worshipped several Gods; *Agni*, the Fire God, had a special place as a medium between man and God. The others included *Indra*, *Mitra*, *Rudra*, *Varuna*, Sun, Moon, Water, Air, Earth, etc. *Homa* and *Yaga* (the sacrifice of cattle) were the modes of worship. Meat and dairy products, and verses of praise, that is, mantras were offered. All prayers were usually for longevity of life, protection for warriors, children, cattle and horses for the community as a whole.

The Rigvedic verses were composed over a period of about 500 years or less. It is quite possible that during this period new ideas and practices were imbibed and new Gods were added to the pantheon. No society can afford to remain static or isolated over such a long duration. The interaction of Rigvedic people with other ethnic groups and the non-Rigvedic tribes would have certainly hastened the process of mutual assimilation of cultural traits and development of composite culture. It is assumed that some of the *rishis* who composed the Vedic verses were from other ethnic communities. Sanskrit verse writers need not necessarily be of the same racial or ethnic stock. However, an elitism based on the knowledge of Vedic mantras did emerge and continued for nearly three millenniums which was shared by people of diverse backgrounds.

Upanishadic Period: 1000 BC to 300 BC

Two major religions, Buddhism and Jainism, originated from India in this period, as also the Upanishadic religion, which dominates Hindu philosophy. Though the original form of Rigvedic religion was extinct, its verses were profusely used;

the study of the *Rigveda* (its memorization) was still considered important by the priestly class. Its relevance was lost once these were given the form of a text. As a result, only a few from the priestly class today can now recite the mantras with proper intonation and clarity. The *Rigveda* had few takers while the *Upanishads* were most sought after.

However, during Upanishadic period, the old Rigvedic rituals and mantras were adapted and used in a ritualistic religion known as the Poorva Mimamsa school which was opposed by both Buddhism and Jainism. However, both borrowed ideas from the Poorva Mimamsa school. Centuries later, these religions were completely overshadowed by another religion—Puranic Hinduism. The Puranic religion drew ideas not only from all the above, but also from the native religions based on *bhakti* of God Shiva and Goddess Shakti.

Society

Human societies endure many processes of change. The tribal societies too were no exception. Social anthropologists postulated that social evolution in human history involves four stages—bands, tribes, chiefdoms, and state. The tribal societies changed into the third stage with one difference. The emerging society was not chiefdom in the classic mould but dominated by lineages known as *ganasanghas*. These eventually led to the emergence of the early kingdoms of the Middle Ganga Plains. The first was Kasi which was established around 600 BC. Still, at later periods we find existence of hundreds of kingdoms within the social framework of feudalism in the classic mould.

This period witnessed the formation of new *gotras*—Brahmana, or the priestly class and Kshatriya or the warrior class. The latter assumed the status of kingship and appropriated territories to themselves. The various *gotras* of Brahmanas (36 well-recognized *gotras* as of today) provided religious services to Kshatriyas and Vaishyas. It should be emphasized that Brahmana and Kshatriya varnas of today have nothing to do with the original Rigvedic people. The majority were from other ethnic groups that claimed new status. Many, particularly in the North, think that they are of Aryan ethnic stock. This is pure fiction. Many who claim to be Kshatriya came to India at a much later point of time. The word 'Aryan' is limited to denoting a cluster of languages with no ethnic connotations attached.

The basic division of Indian society in terms of *jati* and varna can be traced to this period. *Jati*, meaning an endogamous group having a name and identity, has its roots in the thousands of tribes that inhabited the subcontinent even before Rigvedic people. These communities multiplied through migration into newer lands and acquired distinctiveness from their parent groups due to changes in occupation, language, food, and even certain religious practices adopted from local communities. Thus the number of *jatis* grew over a period of time. However, each new *jati* did retain some elements of its identity and thus every *jati* even today has several levels of identity.

The varna system has its roots in religion. The major development is the emergence of a new religion based on the *Brahmanas*. A *Brahmana* is a religious text in Sanskrit prose. All the four *Vedas* have one or more *Brahmanas* attached to them. The *Brahmanas* prescribe the procedures for the conduct of *yajnas* and *yagas*. Those who performed the *yajnas* and *yagas* were later known as Brahmanas. The *Brahmanas*—in the sense of texts attached to the *Vedas*—owe their name to the chief priest who supervised the *yajnas* and *yagas*. Angiras was awarded the title of 'Brahmanaspati' because he was considered to be the doyen of the chief priests. In the later Vedic period, the *Taittiriya Upanishad* dealt with the origin of man in the *Purusha Sukta*, which later got incorporated into the *Rigveda* text. The *Purusha Sukta* explains the origin of the four varna system. The varna system formed the basis for the laws of the *Manusmriti* at a still later point in time.

The priestly class of Rigvedic vintage has a special position in the Indian social milieu. It is to them we owe the memorization of all the *Vedas* and other later Vedic texts. Without this memorization, we would never have learnt about the Rigvedic religion or its successors—the Vedantic and the Poorva Mimamsa school. These together constitute the *Shruti*. The priestly class is also responsible for preserving and enriching the Sanskrit language and literature. The study of the *Vedas* and its memorization is not at all easy. Only the families who were well-versed with them could pass it on to their next generation. The priestly class who can recite the *Vedas* in a proper manner can alone claim to have descended from the Rigvedic people. It is to this priestly class that we owe the *Smritis* as well as the Puranic religion. The people of true Rigvedic vintage can hardly be found today. They have formed a microscopic minority throughout history, yet their contribution to the culture and religion is enormous. Hinduism as revealed in Sanskrit texts represent Brahminical Hinduism. There were and are many popular Hinduisms, which are only notionally influenced by the Brahminical Hinduism.

Religion

The Rigvedic *homas* and *yajnas* assumed greater significance and were now performed for the benefit of the family and heads of lineages. The *Yajurveda* and *Samaveda* were products of this social milieu, while the *Atharvaveda,* which is not considered as a *Veda* at all in the *Manusmriti*, focussed entirely on problems of health and other social issues. While *Yajurveda* focusses on the worship of *devas*, *Samaveda* deals with the worship of ancestors (*pitr*). Many of the mantras in the *Samaveda* are taken from the *Rigveda* but recited in a completely different tune. In the *Rigveda* itself there are hundreds of verses praising Angiras and other great poets. They, in effect, constitute a tribute to and even worship of ancestors. The *Yajurveda* introduces new Gods such as the Lord of the Beasts and even the Lord of Thieves among others. All these represent the process of assimilation of pre-Rigvedic cultures into the emerging Brahminical religion. Thus a new religion based on rituals appeared on the scene. The Rigvedic mantras were considered sacred and held in high esteem, even though their literal meaning did not reflect the ground reality. This new development is known as the Poorva Mimamsa school of Jaimini.

The contradiction between Rigvedic mantras and the social reality induced some priests to doubt the utility of the rituals. They withdrew from the society to contemplate on this and this led to the *Upanishads*. Some of the *Upanishads* mention non-Vedic Gods and their worship. There are over a hundred *Upanishads,* of which only 11 are important. The *Upanishads* explored the concept of the Absolute—*Brahman*—the force that created the universe, the Sun, the Earth and all that is known to man. The *Brahman* cannot be perceived by man and it is beyond his ability to define it. Next to the *Brahman*, the Sun was given importance as the objective God. The idea of the Sun being God existed even in Rigvedic times, but now the Sun becomes the *Brahman* or its principal agent that influences life on earth. This led to the discovery that God resided in all living things and man is no exception. It was postulated that God lived in the hearts of men and it was called *Atman*. Further, it was emphasized that *Atman* and *Brahman* are one and the same.

The discovery of the *Atman* gave rise to the concept of rebirth and the cycle of birth and death. Good and bad actions had their consequences in the next life. Good acts led to higher forms of life and bad acts to lower forms, such as animals or birds. This cause and effect principle is now known as the karma theory. These Upanishadic concepts were elaborated upon and cast within the framework of the feudal system characterized by the four division of society at a later point in time. The best example of this is the *Manusmriti* and the *Bhagavad Gita*. It may be noted here that the *Manusmriti* mentions only Vedic Gods, and Vedic *homa* and no epics. It does describe the varna system but not *jati*; the *Bhagavad Gita* also does not mention the term *jati*, which however existed at that time but without religious recognition.

In the 6th Century, the Middle Ganga Plains were in considerable turmoil, both in terms of politics and religious practices. Gautam Buddha was born during this time and he lived for over 80 years. He revolutionized religious thinking and as a result, both the ritualistic Hinduism of the Poorva Mimamsa and the Upanishadic Hinduism received a severe jolt, particularly the former. Buddha denied the existence of both the *Brahman* and the *Atman*. However, he accepted the concept of rebirth and the karma theory. Buddha expounded the principle of equality among all people. This, in reality, was not a new concept as it was a central Rigvedic principle.

Jainism also originated at the same time. Like Buddha, Mahaveera was a Kshatriya and he also opposed the rituals of Hinduism. He emphasized *ahimsa* as the ultimate principle of life. The Jains practised pure vegetarianism, as opposed to Vedic religions according to which meat was eaten and offered to Gods as well. In other respects, Jainism was no different from Hinduism. Pertinently, both Buddhism and Jainism are Kshatriya religions, born more out of rivalry with the Brahmanas or priestly class.

During this period, the Middle Ganga Plains saw the emergence of urban centres, the first one being the city of Varanasi on the banks of Ganga. The number of urban places and kingdoms also gradually increased. A new feudal order with a king at its apex was beginning to emerge. Priests and religious leaders were more or less dependent on the kings and feudal chiefs for support; on the other hand, they did wield considerable influence among the masses and the kings and other feudal chiefs could not ignore them.

Another major event of this time was the discovery of the art of writing. Writing is considered as a pre-condition for the emergence of early cities. A new genre of literary work emerged during this period, which was part religious and part secular. This genre is known as *Sutras*. The *Apastamba Sutra*, which is a *Brahmana* attached to the *Yajurveda*, is an important example. Others include the grammatical work of Panini and Pantanjali's classic work on *dhyana yoga*.

The *Smritis* belong to a still later part of this period. The *Manusmriti* and *Yajnavalkya Smriti* are among the best known beside others which laid down the rules of conduct for the subjects and rulers. They are part secular and part religious. They give us a deep insight of the life of people of this time period.

Buddhism, Jainism, Poorva Mimamsa, and Vedanta continued to thrive along with pre-Rigvedic religions for several centuries (600 BC to 300 BC) in the Middle Ganga Plains, until Ashoka, the Mauryan king, converted himself to Buddhism and spread this religion not only within his vast empire but also abroad.

Puranic Period: 300 BC to 1800 AD

This period is very long from historical angle; it is divided into ancient period (300 BC to 1000 AD) and medieval period (1000 AD to 1800 AD). The latter is generally the predominant Muslim period in Indian history except in South which did not have any Muslim ruler. From the religious angle, it is better to consider this as one period—a period in which Hinduism became closely identified with the *Puranas* and epics, which are really a part of the *Puranas*.

The *Smritis*, in particular the *Manusmriti*, constitute a sort of watershed between the Upanishadic period and the Puranic period. The *Manusmriti* is dealt with elaborately in later chapters and hence characteristics of society and religion as presented in the *Manusmriti* are not discussed here. We may note that the *Manusmriti* does not mention the Gods of the Puranic age or the epics. I have placed the *Manusmriti* at or around 300 BC. It could be a century or two later in its origin, but definitely predates the *Puranas* and it is written after 326 BC.

In the first few centuries of this period (300 BC to 200 AD), Buddhism and Jainism were clearly more dominant. They, however, constantly fought against each other; not physically but verbally. Hinduism of the Brahminical and native varieties, however, flourished at the village level, while Buddhism and Jainism made their presence felt at the courts of kings. This was true of North India as well as South India. Kanchipuram, the capital of the Pallavas, became a centre for both Jains and Buddhists. Yet another such centre was Nagarjunakonda in Andhra Pradesh. Both these religions made a significant impact on contemporary Tamil literature, popularly known as Sangam literature. *Tirukkural*, a very famous work of this period in Tamil, is a good example of the absorption of Buddhist and Jaina values, in what is essentially Tamil culture and idiom.

This intervening period also witnessed the emergence of *bhakti* or faith from obscurity, based on the worship of Shiva and Shakti, whose roots may be traced to the Harappan culture. These pre-Rigvedic religions find mention in the Buddhist, Jaina and even Sanskrit literatures of this period. The worship of Vishnu also has its roots in this period. However, unlike Shiva and Shakti, worship of Vishnu owes its origin, in part, to the later Vedic religions. In later Vedic literature, Vishnu is equated with Prajapati, Purusha, etc. All these later Vedic Gods did not exist during Rigvedic times.

Society

In 300 BC, India was ruled by numerous kingdoms both in the North and South. In North India alone there were over 200 kingdoms. Most of these were, during the period of Mauryas, a part of its vast empire. However, in reality the local kings enjoyed full powers and were only notionally subservient to the so-called *samrat* or emperor.

The society at this time was essentially feudal in nature, ruled by kings and nobles, with administrative machinery supported by the police to collect taxes and punish the guilty. The Indian society, mainly in the North, was divided into four varna system. In reality, each varna was further divided into *jatis.* The upper three varnas had fewer *jatis* within—in terms of hundreds—while the fourth or Shudra varna had thousands of *jatis.* In the South, the migrant Brahmanas from the North introduced the varna system, in which the Kshatriya and Vaishya varnas were recruits of *jatis* from the local population. According to Kanchi Acharya, there are only two varnas in the South—Brahmanas and the non-Brahmanas or Shudras (This word is disliked all over India today and therefore may be avoided). The word Shudra is a creation of religious texts, while the names of *jatis* are popularly accepted with pride by one and all.

Even in the North, true Kshatriya kings ruled only till about 300 BC. According to one historian, the last of the truly Kshatriya kings were the Nandas of Pataliputra. The Mauryas were Shudras, while a host of other post Mauryan dynasties were all Brahmanas—starting from the Sungas, Kanvas, and others in the North, the Rashtrakutas, Satvahanas, Chalukyạs, and Pallavas in the South. The Pallavas claimed to belong to the Bharadwaja *gotra.*

Another important feature of this period (300 BC to 1000 AD) is the successive invasions and settlement of Central Asian tribes in Northern India. These newcomers constitute a majority of the population of the Punjab and western Uttar Pradcsh, Rajasthan and other adjoining areas today. Alexander's invasion of 326 BC influenced Hinduism in many ways. It introduced new concepts in art and architecture, besides astronomy, astrology and scientific thinking. Later invasions were on a massive scale in terms of numbers, but they stayed behind and today constitute significant numbers of Northern India's elite population. The Rajputs of Northern India are believed to be Hunas or Huns of Central European origins, while the Jats, who constitute over 50 per cent of the population of Punjab and Haryana and a significant population in western Uttar Pradesh and northern Rajasthan are believed to be the descendents of Scythians, who came to India from Central Asia towards the beginning of the first millennium AD. While the Rajputs are accepted as Kshatriyas, the Jats have claimed and received recognition as belonging to the backward classes, much to the embarrassment of many educated and professional Jats. The Jats are perhaps the best-known farming community of India, and during the British period, they were recruited into the army in large numbers. Unlike the Rajputs, the Jats were never fully accepted by other Hindus and hence perhaps the legitimacy of being named as belonging to the backward classes.

The influx of people from outside had serious consequences; the anarchic conditions that prevailed in most parts of the Ganga Plains resulted in large scale migrations of people—mainly belonging to the Brahmana varna—to the South where conditions were better. The kings in the South, particularly the Pandyas and Cholas, welcomed this influx. Hundreds of *agraharams* in Tamil Nadu and elsewhere in the South are actually land-grant villages given to groups of Brahmana immigrants from the North. Cholas are credited for giving them freedom to rule themselves through charters inscribed in copper plates. These are often mentioned as village democracies of the South. These Brahmana settlements of the far South belong to two main groups—the Smarthas and the Srivaishnavas.

Religion

Under the combined influence of Buddhism and the rise of the Mauryas under Ashoka after the Greek invasion of India, Hinduism had to adapt itself and redefine its basic concepts in order to appeal to the masses. It also had to reflect upon the changed social system now firmly in the hands of non-Kshatriya, or even foreign rulers; as is denoted by the repeated use of the word *Yavana.* The *Manusmriti* uses the term 'degraded Kshatriyas' to denote the new class of kings. Under these adverse circumstances, the Hindu priestly class was marginalized and had to invent a new mechanism by which they could regain their influence.

The Buddhists and Jainas were good storytellers and the stories of the hundreds of incarnations of Buddha had prepared the minds of the people for a different kind of religion. The Buddhists and Jainas, in fact, rejected the elitism of the Brahmanas and mixed freely with all sections of the pre-Rigvedic people. They also absorbed their legends and other cultural practices. For the first time, the Buddhist and Jaina literature gives us evidence of the existence of pre-Rigvedic cultures, their Gods and their religious values. The marginalized Brahmanas saw a golden opportunity in this complex situation. Their response was to Sankritize the pre-Rigvedic legends to give them a new shape by including Rigvedic Gods and poets and to cast all these within the then current feudal framework. This gave rise to the two great epics, *Ramayana* and *Mahabharata,* and the *Puranas*. The epics introduced two important concepts—Gods in human form and the ten reincarnations of the principal God, more or less akin to births of Buddha. In the epics, the God is born into a royal family; this reinforced the feudal system with the king at the top and it was acceptable to the ruling class as well as the masses, which feared and respected their king. We may note here that Gautam Buddha was also born into a royal family. The acceptance of God in human form and the worship of human idols owe their allegiance to Buddhism.

The Greek influence was noticeable in several respects. It did not end with Alexander's invasion as many Greeks stayed back and ruled Indian lands for a few more centuries. The *Ramayana* has a close affinity to Homer's *Iliad.* The multiplicity of Gods and their constant interface with humans in our epics is equally true of the Greek pantheon and the Greek epic. The Brahmi script, the first and the mother of all scripts in India, bears a close resemblance to the Greek alphabets. The art of sculpture taught by the Greeks, known as the Gandhara art, led to the worship of idols and finally temple worship. This does not mean that we owe everything to the Greeks, but to deny their influence would be wrong. As always, cross cultural contacts enhance the quality of civilizations. It may also be noted here that the Upanishadic concepts of an abstract God and mysticism found their way to Europe through the Greeks.

The great epics were created from numerous stories in the Buddhist literature and some of these have found their way to Southeast Asia. While we can take credit for the spread of Indian influences in other parts of Asia, we should also recognize the contributions of other cultures to our own. Likewise, Puranic Hinduism owes a lot to Buddhism and Jainism.

The *Puranas* and the Epics

In this period and even up to the present, the two epics and to a lesser extent the *Puranas* form the core of the religion of the masses. *Manusmriti* has already given moral authority to the kings by attributing divine qualities to this new class and legitimized the feudal social order. The Brahmanas had a privileged position in this order as the true interpreters of the laws of Manu. The varna system was not only morally justified but it was expected to be enforced by the state, often very ruthlessly. The Hindu kingdoms were theocratic states, in the sense that Manu's laws formed the basis for governance. The Brahmanas and the Kshatriyas or the ruling class had a very privileged existence, at least in theory. It may be noted that the Shudra kings respected the Brahmanas even more in return for their recognition of them as true Kshatriyas. This marriage of convenience suited both groups, although probably neither had true legitimacy.

The *Puranas*, although held in less esteem when compared to the epics in popular perception, were actually more important from the religious point of view. There are 18 *Puranas* in total. An interesting aspect of the *Puranas* is that they were not fully aware of the South. Only a few places in the South are mentioned in the *Puranas*, while the Buddhists and Jaina monks had come to the South as early as 300 BC. Even Chanakya mentions about Madurai and the Pandyas. The Jainas introduced the Brahmi script in Tamil Nadu; we have epigraphic evidence to support this. In these rock inscriptions we have a combination of Brahmi script, Tamil language, and Jaina principles.

The *Puranas* are basically textbooks used by eminent scholars to instruct their students. They have chapters devoted to cosmology and cosmogony, history as revealed by the epics, elaborate discussion on cultural practices, and jurisprudence. The *Puranas* are always cited as the authority on various customs and practices. Gods not mentioned in the *Puranas* have no authenticity. The *Puranas* introduce us to all the Gods of the Hindu pantheon, their inter-relationships and stories about their powers and the mode of their worship. The *Puranas*, therefore, represent the *Bible* of the literate and through them the masses. Again the *Puranas* written in Sanskrit were clearly the work of Brahmanas. The *Bhagavad Purana* is the oldest and the most important of all the *Puranas* and it includes the two epics, that is, *Ramayana* and *Mahabharata*, as well. The *Puranas*, however, do not reflect the whole picture, since some of the important branches of Shivaite and Shakti sects are not fully highlighted here. They have their own independent literature. In particular, the Shivaites and Shaktas do not recognize the 10 avatars or incarnations of Vishnu. The epics have no meaning to Shivaites or Shaktas. In fact, true Shivaites or Shaktas will not even read the epics if a copy is given to them. However, not all *Puranas* focus on the epics; some reflect the other religious sects as well. The emphasis on specific religious sects depends on the author of each of the 18 *Puranas*.

Hindu Pantheon

The principal Gods of the Hindu pantheon during the period and later are Shiva, Vishnu and Shakti and to this we may add Kartikeya, the Sanskritized name of Muruga, the Tamil God. The two principal avatars of Vishnu, namely Rama and Krishna, are perhaps the best known Gods. There are numerous Gods of lesser order and we have almost thousands of names for the principal Gods. The acceptance of many names for each God made it easier to absorb tribal faiths into the mainstream. Thus, the Gods and Goddesses of all tribal communities of the past and present were integrated into this system. For example, Amman, Mariamman, Kali, Durga and Bhagavati all represent the female Goddess Shakti.

The tribal gods of Orissa were later Sanskritized as Lord Jagannath, Balabhadra, and Subhadra of Puri. Even today, the idols in the temple are made of wood by the same tribal community and they also have the right to install and perform rituals in this temple for a limited period of time. The original temple priests of Tamil Nadu, known as *Kurukkals*, did not belong to the Brahmana varna; the Smartha Brahmanas were never involved in temple pujas; they specialized in Vedic rituals. The worship of idols in temples made it possible for the priestly class of tribals to get into the Brahmana varna. Acquisition of basic knowledge of Sanskrit and the ability to recite a few mantras, even without understanding their meaning, was only needed. On the other end, some of the original Brahmana groups became temple priests and even specialized in this new profession, as it was more lucrative. This practice is at variance from Manu's prescriptions.

Modes of Worship

The Vedic religious practices were more or less confined to Brahmanas, particularly in the South, while in the North these became practically extinct during the Muslim period. In the South, the Smartha Brahmanas are credited with the preservation of the Vedic tradition almost intact. This is asserted by no less an authority than Max Weber in his *Religion of India*, a classic by all means.

Worship of the Puranic Gods in homes and temples followed local traditions; the concept of temples for Gods has its origin in pre-Rigvedic times and it is acknowledged in the *Manusmriti*. Temple traditions are actually borrowed from the Shudras and then Sanskritized to make it appear as though it is a true product of Vedic vintage. The principal form of worship was the puja or offering of flowers to the deity. *Bhajans* or singing of songs in praise of the deity was another mode. All these were supplemented by festivities associated with the temple. Each temple has its own legends or *Sthala Puranas*. All these practices demonstrate that the Puranic religion has more to do with the pre-Rigvedic cultures of India. The worship of idols of Gods in temples or at home has nothing to do with the Vedic religion. The *shlokas* describing Puranic Gods used in pujas is a new practice and it is a key element of the Sankritization process involved in the Puranic religion. In the Vedic religion, *Agni* is the sole medium between man and God and all offerings are made to *Agni* alone. Only Vedic mantras can be used for *homas* and *yajnas*. *Shlokas* and mantras refer to verses in Sanskrit; but they belong to entirely different time periods and relate to two vastly different religions.

Hindu Religious Sects

The worship of the three principal Gods resulted, in course of time, in three distinct sects within the fold of Hinduism—Shivaite, Vaishnavite and Shaktas. In addition, we also have Kartikeyas or more popularly known as *Muruga bhaktas* in Tamil Nadu. Srivaishnavites of Tamil Nadu, popularly known as Iyyangars, and the Veerashaivites of Karnataka, popularly known as Lingayats, are perhaps the best recognized religious sects of India. There is an excellent book on Hindu religious sects written by an Indian sociologist. There were many subdivisions in each of the religious sects; most of which are now extinct. The rather sharp differences in faith among the religious sects and their open animosity are now a thing of the past. For example, in the past the Srivaishnavites would not even pronounce Shivaite names and vice versa; now they entertain no such acrimony.

Bhakti Movement

While the *Puranas* are distinctly North Indian in origin, the *bhakti* movement has its roots in the South. *Bhakti* did exist in the North in the early Puranic period and this is exemplified by the presence of Bhagavatas and Pasupatas. The principal Gods in Tamilazakam, which in Sangam times (200 BC to 200 AD) included the whole of South India, were Murugan and Mariamman. The forms of worship of these Gods were also well entrenched. The Tamil bards sang songs in praise of their Gods in Tamil. The literary style in Tamil is characterized by the basic concepts of *akam* and *purram* (the inside and the outside), and their concomitant concepts of seasons, landscape, moods and so on. Devotion or *bhakti* is a natural concomitant of Tamil literary ethos which is highly emotional in nature. When the North Indian religions of Buddhism, Jainism and later the Vedic religion came to the South from around 300 BC, they were assimilated into the Tamil idiom and the *bhakti* movement took shape here. The new Gods added to this genre were principally Shiva and his consort and Vishnu with his avatars and so on.

Tamil Nadu has a long and vibrant history of *bhakti* movement, starting from 500 AD or even earlier and climaxing during 1200 AD and 1300 AD. The 63 *Nayanmars* and 12 *Azhwars* represent the Shivaite and Vaishnavite sects, while the former were almost entirely from the non-Brahmana communities, the latter were predominantly from among the Vaishnavite Brahmanas of the South. The *Nayanmars* and *Azhwars* were poets and they composed devotional lyrics in Tamil in praise of their favorite Gods. The Tamil language is very rich in devotional lyrics and songs and these belong to different sects; each having its own distinctive style.

We should give due credit to Tamil poet for presenting the *Ramayana* in Tamil; the *Kamba Ramayanam* is the earliest version of Valmiki's *Ramayana* in any modern Indian language. It was written in 900 AD, while *Ramacharithamanas* of Tulsi Das written in Hindi belongs to 1600 AD.

Temples and *Agamas*

South India also has a rich temple tradition. The earliest temples were those built by the Pallavas between 500 AD to 800 AD. This was followed by the Cholas from 900 AD to 1200 AD. In the Kannada land, the Gangas and Hoysalas, the Chalukyas, and numerous other Southern dynasties built temples of exquisite beauty. Temples of great beauty were also built further north, in what may be described as northern Peninsular India, but in the Indo-Gangetic Plains they are conspicuous by their absence.

All temples in the South were supported by generous land grants from kings and big landowners. The temple walls are full of records of such donations and other contributions. The temples were administered by a committee of prominent individuals. The Southern temples offered free lunch to poor Brahmanas and others during most of the historical period. After Independence, temple lands were taken away and all temples (except the very small ones) are now maintained by the state governments. Today the temple priests receive their salaries from the government, although they are not considered as government servants. The temple tower is still the principal hallmark of the Southern cities. In all villages and towns of the South, the temple was the focal point of social and cultural activities throughout the historical period and to a lesser extent even today.

The temples in the South were constructed on the principles of *vastu shastra* which was brought here by the Buddhists. However, the architects and sculptors were all from South India and thus they wrote down the *vastu shastra* in Tamil and other Southern languages with diagrams and so on. These in fact continue to be the basic texts on town planning and temple planning. All the major temple towns of South India were built on a pattern of concentric squares, with the temple occupying the central square. The successive rings around the temple were occupied by Brahmanas, Kshatriyas, Vaishyas, and finally Shudras. This form of social organization, with minor modifications, still exists in many temple towns in the South.

During the medieval period only the Southern architects based on *vastu shastra* survived. After the Mughal period, the Southern *stapathis* (sculptors) were invited to Northern India to build temples. The temple and palace complex in Alwar in Rajasthan is one such temple.

The textual code for temple rituals and practices is given in over one hundred *Agamas*. There are both Shivaite and Vaishnavite Agamas, the former being far more numerous than the latter. They are in Sanskrit language. The *Agamas* are more like the *Puranas*, in that they also contain a variety of other material including mythology and Vedic philosophy. The *Agamas* are still followed in major temples of South India, where the chief priests are fully trained in the system. The *Agamas* clearly spell out the daily rituals to be performed in temples and the procedures to be followed during festivals and various other issues relating to temple management. The *Agamas* are held in far greater esteem than the *Puranas* by Shivaites.

The *Agamas* were written in Sanskrit and at present, temple worship in the South is also performed in Sanskrit language. In ancient times in Tamil Nadu, the temple priests did not know Sanskrit and worship was performed in Tamil. It may be noted that temples for worship of Gods is based on pre-Rigvedic cultures. Even in the *Manusmriti* there is a brief reference to temples outside the villages. These temples were for non-Vedic Gods. This practice had and still has nothing to do with the Vedic religion. Later, the Gods and the forms of worship in temples were all Sanskritized. However, in recent years, the government of Tamil Nadu is trying to bring back Tamil as the language of worship in temples. It is ironical that the priests trained in Sanskrit (some of whose forefathers were priests who worshipped Gods in Tamil) now object to the restoration of their original practices.

The *Bhagavad Gita* and Adi Shankaracharya

The Puranic religion, as exemplified by the *Bhagavad Purana* and the two great epics, would be incomplete without mentioning the *Bhagavad Gita* (400 AD) and its great interpreter Adi Sankaracharya (800 AD). The *Bhagavad Gita* makes a complete departure from the general trend of the times. The Upanishadic and Vedic religion was largely sidelined during the early Puranic period. The *Bhagavad Gita* is in fact a later addition to the *Mahabharata* epic. The *Bhagavad Gita* makes a valiant attempt to revive interest in the *Upanishads* by sugarcoating it with the Puranic tradition of storytelling and *bhakti*. It succeeded to some extent in this. The vital question is what prevailed at the end. My own view is that *bhakti* triumphed over *jnana*. The Upanishadic content in the *Bhagavad Gita* is often misunderstood or deliberately ignored.

Centuries later Adi Shankaracharya battled with divergent viewpoints put out by Tantrics and other sects to establish the supremacy of Upanishadic religion. His most notable commentaries were on *Brahma Sutra* and the 11 *Upanishads* selected by him. He used the *Bhagavad Gita* to support his view point; this was more palatable than the obscure question and answer mode adopted by the *Upanishads*. He redefined the *Vedas* virtually as the scriptures for which he wrote commentaries.

He never mentioned the *Rigveda* anywhere in any specific way, nor has he written a commentary on any of the *Vedas*. He was notionally opposed to the Poorva Mimamsa school of thought. However, Shankaracharya's contribution goes beyond the *Upanishads*. He was a cultural and social reformer as well. His own work addressed to the householders of his time—the *Bhaja Govindam*—is a reflection of his dual approach, a combination of *bhakti* and *jnana*; *bhakti* for the ordinary people and *jnana* for the selected few. He is credited with the revival of Hinduism and its integration in the whole of modern India. He established the four well-known *Mutts* in the four corners of India, thus defining its east-west and north-south geographical limits.

Hinduism under Muslim Rule

For about 600 years, Northern India was ruled by Muslims (1200 AD to 1800 AD). During this period many Hindus were converted to Islam. An overwhelming majority of people of Pakistan (98 per cent) and Bangladesh (85 per cent), who were earlier Hindus, became Muslims. However, in India, particularly North India, the level of conversion was low, even though Delhi and Agra were the chief capital cities during this period. The proportion of Muslims in India today is only 11 per cent and this is more or less uniform throughout the country.

Apart from conversion, Muslim rule did affect the practice of Hinduism in many ways. Hindu temples were destroyed in large numbers in North India, especially during the rule of Aurangzeb. All the temples in Varanasi were rebuilt after the Aurangzeb era, which ended in 1707. Through out this period, Hindus had to be very discreet in the practice of their religion so as not to attract attention. The Bhakti Movement with *Tulsi Ramayan* and the *ras leela* of *Gita Govindam* became focal aspects of religion only after the death of Aurangzeb. The Rama cult in the Hindi belt is a post-Aurangzeb phenomenon, although *Tulsi Ramayan* was written during the reign of Akbar (1600 AD).

Some Brahmana communities of the Indo-Gangetic Plains gave up the traditional rituals and accepted farming as their primary occupation. The Bhumihar Brahmanas became actual tillers of the soil (as contrasted with absentee landlordism practised elsewhere in India). They form an important group in Bihar and Uttar Pradesh. In western Uttar Pradesh, they use the surname Tyagi, clearly indicating that they had given up their *varna dharma*. In western Uttar Pradesh and further west, Brahmanas form a smaller percentage of the population; they are also relatively poor. Their knowledge of Vedic practices is little as a result of centuries of neglect under adverse circumstances. Further, and possibly for the same reasons, they were not much respected by the Kshatriyas and others. The Kashmiri Pandits, however, have enjoyed a higher status among Brahmanas in the North and together with the Kshatriyas they enjoyed special privileges in the Kashmir Valley, until a few decades ago. In Jat villages—in Punjab, Haryana, and western Uttar Pradesh—Brahmanas are generally absent and the Jats traditionally have had no respect for Brahmanas.

Reading of the scriptures and their preservation was impossible in North India during the medieval period. During the 1900s, when the European Indologists looked for manuscripts of our scriptures, they could find them only in South India (75 per cent) and in the Himalayan belt, especially, Nepal (25 per cent). South

India, particularly Tamil Nadu and Kerala, escaped Muslim rule and in these states Brahmanas were highly respected. They were economically better off due to income from agriculture and they managed to preserve the Vedic traditions.

There were some Muslim scholars who were sympathetic to Hinduism and Hindu philosophy. Feeble attempts made to integrate these two widely-different religions miserably failed. Sufism and Sikhism succeeded to some extent, but their influence was very limited.

Modern Period: 1800 AD to Present

Between the collapse of the Mughal Empire after the death of Aurangzeb in 1707 and the advent of the British, there was total chaos in North India. The British, however, established themselves firmly in India by 1800 and their rule extended all over the subcontinent of South Asia.

The British brought about wide-ranging changes in administration and law; education along modern lines was promoted and the country witnessed the introduction of the railways which facilitated the movement of people. Indians got to know themselves better than before. Ironically, it is the British who showed interest in Indian languages and in our religious texts. They retrieved the manuscripts which would otherwise have been lost to posterity and developed a distinct subject—Indology. The Max Mueller Bhavan and the Bhandarkar Institute in Pune stands testimony to this. Bhandarkar, well known for his classic books on Sanskrit grammar, was an outstanding Sanskrit scholar of the 19th Century. He studied in England and was well versed in English. His books were published in 1864.

The British administration was secular since in England itself the Church has been separated from the state. The laws of British India, therefore, were secular in nature. However, there were laws that recognized the traditional practices of Muslims and Hindus. Strictly speaking, these are not religious laws, only religion-based laws.

Without doubt, Hinduism was better off under the British than the Muslim rule. The Christian mission in India did try to convert the local population to Christianity, but this was not supported by the state. After 150 years of British rule, less than two per cent of the people of India are Christians. Still, the Christian missionaries were aggressive and criticized Hinduism sharply. This aspect is discussed in more detail in the subsection on religion.

India became independent in 1947 and it is now overwhelmingly a Hindu state. Yet our Constitution and our national leaders believed in a secular democratic state. The Constitution guarantees religious freedom. After six decades of Independence, we can proudly assert that we are a free, secular, democratic, plural society. The religious freedom that we have enjoyed in the past and especially after Independence has no parallel.

Society

India today is a plural society where people professing various religions, speaking different languages and belonging to different ethnic groups, *jatis* and *varnas* coexist in a more or less peaceful manner. Every citizen is equal before the law and the state provides for equal opportunities in education and work to all.

There is affirmative action in favour of the minorities and the underprivileged segments of the population. Untouchability has been abolished and its practice made punishable. Laws on marriage, divorce, and inheritance have undergone change. The *Manusmriti*, in particular, has become *persona non grata* in the eyes of the educated and the ruling class.

In schools, colleges, and places of work and business, people intermix with each other regardless of religion, caste, or language. English continues to be the language of advancement and is favoured by parents and students alike. There are more number of English knowing citizens today than before Independence. The majority of the population is now literate, although female literacy is still lagging behind. The birth and death rates have come down and medical facilities have improved by leaps and bounds. The expectation of life at birth has jumped to over 60, from 35 before Independence.

Remnants of the feudal age have vanished. There are no kings and nobility. Money continues to be an important goal and perhaps the only measure of respectability. *Sarve gunah kanchanam ashrayante,* meaning that 'all good qualities depend on gold', is truer now than ever before.

Religion

During 1900, Hinduism was attacked relentlessly by Christian missionaries using the church as their launching pad. They particularly attacked the caste system, untouchability, the notion of purity and pollution practised by various castes, the multiplicity of Gods, Gods in human and animal form, child marriage, Sati, the treatment of widows and so on. At the same time, the Indologists, mainly from Germany and England, had high praise for Hindu philosophy and scriptures.

There were several kinds of responses. The first was a tit for tat response which counter-attacked Christian beliefs and practices. The more substantive reactions were those of the Brahmo Samaj of Raja Ram Mohan Roy and the Arya Samaj of Swami Dayananda Saraswati. The former was more or less Western in its outlook and reformist in nature, while the latter redefined Hinduism as Vedic Hinduism in which the *Puranas,* epics and the *Smritis* were totally rejected. The Arya Samaj is still a vibrant force in North India and there is considerable sympathy for its viewpoint. The Arya Samaj introduced the concept of conversion (*shudhi*) into Hinduism for the first time in India. Earlier, we had informal processes of adoption of a religion and assimilation of a person or groups into a sect or religion. The conversion of people from Buddhism and Jainism, or vice versa, was of this nature. The criticism of the caste system has had a long-term beneficial impact. No one supports it today, at least openly.

Till the time of Independence, Hinduism and related religious practices were observed in a reasonable manner and people, especially the Southern Brahmana communities, were fully aware of the scriptures and the prescribed practices. Religious awareness has fallen to abysmally low levels after Independence, especially among Brahmana communities in the South. The reference here is to Sanskrit scriptures and Vedic rituals.

In rural and tribal India, we have an entirely different situation. In the tribal areas, we have tribal religions with some input from mainstream Hinduism. In some areas, such as the North-East, Christianity has made significant inroads. In rural India, we have an amazing variety of religious practices and beliefs. Even within a village, there are 10 or 20 different *jatis*, each having its own religious practices. Most of these practices are hundreds if not thousands of years old. Although all of them are considered to be Hindu practices, most Hindus may not endorse them, for example, the practice of sacrificing goats, fowls, garlanding mother goddess with the intestine of goats, etc. The mainstream Hinduism exists only notionally in rural India. This also explains the reason why we do not have even a single common religious festival in India. Even festival like Deepavali that is celebrated widely is interpreted differently in various parts.

Hindus are a most confused lot. The Vedic practice of *nitya karma* is hardly practised by anyone. The *pitr karmas* are performed by a few. The Hindu priest, trained in Vedic rituals, is not treated respectfully but as a daily wage earner. At the same time, most Hindu priests are not well trained and their knowledge of Sanskrit is weak. They have never read or understood any of the Hindu scriptures. The priest has become just a performer of rituals and not an instructor in religion. The social status of the temple priest is even lower. These issues need to be addressed with urgency. For a common man, various religious texts are available in many languages including English. One may need sustained effort to understand and digest them and people do not even have any inclination or time to read them. The religious *Mutts*, in vast numbers in South India, represent a variety of sects both old and new. They, however, have no mass appeal and their dictates do not rule.

Nevertheless, there is no dearth of enthusiasm and people are ready to spend money on Hinduism. Some money goes to a few well-known temples and the rest to religious institutions built by emerging neo-religious leaders. There are many educational institutions and hospitals and more recently old age homes. This approach probably was started by the Ramakrishna Mission, modelled on educational institutions and hospitals built and run by Christian missionaries. Almost all such institutions are headed by individuals having absolute power.

Of late, there is considerable interest in recent cults, the Ayyappa cult and the Saibaba cult, for example. Both have no validity in the *shastras*. While the varna system has broken down totally, *jati* persists especially among the poor. To some, Hinduism, particularly the practice of yoga and meditation, has become a kind of psychotherapy rather than a religious practice. For this, they are willing to spend a lot of money. For most, religion is not an important part of their daily life and some disclaim attachment to any religion.

Despite the above, religion now plays a greater role in politics. Religion was always present in politics in India; it was planted by Mahatma Gandhi. Now there are several recognized political parties and quasi-politico-religious organizations wedded to the promotion of Hinduism and other religions. Recently, religion is being used for violent activities. The roots of this phenomenon may be traced to foreign lands. This tendency has done considerable harm.

Summary

In the past, the people of India adapted their religion to suit the changing social conditions of the time. Thus, we have the Rigvedic religion suited to a tribal society, where everyone is an equal member and where the society functioned as a unit.

Later, the tribal way of life gave way to a peasant agricultural cum cattle rearing economy in which lineages, families, and individuals had distinct roles. The later *Vedas* (*Yajurveda*, *Samaveda*, and *Atharvaveda*) and the *Upanishads* reflect these changes in society.

Still later, we find mature feudal societies with a king at its apex. In this society, all human relations were based on the scheme of master and servant. The servant of a householder becomes a master in his own household. A person's conduct changes with the situation. This period also saw many Gods who were dressed like kings and were often equated with them or considered at a higher level. People were expected to be suppliant to Gods and surrender themselves to their favourite God in order to obtain his favours. Thus, the Puranic religion was ideally suited to a feudal society. This conformed to the social ethos of the time. We have not altogether given up the feudal outlook even today, although there are no kings and queens anymore.

Today, India is a free, democratic, and plural society. The old Puranic religion is no longer in conformity with our present ethos. We now focus on equality among all people. In some ways, we are closer to the Rigvedic ideals of unity, equality, common understanding, and the welfare of all people. Though there are differences, we have to move forward without totally discarding the past.

This study of the evolution of Hinduism through history highlights the fact that Hinduism is a dynamic religion capable of adapting itself to changing social circumstances or conditions. Hinduism should continue to move along the path of *sanatana dharma*, emphasizing its permanent and lasting values.

Three

Introduction to *Rigveda*

Introduction

The *Rigveda* is the oldest and in fact, the most sacred of all the religious texts of Hindus. Composed by as many as 50 poets almost 3,500 years ago, it consists of over 10,500 verses compiled over a period of several centuries. These verses were constantly chanted by lineages and disciples of the Rigvedic poets so as to memorize them. Once the art of writing was invented many centuries later, they were then written down on dried barks of trees, leather, or pieces of cloth. Such writings made it possible to put together all the segments of the Rigvedic verses in one place and give it the form of a compiled sacred text. It was no mean task, for in those days the Vedic mantras were kept as a secret and families would not easily part with their belongings.

Shruti Texts

Sacred religious texts of the Hindus fall under two basic categories—*Shruti* and *Smriti*. *Shrutis* include the four *Vedas* and the *Upanishads*. *Manusmriti* and the *Puranas* are *Smritis*. The *Smritis* were composed when the art of writing was already in vogue and hence there was no need to memorize them or compile them at a later stage. On the other hand, *Shruti* texts were composed when writing did not exist and hence they had to be memorized and later put on together as a text. Also the *Shruti* texts often had multiple authors and they were transmitted in a fragmented form, which made compilation very difficult. These fragmented texts were scattered among numerous families living in diverse regions. In this process, sections of various *Shruti* texts got mixed up. Some of these were deliberate and some accidental. Legend confers the honour of compilation of the *Vedas* to Veda Vyasa but historians opine that it may not be the real name of the compiler but a conferred on him as the name Veda Vyasa means 'compiler of the Vedas'. The *Smritis* were conceived and simultaneously composed unlike the *Shrutis*. Hence *Smritis* are very well organized as a text, like any modern literature, for example, *Manusmriti*.

Compilation of Rigvedic Text

Considering the volume of work, hardship and the span of time involved in the process, one can speculate that the *Rigveda* and other *Shruti* texts could not have been compiled by any one person but by a number of persons at different times. This explains the circulation of multiple versions of the same text.

The first compilation of the *Rigveda* probably took place around 400 BC, preceding the *Smritis*. Interestingly, the author of the *Yajnavalkya Smriti* is also the compiler of the more popular version of the *Yajurveda*. There were repeated recompilations of the *Vedas* in succession to safeguard against their loss or destruction but none of them survived in its original form as of now.

During the 1900s, the present day Rigvedic texts and other scriptures were recompiled under the guidance of Western Indologists. The source material was derived mainly from Southern India, where Brahmana families had preserved the ancient Rigvedic texts and practices. In Tamil Nadu, the Brahmanas wrote down the Vedic texts in *grantham* script on palm leaf. It was replaced by the Devanagari script in the year 1900.

Reality Versus Inferences

The foregoing statements are inferences based on evidence. What actually transpired during the period is unknown and we can only deduce. The basic questions that arise are:

1. How do we know that the Rigvedic verses originated around 1500 BC?
2. How do we know that the Rigvedic people were pastoral nomads?
3. How do we know that the Rigvedic people lived in the Indus valley?

We can ask many more such questions but these can be answered only in terms of credible inferences from available evidence. What are these evidences? They include archaeological evidence, historical evidence, and textual evidence. We shall examine these in a very concise form below. The purpose is to illustrate the method.

At the outset, we need to stress that in an enquiry of the historic and pre-historic past, it is important to consider all available evidences in their totality. The following discussion, therefore, looks at the nature of evidences in brief.

Archaeological Evidence

It is rather incongruous to talk about archaeological evidence with respect to the Rigvedic people. Those pastoral nomadic people living in temporary settlements could hardly be expected to leave behind any signs of buildings or settlement.

Ancient Indian history and pre-history are found on three major archaeological discoveries of the 20th Century. They are:

1. The discovery of the Harappan civilization dating back to 2500 BC to 1800 BC,
2. The discovery of the Painted Grey Ware culture of 1200 BC to 800 BC, and
3. The discovery of the Northern Black Polished Ware culture of 600 BC to 300 BC

Dating the pre-historic period and even early historic periods is done on the basis of the well-known radio carbon dating method. This method has a difference in accuracy of plus or minus 100 years. Further, the conclusions based on this method have been arrived at by examining data from a large number of sites. Therefore, the radio carbon dating method is considered to be fairly reliable.

The Harappan civilization is the oldest and most extensive of the archaeological discoveries. Ample evidences of the existence of this civilization have been found in thousands of rural and urban habitations, covering the whole of Punjab and Sind in Pakistan, Gujarat, Rajasthan, Haryana, Punjab, Delhi and parts of western Uttar Pradesh in India. The Harappans had a very advanced culture compared to Mesopotamia and the Nile Valley and had extensive trade relations with the Sumerians. They seem to have nothing in common with the Rigvedic people and it is, therefore, assumed that the latter came to the subcontinent at a later point in time, probably at around 1500 BC. The Harappans worshiped both male and female Gods and it is possible that God Shiva and Goddess Shakti have their origins in the Harappan culture and religion. Although the Harappan civilization declined and the urban aspect of their culture disappeared from the scene, Harappan people continued to live in more scattered rural settlements, practising agriculture and animal husbandry. They also retained most of their religious beliefs and practices.

The post-Harappan period of this region is very pertinent but there are no major new discoveries until we approach 1200 BC. At this stage, we have archaeological evidences of a new distinctive culture which has been named as the Painted Grey Ware culture, based on the attributes of pottery used at that time around Delhi and on either side of the Yamuna River. This rural agricultural society used iron tools, even though small in numbers. There is no evidence of urban settlements. This is a pre-literate society with no kings or kingdoms and associated capital cities. The Painted Grey Ware culture more or less fits the type of society portrayed in the later Vedic and other related texts such as the *Yajurveda, Samaveda*, and the *Upanishads*. Over 300 rural settlements of this period, dating 1200 BC to 800 BC, have been excavated and evidence relating to this culture is fairly exhaustive.

At a still later point in time, from 600 BC to 300 BC, we have fresh evidence of a new culture which is characterized by incipient urbanization. Amidst a large number of rural settlements we also have a few urban settlements; the most notable being Kasi which is accepted to be India's oldest surviving city. This urban culture known to historians as the Northern Black Polished Ware culture extends over a vast area from Allahabad in the west to Patna in the east. The post-Vedic literature, starting with the *Sutras*, indicates an urban culture with kings and kingdoms and their names. The Northern Black Polished Ware culture is generally identified with the literary age of the *Sutras* when the art of writing dawned. This culture stands in contrast with that of the later Vedic texts. Historians have chronicled the events including the migration of people from west to east. Thus we have both archaeological and textual evidence for this period. They corroborate each other.

The archaeological evidences, though in skeletal form, are substantial enough to draw firm inferences as to the historicity of later Vedic texts and literature.

Historical Evidence

The historical method involves comparison and juxtaposition of various sources of information. In ancient Indian history, we have both foreign and domestic sources in several instances. The earliest external source available is information from Alexander's invasion of India in 326 BC. This has come to be accepted as an important historical datum line for judging other dates and periods in ancient Indian history.

Thus, Gautam Buddha's year of birth is placed at 560 BC. We have a heap of information on the Buddhist period from both Indian and foreign sources. Further, this literature leads us to the premise that the later Vedic period was partly contemporaneous with the Buddhist period. Thus, historians have placed the later Vedic period to the time when other *Vedas* and *Upanishads* were composed at around 1000 BC to 500 BC. The Rigvedic age is obviously earlier, roughly around 1500 BC to 1000 BC.

Textual Evidence

The Rigvedic text in itself is a massive source of authentic information on the society, habitat, livelihood and evidence on the life and time. Though the *Rigveda* is primarily a religious text, fortunately it contains lot of secondary non-religious details that prove very helpful in a study of this kind. The geographical and chronological information is rather scanty and tenuous. The textual evidence is still important and has to be examined in much greater detail and care than done in the past. In the past, people have jumped to conclusions. The study of textual evidence from the *Rigveda* requires expertise in human ecology; geographers and social anthropologists are best suited for this task.

In interpreting the Rigvedic texts, one requires versatile skills, complete mastery over Sanskrit, ability to decipher ancient scripts, flair and a lot of empathy for understanding the traditional meanings and interpretation of the Rigvedic texts and a foundation in the academic disciplines of history, geography, philosophy, linguistics, archaeology and social anthropology. It is humanly impossible for any individual to acquire all these skills and yet a firm rooting in these or even more is necessary to understand Rigvedic texts.

Rigvedic Society

Before we proceed further, it is appropriate to quote a well-known Rigvedic mantra that gives a fundamental insight into the lifestyle of the Rigvedic people:

> मा नस्तोके तनये मा न आयौ मानो गोषु मानो अश्वेषु रीरिषः।
> वीरान् मानो रुद्र भामितो वधी हविष्मन्तः सदमित् त्वा हवामहे।।

(*Rigveda*, Chapter 1, Section 114, Verse 8 by the poet Kutsa Angirasa in the *Jagadi* meter as a prayer to God Rudra)

This translates as:

> "Oh radiant Rudra! Do not hurt our sons and children, do not hurt our lives, do not hurt our cattle and our horses. Do not kill our warriors. We offer you all the sacrificial material placed here."

It is apparent that the Rigvedic people constituted a tribal community, whose main possessions were their cattle and horses. Their warriors too were important for their safeguard. This is clearly a pastoral nomadic society. This mantra is considered to be extremely important and sacred and even today it is commonly used in rituals as a protective prayer. The references to warriors are to a group of able men on horseback who provided security and protection to the Rigvedic people and their cattle. It is purely a defensive force.

The characterization of the Rigvedic society as 'tribal' should be considered in a positive light. Social anthropologists long ago gave up the adjective 'primitive' in connection with the word 'tribal'. They have emphasized the fact that tribal cultures were as advanced as any; in some ways tribes were more 'cultured' than some modern societies. The Rigvedic society had made great strides in religious thinking; the thoughts and values enshrined in the Rigvedic verses have lasting value and they hold good to humanity as a whole even today. This will become apparent as we reach the closing verses of the *Rigveda* in a later chapter.

Organization of Rigvedic Text

The Rigvedic text is very unique in many respects. It was composed by several poets who lived at various points in time, spanning centuries. Yet, it is not chronologically organized. Each verse is more or less independent of the other. Verses are unified author-wise or subject-wise (or both) which in most cases refer to a particular God or theme. Even in some cluster of verses obtained from a specific lineage of poets, the pattern lacks uniformity throughout. It is necessary to examine further to understand the complexities of the Rigvedic text as we know it today. The organization of the Rigvedic text is something that has been imposed upon from outside by the compilers.

Chapters

The *Rigveda* has a total of 10,552 verses which are divided into chapters, sections and verses. We have two independent systems of organization, namely the *ashtaka* and *mandala*. In *ashtaka*, the text is divided into eight chapters, which are sub-divided into eight *adhyayas*. The number eight was mystic in the days of the *sutrakaras* or poets who composed *sutras* or aphorisms. Panini's *Ashtadhyayi* and Pantanjali's *Ashtanga Raja Yoga* are well-known examples. One may note here that the *gayatri mantra* consists of 24 syllables divided into three parts of eight each. The significance of numbers eight and three is clearly emphasized here. Our study follows the *mandala* system in which the text is divided into ten *mandalas* or chapters, which are then sub-divided into 1,028 *suktas* or sections containing a variable number of verses.

At this stage one might ask the reason behind dividing the text into 10 *mandalas*. The answer is not clear, but there are a set of possibilities. An obvious choice of criteria would be the chronological order of either the verses or their authors; since the available information is inadequate, much of it is inferential in nature. A second possibility is to organize the chapters in terms of lineages of authors. There are several prominent lineages of authors or poets; the most notable one being Vashishtha. Chapter 7 of the *Rigveda* is entirely devoted to verses composed by poets from this lineage. In Chapter 5, the poets of the Atri lineage are predominant. The rest of the chapters have poets drawn from several lineages. The problem is that the verses came down the generations either through father-son path or teacher-student line. In tracking down the agnatic line, we face the problem of kinship; all marriages were between inter-lineages (later called as *gotras*) and never from within, and as a result, members of different lineages were closely knit. It is well known that the *Rigveda* came to us from families of different *gotras*. However, the verses remembered by them relate to poets of different lineages or *gotras*. A third possibility is to organize the text in terms of the gods to whom the prayers are addressed. The problem here is that *Agni*, the Fire God, would occupy a lion's share (40 per cent) followed by *Indra* who would take about one-fourth. There are several hundred verses devoted to Brihaspathi, the father of the Rigvedic religion. Other senior poets such as Vashishtha, Bharadwaja, Jamadagni, Atri and others also have a large number of verses addressed to them. Besides there are other Gods, including the sun, the moon, earth, water, air and so on. The chapters would be far too numerous and very unequal in size in this method.

The present organization of the *Rigveda* into ten *mandalas* is a compromise framework and it should be looked at from the point of view of the compiler who had a difficult task in hand.

At the outset it may be mentioned that while some chapters are clearly organized, others may be considered as expedient collections. Furthermore, it is important to note that the opening and the closing sections of the *Rigveda* have been very carefully selected. The opening verses depict the importance of *Agni*, the focus of the Rigvedic religion, and the closing verses consist of a parting advice by a poet-teacher of perhaps the post-Rigvedic period in which the value of the Rigvedic learning and its objectives are stressed.

Sections

The sections within a chapter in the *Rigveda* stand apart as independent entities in themselves; there is no particular order in presentation. The sections by and large represent a cluster of verses that were memorized and recited together. They often have one author or sometimes more who hail from the same lineage or are inter-related in terms of kinship or student-teacher relationships. They are also devoted to a specific God(s) who are similar in some way or the other.

The most common system of sections is called *suktas*; the alternate one is known as *varga*. There are some other types of sections as well. In the text followed here, the chapters are divided into *suktas* and each *sukta* has a number of verses. *Sukta* literally means well said. The heading for each *sukta* includes the name of the author(s), the name(s) of the Gods, and the meter(s) in which the verses are composed. These *suktas* have come to us from a specific source in each case and are not a collection of verses from different sources or families. However, often several families would recite the same, since these have come to them in similar way, from generation to generation.

Some *suktas* have high ritualistic value. They focus on a theme or God or a natural phenomenon. Most *suktas* also have only one author, a *rishi* or poet. The term *rishi* here is specific to Rigvedic poets and should not be confused with those of Puranic literature, as in Puranic literature *rishis* appear as legendary characters who are immortal. It is very important to emphasize and remember this point always.

Verses

The word *'rik'* in the *Rigveda* actually means a verse and thus *Rigveda* means knowledge in verses. The verses are also known as mantras which in literal terms means advice or instruction. There are many verses that are renowned and held to be extremely sacred. One such mantra is the *gayatri mantra* which is an invocation to the Sun God; this mantra is held to be the key to the whole of Rigvedic knowledge. The verse is as follows:

तत् सवितुर्वरेण्यं। भर्गो देवस्य धीमहि।
धियो यो नः प्रचोदयात्।।

(*Rigveda*, Chapter 3, Section 62, and Verse 10)

This translates as:

> "That which belongs to the sun is highly desirable, the radiance of the God is most illuminating, that which you (the Sun) possess, let that inspire us."

The above verse appears repeatedly in various chapters of the *Rigveda* and other *Vedas*, signifying the reverence attached to this mantra. It is important to note that in all compiled works (*Shruti* texts) there is considerable repetition; one may hazard the guess that the verses which are repeated most often are the ones held to be highly sacred than the others.

We have seen that each verse in a section is more or less independent and can be interpreted without reference to other verses. The linkage, if any, with subsequent verses is indirect. Each mantra expresses a wish or a prayer and highlights an aspect of a natural phenomenon. These subtle poetic expressions give us deep insight into the relationship between man and God and natural phenomena. The mantras are also valuable in understanding human ecology during the Rigvedic period.

The Rigvedic verses are composed in one of several meters. The discovery of the oldest and the most sacred *gayatri* meter by Angiras is probably the most important event that has made the *Rigveda* an outstanding text of all times. Nothing can even remotely match the *gayatri* meter verses in their eloquence, splendour and style. Although a total of 19 meters are used in the verses, three stand out, as they account for 75 per cent—*thrishtup* over 40 per cent, *gayatri* about 23 per cent, and *jagadi* about 13 per cent. Of the remaining, other five meters like *anushtup*, *pankti*, *ushnik*, *brihati*, and *dwapada virat* account for between 100 and 1,000 verses. The progress in terms of discovery of new meters was perhaps quite slow.

We need to emphasize that all the verses may not belong to the Rigvedic period. A considerable number was probably introduced in the later Vedic period, particularly to justify newer ideas which in fact have nothing in common with the *Rigveda*. The *Rigveda* is always quoted as the authority on every subject. Obviously, many important and great ideas originated at later points in time and although their authors were indeed great men, the acceptability of their ideas was easier if they are traced to the *Rigveda*. The authors of many great works did not even bother to mention their names for the same reason. For example, the authors of the *Upanishads* and the *Bhagavad Gita* did not append their names to their work.

How can we determine whether a verse belongs to the Rigvedic period? Fortunately, there is a clear rule of thumb. If a verse has the pronouns 'us' and 'we', it most likely belongs to Rigvedic period. On the other hand, if a verse emphasizes the pronoun 'I' it most likely belongs to the later Vedic period. These pronouns reveal the transformation from an egalitarian tribal society to an individualistic feudal society.

Conclusion

The *Rigveda* is perhaps the least read or understood of all our sacred scriptures. It is often cited as an authority but no actual references to verses are given. The Rigvedic text, unlike the sacred texts of other world religions, is not readily available in book shops. Sanskrit text of the *Rigveda* is available only in a handful or very specialized book shops in a few major cities of India. The *Rigveda* is often considered to be very voluminous and tedious to read. The fact is that no one has cared to make this sacred work available to the public and in a simple form. It is true that this will require a large investment and equally large subsidy.

There are a few interpretations of sections and individual verses of the *Rigveda* which focus on the spiritual side. My own view is that some of these spiritual interpretations distort the meaning of the verses and do little justice to the poetic work of the great *rishis*. Popular perceptions of the *Rigveda* reach euphoric heights, but they are not based on facts. Mere sentiment is not adequate justification for true understanding of a great text.

The problem is that those who know Sanskrit have little or no knowledge of ancient Indian history or its siblings like social science disciplines. A good knowledge of social science is a prerequisite for understanding the *Rigveda*. Mere religiousness and knowledge of Sanskrit are not adequate. On the other hand, the great majority of historians and social scientists in India do not have adequate knowledge of Sanskrit and hence are unable to comment on relative issues. We need to bring the knowledge of Sanskrit with an understanding of the methodology of social sciences to arrive at a true evaluation of the value and meaning of the Rigvedic text.

Names, words and even verses found in the *Rigveda* are occasionally wrongly used in the Puranic and later literature. For example, the word *ganapathy* used in a very famous verse in the *Rigveda* in praise of Brihaspathi is equated with Lord Ganesh, a God of recent origin, giving the impression that this God is of Rigvedic origin. But this is certainly not true. There are many such examples. One has to be very skeptical of recent interpretations of the *Rigveda*.

The *Rigveda* is an outstanding and incomparable work of art created by people of exceptional merit who lived a long time ago. Nevertheless, it is about very simple people who lived with nature close to their heart. It is not possible to describe the *Rigveda* in great detail in this book. However, after reading it entirely, I have come to the conclusion that it is best explained by studying the cluster of opening and closing verses. In the following two chapters, I have tried to bring the essence of the *Rigveda* by quoting these verses in original and explaining their meaning.

Four

Opening Verses of *Rigveda*

Introduction

Rigvedic verses are prayers addressed to various Gods that represent natural elements which impact the lives of the people significantly. They basically describe how the Rigvedic people perceived the geographical environment and responded to it. Nature was seen both as provider of food and means of sustenance and a powerful catastrophic force. They admired and feared this phenomenon.

A little over of one-third of the Rigvedic verses are devoted to fire, or *Agni*. The word encompasses both natural and man-made fire as well as the Fire God. The compiler of the *Rigveda* begins with nine verses in praise of God *Agni* composed by Madhuchanda Vishwamitra, a descendent of the prominent Viswamitra lineage, in the *gayatri* meter. We already know the sacredness and importance of this meter and *Bhagavad Gita,* pronounces it be dearest to Lord Krishna. The first nine verses by no means are the oldest and probably belong to the middle phase. The Rigvedic poets span over 20 generations and an intervening time period of about 500 years. When the *Rigveda* was being actually compiled several centuries later, *smriti* age had already blossomed.

The nine verses on *Agni* describe the role of *Agni* in the ordinary life of the Rigvedic people. They appear below in the Devanagari script, followed by a literal translation and an explanatory note aimed to present a very simple and straight forward meaning.

Verse 1

अग्निमीडे पुरोहितं यज्ञस्य देवमृत्विजम्।
होतारम् रत्नधातयम्।।

"I praise *Agni*, the *purohit*, the God of *yajna* and *ritwik*, the *hota* or reciter of Vedic verses, verses that are the very best gems."

While the *purohit* makes all preparations for the sacrificial ceremony called *yajna*, the *ritwik* performs the physical acts, as for example, the offering of the oblations. Other categories of priests are not mentioned here but they are 16 in number and the same person can perform one or more duties that are interchangeable. The Brahman is the senior-most or chief priest who supervises the *yajna*. He is the master of the ceremony and sits on a high pedestal. His instructions are to be implicitly followed. The word Brahmana is not to be confused with other connotations of the word in subsequent times. These categories should also not to be confused with surnames or *gotras* of the present times.

What this mantra says is that *Agni* being a priest himself, represents all categories of priests. In this case, *Agni* is equated with Angiras, who was the first priest poet among the Rigvedic people. Sometimes a father-son relationship is imputed to them.

In Rigvedic verses, every God has many names and the same descriptive name is applied to different Gods as well. Thus the word *vrishan* may be of *Agni*, *Indra*, or *Soma*. This casts doubt and leads to multiple or contrasting interpretations or inferences. Such usage is common in India even now, causing considerable confusion to layman.

Verse 2

अग्निः पूर्वेभिर्ऋषिभि रीडयो नूतनैरुत।
सदेवाँ एह वक्षति।।

"*Agni* was praised by our ancestors and *rishis* (poets) and also by present day men. He, *Agni*, grows powerful like the Gods."

This verse tries to emphasize the importance of *Agni*, first by saying that it has always been held in high esteem by the ancestors and equally by the poets. The poets or *rishis* were part of the tribal community and everyone enjoyed more or less equal status in a tribal society. Poets find mention as they held a special place in this community. After all, it is the poets who praised *Agni* with their verses. For the sake of continuity, the contemporaries of the poet Madhuchanda Vishwamitra are also mentioned as having high regard for *Agni*.

Is *Agni* praise worthy? Why? The reasons given are that *Agni* is both God and friend; it has many fundamental uses for mankind; it is the only medium between people on earth and the Gods above; and it has the potential to become very powerful like other Gods. However, Rigvedic people believed that *Agni*, the God, took pity on men on earth and agreed to be domesticated for their use. Rigvedic people knew how to produce fire by rubbing stones. This was the method in vogue for thousands of years. While *Agni* is considered docile in the domestic and ritual situations, the wild *Agni* becomes very powerful and destructive. People can set fire to grass and even trees and use fire as a weapon or powerful tool against enemies.

Verse 3

अग्निना रयिश्रवत् पोषमेव दिवे दिवे।
यशसं वीरवत्तमम्।।

"Eating food cooked in fire is very nourishing day after day. It is very tasty and most strengthening."

The first and foremost use of *Agni* is for cooking food. Raw food is definitely less attractive than cooked food. Although this might sound mundane, it is very relevant in the context of the Rigvedic people having not used spices or even salt. Throughout the Rigvedic text there are numerous simple statements; they are factual and easy to understand; some are witty and others refer to common human acts that are nowadays not publicly expressed.

Verse 4

अग्ने यं यज्ञमध्वरं विश्वतः परिभूरसि।
स इद् देवेषु गच्छति।।

"In *Agni,* the oblations that are fully and meticulously offered, certainly reach the Gods."

Agni is the courier and messenger between man and God. But the question arises that who is 'you' in *paribhurasi*? The answer is the priest or *ritwik*. This is an instruction to the priest to carry out his duty with utmost care and only then the message will reach the Gods. This verse can be construed as a rationale for the performance of sacrifices in fire. It assigns a central role for *Agni* which is so unique to Rigvedic religion. In Islam and Christianity also we find a messenger of God in human form. In Puranic times, India also has seen many God men possessing supernatural powers on earth or who were acclaimed to be God's representative. *Agni* is a natural phenomenon and is impersonal. *Agni* is described as follows in a very famous Rigvedic verse:

चत्वारि शृङा त्रयो अस्य पादा द्वे शीर्षे
सत्प हस्तासो अस्य।

(*Rigveda*: 4.58.3)

"Four horns, three feet, two heads and seven hands he has!"

This verse is invariably used by the priest while kindling the sacrificial fire. It is a numerical description of the Fire God and the concept probably is inspired by the visual image of burning fire in the *homa*. The above verse is also significant since it assigns a form or shape for a God with an embodiment of nature.

Verse 5

अग्निर्होता कविक्रतुः सत्यश्चित्रश्रवस्तमः।
देवो देवेभिरा गमत्।।

(*Rigveda*: 1.1.5)

"Verses recited in front of *Agni* are brilliant, true and most famous. They are received by the Gods and responded to by them."

Agni conveys to Gods the messages which may consist of praises of Gods or prayers to them. *Agni* also brings back gifts from the Gods. *Bhagavad Gita* mentions the two-way relationship between man and God; they contribute to mutual welfare (Chapter 3, Verses 10 to 19).

Gods accept oblations and praises of their deeds and powers and are pleased by these actions of man. In return, they provide rain, ensure fertility of the soil and plentiful supply of grass for the cattle, and thereby take care of the welfare of people.

The verses composed by *rishis* are very important as they provide a sacred language that is understood by the Gods. It was believed that nothing can match the beauty, magic and mystic of the verses. The Rigvedic verses are as important as *Agni* itself in the Rigvedic religion.

Oblations are things offered as sacrifice to the Gods. What were these oblations in Rigvedic times? These were mostly meat, which was obtained by sacrificing cattle (the male calf) tied to a sacred tree or pole. Milk, sour milk or yoghurt, and clarified butter were also offered. The Rigvedic people also offered *soma ras*, the juice of the *soma* plant. The plant has not been identified so far since its use was discontinued a long time ago (before 1000 BC). Among all the items mentioned above, only clarified butter is offered currently as per the Vedic rituals. Basically, the oblations consisted of the food items that the Rigvedic people normally took. There is no mention of grains in the Rigvedic verses. Centuries later, cooked rice was offered as oblation or *bali* in place of meat that probably answers the criticism of Jainism and Buddhism on Hindu religious practices.

Verse 6

यदङ्ग दाशुषे त्व मग्ने भद्रं करिष्यसि।
तवेत् तत् सत्यमङ्गिरः।।

> "Whatever you offer to *Agni* should be done very carefully, and must be true to Angiras."

All forms of worship and sacrifices should conform strictly to what Angiras has prescribed. The following Rigvedic verse dedicated to Brihaspathi (Angiras) is invariably recited even today in all Vedic rituals:

गणानां त्वा गणपतिं हवामहे कविं कवीनामुपमश्रवस्तमम्।
ज्येष्टराजं ब्रह्मणां ब्रह्मणस्पत आ नः शृण्वश्रतिभिः सीढ सादनम्।।

(*Rigveda*: 2.23.1)

> "You are the greatest and the most incomparable poet of all. Your are the leader of the collegiums of poets. You are the doyen of the chief priests and their lord. Alas! Your voice and its effect are like the sound produced by the *vajra* (the weapon of the Vedic God *Indra*)."

The reference here is to thunder and lightning.

Angiras has a very special place in Rigvedic religion. He is often equated with *Agni* and the process of transforming historical and real persons into Gods or legendary characters had begun in the Rigvedic period itself, but this is restricted to the chief poets.

In Puranic literature, Brihaspathi is shown as the preceptor of the Gods (*devas*) while Sukracharya is the preceptor of the *Asuras* or demons. Brihaspathi, people still believe, knows everything—the past, the present, and the future. He is an embodiment of all knowledge and yet detached. He is teacher or guru supreme. He is the father figure of the Hindus. Thus, the *Puranas* have only enlarged the legends of the *Rigveda* in this case.

Verse 7

उप त्वाग्ने दिवे दिवे दोषावस्तर्धिया वयम्।
नमो भरन्त एमसि।।

> "Oh *Agni*! We are placed under very hard times. We worship you day after day. You are the way filled with food."

This verse focusses on the hard times of the Rigvedic people. What is meant by hard times? What is the role of *Agni* then? In the Rigvedic times, the community depended on grass for feeding cattle and horses. The end of the summer season before the onset of monsoon was the hardest time of the year. Food and water for cattle and man were really scarce. At this time, ironically it might appear to be, the practice was to deliberately burn the remaining dry grass and then wait for the rains. When rains come, grass grows luxuriously and provides food for cattle. The verse is an allusion to this age-old practice. The world over people have used fire to remove weeds and dead grass to provide fertilizer to the soil. *Agni* does play an important role here. This practice brings food in plenty after the rains and hence *Agni* is the way filled with food.

After the grass had been set on fire, the Rigvedic people performed rituals in front of *Agni* invoking *Indra* and *Varuna*, the God of thunder and clouds, and the God of water or rain respectively. In a short while, thunder, lightening and rain followed by way of summer showers. The prayers of the community have been answered. If not, they would assume that they have committed error in their prayers and the Gods are not pleased. Their only choice then is to perform the sacrifices meticulously again.

Verse 8

राजन्तमध्वराणां गोपामृतस्य दीदीविम्।
वर्धमानं स्वेदमे।।

> "Resplendent *Agni*! Protector of immortality, glowing furiously with the oblations, you grow even more powerful when attempted to control."

When fuel is added to fire, it becomes bigger and very difficult to control. Similarly when grasslands are set on fire by people in the Rigvedic age, no one could control it. *Yajna* and the oblations offered to *Agni* make it so powerful beyond the power of man. This is good for the performer of the *yajna* and bad for the enemies by implication. The burning fire of the *yajna* is a symptom of the success of the worship of *Agni*. *Agni* is to be worshipped only when the flames are fully visible.

Verse 9

स नः पितेव सूनवे ऽग्ने सूषायनो भव।
सचस्वा नः स्वस्तये।।

> "He (*Agni*) to us is like a father to his children. Oh *Agni*! Please cause births to take place. Assist us in our welfare."

This verse makes a general appeal to the fire God to help the tribal community in its welfare. This is appropriate as it is the last verse of this introductory section of nine verses.

Agni here is portrayed as a father figure much like the stud bull in a herd of cattle. The symbolism of the bull is very important in the Rigvedic culture and word *vrishan* (the bull) appears time and again in the verses. The role of the bull is to cause the birth of calves and increase the size of the herd. The number of cattle is a measure of wealth to the Rigvedic people and is very much desired. So also the Rigvedic people desired children so that their number would also increase. A larger community having many warriors can defend itself better and is less vulnerable to attack. This verse appeals to *Agni* the God, rather than *Agni*, the natural phenomenon.

Invocation to *Agni*

The opening verses of the *Rigveda* highlight the role and importance of *Agni*, the Fire God and the natural phenomenon. The very fact that the original compiler thought it appropriate to start with these verses on *Agni* is significant. It is an impressive and most appropriate introduction to the text containing 10,552 verses.

It is in the fitness of things to conclude this section with an invocation to *Agni* with another verse taken from the first chapter of the *Rigveda*:

अग्ने नय सुपथा राये अस्मान् विश्वानि देव वयुनानि विद्वान्।
युयोध्यडस्यमज्जुहुराणमेनो भूयिष्टां ते नमउक्तिं विधेम।।

(*Rigveda:* 1.89.1)

"Lord *Agni*! Lead us along the right paths, the universal paths of the Gods, the illuminated paths of learned men. Destroy our sins and crooked acts (acts of omission and commission). We offer you plenty of food and praise."

This verse is recited during all Vedic rituals. *Agni* is the beacon of light; all men depend on it.

Five

Closing Verses of *Rigveda*

Transition from Tribal to Feudal Society

The concluding verses of the *Rigveda* reflect the drastic departure from a tribal nomadic society wedded to community welfare to that of a semi-feudal society lorded by lineages of priests, warriors, agriculturists and others. It was inevitable since the Rigvedic people migrated to an area inhabited predominantly by other agricultural communities. There was no room for isolation as the competition for land for grazing and farming was severe and there was little scope for shifting to newer pastures as the lands further to the east were dense forests.

Rigvedic people had already moved from the Indus basin towards the Yamuna region where a new plural society centering on agriculture was emerging as evidenced archaeologically. This society was the Painted Grey Ware culture. The later verses of the *Rigveda* were probably composed in this region when the society lost its tribal character and was marching towards a stable peasant agricultural society.

In this situation, lineages were a social frame. The other lineages such as poets and priests, warriors, farmers, cattle herders, and a host of others like potters, weavers, smiths, etc., who ethnically differed from Rigvedic people, exerted considerable pressure or influence due to their sheer numbers as proved by circumstantial evidence.

The Rigvedic people were webbed into three lineages—priests, warriors, and farmers. Priests enjoyed a unique position due to their mastery of mantras. The notable point is that Rigvedic people lived peacefully with others. These societies ultimately led to the emergence of a feudal system in which *jati* formed the building blocks of society. Indian society at the village level was still a conglomerate of numerous *jatis, ab initio* of pre-Rigvedic times. The *varna* concept emerged in later Vedic times. Here *jati* or caste construes an endogamous group of people by occupation, language, religion, or ethnicity or a combination of all. The later Rigvedic verses indicate this transition comprehensively.

***Gurukula* System**

With the end of the tribal way of life, the role of the priests and poets had to undergo many changes. They specialized in the preservation of the Rigvedic verses and the related rituals and adapted them to suit the needs of the new social order and environment. Three objectives were primary—to protect and preserve the Rigvedic tradition; pass on the knowledge to the newer generation; and provide ritual services to lineages that specialized in other occupations.

The more learned among the priestly class destabilized their lives to establish homes away from the society to practice the traditions of the Rigvedic society. Importantly, they imparted training to those who were interested. The boys stayed with the family of teachers for many years and were treated as an extension of family. Everyone had to do all the chores of life including tending of cattle. Cattle were an important part of this system because it perpetuated the ambience of the Rigvedic times. This is what is known as the *gurukula* system. The more important poets and teachers of later periods continued to emulate Samvanana's tradition.

The students in the *gurukula* came primarily from the priestly class, though some outsiders were also admitted. The criteria of admission were their ability and suitability. Initially, it must have been a self-sustaining entity but with the passage of time, the system needed financial support. However, in Samvanana's time the practice of accepting gifts was absent.

After five to fifteen years of study, the students left the ashram to pursue their career as priests in their places of origin or wherever opportunity presented. Some of the students went to others for further study or specialization as well.

Parting Advice of Teacher

When students left for their homes after completion of training, the teachers formally gave them the parting advice. The closing verses of the *Rigveda* reflect the beginning of this tradition. The concluding part of the *Rigveda* consists of four verses by the poet *rishi* Samvanana Angirasa, a descendent of Angiras. These verses are in *anushtup* and *trishtup* meters of subsequent period. Samvanana Angirasa probably taught the Rigvedic verses he knew and specialized in. He was apparently a well-known erudite.

There were three main sub-divisions of the original lineage of Angiras, namely the Kevala Angirasa, the Gautama Angirasa and the Bharadwaja Angirasa. Samvanana belonged to the first of these sub-divisions.

The compiler of the *Rigveda* chose these verses not only for their beautiful lyrical qualities but also for its intrinsic values. These verses sum up the rationale for the study of the *Rigveda* and the practice of the Rigvedic rituals and as such are even applicable to one and all in the contemporary world. They have a lasting value and are widely quoted without understanding their meaning. They are explained below.

Verse 1

संसमिधुवसे वृषन्नग्ने विश्वान्यर्य आ।
इदस्पदे समिध्यसे स नो वसून्या भर।।

(*Rigveda*: 10.191.1)

"You shall praise and glorify the universally honored bull *Agni*. Most worthy of praise, you offer fuel to him. He will bestow us wealth."

The concluding advice begins with the need to invoke *Agni*, the Fire God. We may note here that the *Rigveda* started with verses pertaining to the role and importance of *Agni*. Also the worship of *Agni* is specifically for wealth or welfare of all. There is no reference to children, warriors, cows, or horses. Samvanana is definitely not thinking of a tribal society when he uses the term 'us', but a more diversified society of priests, warriors, farmers, herders, artisans, etc. Perhaps it meant only the student-teacher community alone and hence the prayer for wealth for all. Nevertheless, the prayer is still for 'us'—a Rigvedic value. Most

Rigvedic verses have time and again emphasized the value of oneness and togetherness. The welfare of the family and individual are never mentioned. All religion is for the community as a whole. This indeed is the core value of the Rigvedic religion.

In the above verse, the poet advises his students to worship *Agni* diligently for the welfare of everyone.

Verse 2

सं गच्छध्वं सं वदध्वं सं वो मनांसि जानताम्।
देवा भागं यथा पूर्वे संजानाना उपासते।।

(*Rigveda*: 10.191.2)

"You all go together, you all speak together, let your minds understand together (have common understanding).
The worship of Gods mentioned earlier is done for harmonious living and common understanding."

The worship of Gods may mean just *Agni*, as mentioned in the first invocatory verse or the entire course of teaching that Samvanana offered. The latter interpretation appears to be more appropriate.

Unity and harmony in words, deeds and understanding are the key values to be cherished by all students graduating from the *gurukula*. The worship of *Agni* and the other Gods is solely for this purpose. The teacher may in fact deprecate the use of the Rigvedic religion for personal gain, a practice that was already gaining ground. The students have been taught not only the verses of the *Rigveda* but also the rules for performance of rituals of *homa* and *yajna*. These were carried out on a daily basis at the guru's ashram. The injunction to students is to use this training properly.

There is also the possibility that the apprehension in mind of Samvanana was abut the wrong interpretations and use of the verses and the competition in society for fame and wealth that he wanted his students to avoid. In the context of rapid social changes, Samvanana re-emphasized the old tribal values of togetherness and harmonious living which was the need of the hour. Samvanana must have been the leading teacher of his time and he probably was dealing with mature and adult students who joined his camp after studying in schools of lower standards. Hence his advice has to be taken very seriously as they represent a very carefully considered view of a learned person

Verse 3

समानो मन्त्रः समितिः समानी समानं मनः सह चित्तमेषाम्।
समानं मन्त्रमभि मन्त्रये वः समानेन वो हविषा जुहोमि।।,

(*Rigveda*: 10.191.3)
"You have received equal instruction. You are an assembly of equals. Your minds and intellects are equal. I counsel to you the principle of equality. With equal measure of oblations, I pray for you all."

It is the duty of a teacher to impart everything that he knew to all students in equal measure. Nothing is to be hidden, for knowledge is for all. Samvanana was instructing his students to practice his preaching when they become teachers in due course. Guru's advice was considered to be mandatory and inviolable.

The emphasis on equality—a word that is repeated often in this verse—has to be judged against the backdrop of the then prevailing social trend which was of increasing inequality among people. The tribal value of equality among men belonging to different lineages and occupations was giving way to unequal powers and privileges. This ultimately led to the feudal system where inequalities were the very manifest and were accepted as normal. The varna system is based upon this feudal principle of inequality. In the feudal system, kings and nobles, wealthy traders, warriors, and administrators stood apart from the common artisans, cattle herders and farmers. The priestly class was marginalized economically and weak in this system; and often it became impoverished and dependent on other segments of society. Their stock with the artisans, farmers and herders were however high, but they received grudging respect from the kings and wealthy traders. Kings were even scared of the priestly class because of the overwhelming influence they wielded among the masses that could be easily used to overthrow them. This scenario belongs to a later time period, different from Samvanana's time when here were no kings and no acrimony between the priestly class and the warrior lineages.

Samvanana's parting advice is more platitudinal in nature and it enshrines nostalgia for the egalitarian tribal life.

Verse 4

समानी व आकूतिः समाना हृदयानि वः।
समानमस्तु वो मनो यथा वः सुसहासति।।

(*Rigveda*: 10.191.4)

"Let your aspirations be equal
Let your hearts be equal
Let your minds be equal
In whatever manner you are made to rejoice."

This is a sublime and ethereal benediction from a learned teacher to his students on the day of parting. This verse and the verses above are often used as invocation in functions of graduating students in Indian universities today.

Samvanana appears to have distanced himself from his students who are about to enter a different society. Teachers in the *gurukula* system always distanced themselves from the society outside, which they detested for its cruel and selfish ways. There is a general weariness of outside world among poets and teachers, and this becomes even evident in the case of the Upanishadic poets and their students.

Samvanana's parting advice stands in contrast to the invocation used by the celebrated poet of the *Kathopanishad* which is as follows:

सहनाववतु। सहनौ भुनक्तु।
सहवीर्यम् करवावहै।
तेजस्वी नाव अधीतमस्तु।
माविद्विषावहै।।
ओम् शान्तिः शान्तिः शान्तिः

"Protect the two of us. Feed the two of us.
Let the two of us be courageous,
Let what we learn be brilliant and famous,
Let the two of us not mistrust each other,
Oh God! Let there be Tranquility! Tranquility! Tranquility!"

This invocation is also often recited in rituals and other occasions. It focuses on the teacher and the student. The 'us' of Rigvedic religion is totally absent. The society outside the student-teacher milieu is ignored. This is indeed highly individualistic in value system for which the *Upanishads* are well known. In the *Upanishads,* the self is supreme, society is irrelevant and something to be abhorred if not altogether avoided. While Samvanana emphasizes Rigvedic values of equality, togetherness, and welfare of all, *Kathopanishad* focuses on self and student.

Furthermore, the line "let us not mistrust each other" is anticlimactic on the whole. There is a wedge between the *Rigveda* and the *Kathopanishad*—a gap of time and social change.

What is the mistrust between the teacher and the student? Around 500 BC, the lineages had weakened. The student of other lineages or none at all spied on the good teachers to extract knowledge and use it for other purposes or for self gain. The teachers were highly protective of their knowledge, for knowledge was power and fame. The students were apprehensive that teachers may not teach everything to them. In the *upanayana* ceremony (the initiation of a child into bachelorhood), the father as guru teaches the *gayatri mantra* as a secret to the child. This is called *brahmopadesam*—advice to the student about the secret knowledge of the Absolute God. The *gayatri mantra* is never to be loudly recited. The net effect of all this is mistrust between the teacher and students.

Unfortunately, with Samvanana the Rigvedic tradition came to an end and individualism and social inequalities with their attendant mistrust came to the fore.

Invocation to Brihaspathi

It is appropriate to conclude this study of the closing verses of the *Rigveda* with an invocation to Brihaspathi drawn from the *Samaveda,* the third *Veda,* considered as his dearest by Lord Krishna in the *Bhagavad Gita.*

Brihaspathi is the founder of the Rigvedic religion and exemplary guru of all Hindus. This verse was composed a long time after the end of the Rigvedic era; it does, however, emphasize the supreme authority of the Rigvedic tradition. The following is the last and concluding verse of the *Samaveda*:

ओम् स्वस्ति नो ब्रृहस्पतिर्दधातु।
स्वास्ति नो बृहस्पतिर्दधातु।।

"Oh Brahman! Let Brihaspathi uphold our welfare.
Let Brihaspathi uphold our welfare."

Six

Vedic Religion

Overview

The following three verses drawn from the *Vedas* define the Vedic religion:

ओम् तत् सवितुर्वरेण्यं। भर्गो देवस्य धीमहि।
धियो यो नः प्रचोदयात्।।

इशा वास्यमिदं सर्व यन्किं च जगन्यां जगत्।

असावादिन्ये ब्रह्म ब्रह्मैवाहमस्मि ओम् खम् ब्रह्म।।

First prerequisite is the complete memorization of the verses and thorough understanding of their meaning. To begin with, one could recite them from the text daily at least for 15 minutes loudly as *japa*. In the initial stage, this may help in focussing the meaning of the statements. Care must be taken to pronounce the verses in proper manner. After complete mastery, they are to be switched over to meditation mode, in total silence as *dhyana*. At this time, the mind is focussed on the *Brahman*, the

Absolute God. Once this is accomplished the self merges with the infinite and attains bliss that will banish the sense of pleasure and pain instantly. Meditation requires diligent and determined practice and its powers can be felt only slowly. Once the goal is achieved, one can have permanent peace of mind. This is the Vedic religion.

Source and Meaning

The three mantras given above are taken from the *Rigveda* and the *Yajurveda*. The first, known to all as the *gayatri mantra* (*Rigveda:* 3.62.10), is very sacred and is believed to represent the *Vedas* in a nutshell. It is repeated during the *sandhya vandana* or the daily ritual of Brahmanas (*nitya karma*).

The mantra is prefixed by the *akshara* 'Om' which signifies the Absolute God or the *Brahman*. This practice was introduced after the Rigvedic period, but has been followed ever since. The *gayatri mantra* translates as follows:

> "That which the sun possesses is highly desirable. The God's radiance is highly enlightening. Oh Sun, that which you possess, let that inspire us and take us forward."

This mantra is obviously addressed to the Sun God. The word 'us' includes everyone. Here the world is but one family—*vasudaiva kutumbakam* or universal family.

The second mantra is from the *Yajurveda* (40.01) and it is the first of 17 mantras, most of which are taken from the *Isavasyopanishad* and a few from the *Rigveda*.

The mantra means that God resides in whatever that lives or moves in this world.

This is a basic principle that all living things deserve equal respect since God resides in each one of them.

The third mantra is also from the *Yajurveda* (40.17). I have used a later modified version as it is recited in the *sandhya vandana* rituals instead of the original verse.

The meaning of the mantra is in two parts: in this sun *Brahman* exists; that *Brahman* is me (note: not in me but me). The sky or the cosmos is Brahman.

This statement is central to the spiritual realization of the Atman (or the self) and *Brahman* (the Absolute God), which are one and the same. This realization leads to permanent happiness.

Sun as Objective God

Agni and Sun (as divine objects) occupy a central position in the Vedic religion. *Agni* is the representative of the Sun on Earth. Both provide light and heat and are basic to human life. Only man among animals has a measure of control over *Agni* in the sense of fire and he alone has a concept of God. Fire is a phenomenon and not really an object, while the Sun is an object that one can see but beyond human control. The Sun is distant and unapproachable, but infinitely more powerful and important than fire. Hence, even while fire is worshipped, its essential function is as a medium between man and the Gods. The worship of fire is not an end in itself but a means to an end. In the daily rituals of the Hindus, the oil light represents the God *Agni*.

The *gayatri mantra* places the Sun as the objective God next in importance to the Absolute God or Brahman, which is abstract, and beyond human cognition. It may be noted here that the Brahman is infinitely more powerful than the Sun, and there are several billion stars like the Sun in the universe.

At a level below that of the Sun, *Agni* is a God that is both a master and servant. It is believed that *Agni* came to Earth to serve man.

The Sun is the most important object in the universe from human point of view. Life on earth is made possible by the sun and it influences our lives on a daily basis. Morning and evening, day and night, summer and winter determine life rhythms. Sun's influence is essential to all life and especially to vegetation. Animals depend on vegetation. There is what is known as the food chain which ultimately depends on sun rays.

The Sun is responsible for the origin of life on earth and the evolution of species. Sun's ultraviolet radiation is the key to mutation of genes and the origin of new species and higher forms of life that we cannot even see with the naked eye. The intricacies of the basic unit of life, the DNA, is as complex as the universe itself. The micro and macro factors represent *terra incognita*, awaiting future exploration.

The Sun is the source of energy to plants and animals alike. Coal, petroleum and natural gas are but derivatives of solar radiation. Hydroelectricity is a by-product of the atmospheric processes. Ocean currents, atmospheric circulation and the hydrological cycle are dependent on the Sun. Thus all atmospheric phenomena depend on the solar system.

In spite of the above, the Earth actually harnesses only a tiny fraction of Sun's radiation and the rest goes to all other planets and outer space. One can imagine the magnitude of Sun's energy resource. The Sun has been emitting its energy for billions of years and will continue to do so for another billion years at least. Thus, the Sun is *nityam* or everlasting—a concept that is so important in the delineation of the *Brahman*. The Sun, then, is veritably the *Brahman* itself.

God Exists in All Living Things

We have said that the Sun had a role in the origin of life on earth and it continues to sustain life on them. The Sun represents the Absolute God (*Brahman*) at the macro level and micro level or the lowest order of life. And one can call it the soul or Atman or by any other name. The Vedic people knew that God exists in all living things.

The Vedic people were not aware of the origin of life or the evolution of species. Nevertheless, the total dependence of all life forms on the Sun was easily discernible. It is this basic fact that underlines the notion of God residing in every living object.

All life is in effect sacred and in equal measure. All living things on earth live in a symbiotic relationship—a sort of balance of nature. Disturbing this balance can cause species to become extinct. Man has altered the face of the earth a great deal and has caused considerable harm to the soil, vegetation, and animal life. Man's numbers have increased manifold and his desire to live in greater and greater comfort is causing harm to ecology. The fear is that this may lead to his destruction in the long run.

Man should respect all life and given his knowledge, he has the responsibility to protect all living things and thereby ensure his own survival and the survival of the earth habitat that the Sun (*Brahman*) has created.

Look for God Inside

Man is by nature selfish. All living beings are selfish; their first duty is to protect themselves. By this selfishness they are also protecting the world. Animals and plants do not intentionally harm other life; man does. This is the notable difference. Knowledge can eliminate the tendency in man to harm other life, both directly and indirectly, and protect the world.

Man should realize that God is present in every living object and that God is the same as the God that resides in him. This will elevate him to a new level and his tendency to harm others will vanish. This realization will bring peace and happiness to him.

When the third mantra asserts that the *Brahman* that resides in the Sun is me, it opens up a new dimension. *Brahman* that resides in me is me. Here the self gets elevated from being selfish to being selfless. This discovery is of paramount importance. Once this understanding has been reached all differences vanish and everything fits into a unified whole. There is no duality. I, you, and living things are the same. There is no difference. This is the ultimate knowledge.

Knowledge is Bliss

To know *Brahman*, the Absolute God, is knowledge or more precisely *jnana*. A person who knows the *Brahman* is, therefore, a *jnani*. However, *Brahman* is not knowable, as it is beyond human cognition. Then how can one know the *Brahman*? The sage Patanjali and later Adi Shankaracharya say that it is possible.

Knowing the *Brahman* that resides in the sky is infinitely more difficult than knowing the *Brahman* that lives in one's body. Both are same; yet, it is a lot easier to discipline the body organs (the *indriyas*) and the mind. Thereafter, one can focus on the *Brahman* or more appropriately the atman. This is done through *dhyana* or meditation. Through meditation one can discover the inner self or atman. This state is known as *samadhi*. One who attains *samadhi* is a *jnani*. However, *samadhi* is attained only for short periods of a few minutes initially and this increases progressively to about 30 minutes, they say. The bliss that is the accompaniment of *samadhi* continues in the person even when he is awake and active after meditation. *Samadhi* can be a repetitive experience and can continue throughout one's life.

The ancient *acharyas* insist that while the knowledge of *Brahman* is personal, one requires the guidance of a guru to attain it.

Know the Atman/*Brahman*. Knowledge is bliss.

Seven

The *Bhagavad Gita: Jnana Yoga*

Introduction

The *Bhagavad Gita*, written around 400 AD and included in the epic *Mahabharata*, consists of 700 *shlokas* of two lines each in Sanskrit. My copy of the *Bhagavad Gita* is in the Devanagari script with Adi Shankaracharya's *bhashyam* in Sanskrit prose. This volume also contains a Hindi translation of the *bhashyam*. I have followed the original Sanskrit *shlokas* and the Acharya's explanation in Sanskrit prose and referred to the Hindi translation only when needed. I took a year for my first reading of the *Bhagavad Gita* and thereafter I have read it twice to get a firmer understanding of the text and its contents.

The 700 *shlokas* are in 18 chapters of unequal length; the second chapter has 72 *shlokas* while some have only 20. Each chapter is named as *yoga*. In this section, I shall focus only on the first three chapters of the *Bhagavad Gita*, namely *Arjuna Vishada Yoga, Sankhya Yoga* and *Karma Yoga*. Chapters 2 and 3 are the most important ones and hence merit special attention. Other chapters are more or less elaborations on the two chapters.

It is important to note that the *Bhagavad Gita* and *Manusmriti* complement each other very well. They dictate religious doctrines, and social and moral values (ethics) respectively. We already know that they represent the two schools of Hinduism after the breakup of the tribal Rigvedic society. The *Bhagavad Gita* is replete with several indirect references to the *Manusmriti* of pre-Puranic origin.

Both these scriptures affirm the four varna system of Hindu society and consider it as sacrosanct. In fact, it is emphasizes that it is the duty of the Brahmanas and Kshatriyas to protect this system for its perpetuation.

In his *bhashyam,* Adi Shankaracharya makes it clear that the *yogas* prescribed in the *Bhagavad Gita* applied specifically to the first three varnas, although *karma yoga* was practised even by fourth varna in the epics. The basics of *karma yoga* is a strict deference to the *varna dharma*. In recent times, the *jnana yoga* and *bhakti yoga* are also practised by all. Further, the specific occupations of the four varnas are no longer followed. In other words, *varna dharma* has totally lost its relevance. As a result, the foundation on which the *Bhagavad Gita* and *Manusmriti* were built has tottered. This needs to be kept in mind all the time. The content of the *Bhagavad Gita,* which is based on the *Upanishads,* is independent of the social system; it is, therefore, valid at all times and can applied to all societies.

In my analysis, I shall not quote the original *shlokas* as this will distract our main aim. However, reference to the *shloka*(s) under discussion will be given at the end of the sentence or paragraph in brackets. I would assume that the reader has already glanced a copy of the *Bhagavad Gita* or has access to it. If not, he is well advised to read this overview which is self-explanatory.

Prelude

The introduction to the *Bhagavad Gita* is pretty long—57 *shlokas*, whole of Chapter I and initial part of Chapter II. Shankaracharya's *bhashyam* begins only after the 11th *shloka*, which according to the Acharya merely illustrates the wrong reasoning. In other words, the Acharya totally dismisses contextual significance of the *Bhagavad Gita*.

What is the confusion? Arjuna, a courageous soldier, sulks not on account of fear of the enemy and death, but because of genuine grief over the potential death of dear and near ones and the need to kill his guru and great grandfather. He seeks Lord Krishna's help. Arjuna was aware that if he refused to fight, he will be declared as a coward for ever and death would be preferable to living in shame. Still, he had doubts about the morality of war and his own role in it.

The *Bhagavad Gita*, as do most of the *Upanishads*, follows the question and answer format style, in which the student asks the questions and the teacher responds to them. The teacher here is God himself in human form while the student is a well-known kshatriya. The choice of the student (as also of the teacher representing God) is rather enigmatic. As we will see later, the student is not qualified for *jnana yoga*, and he, in fact, is just a householder performing *varna dharma*, and not really even a *karma yogi*. Nothing much is promised when one becomes a *karma yogi*, for a *karma yogi* will have to be born again and he will have to take several births to attain *moksha*.

Sankaracharya's *bhashyam* gives the literal as well the real meaning and significance of the *shlokas*. This is followed by a question and answer discussion, where the questions raised are by hypothetical opponents (possibly this refers to earlier *bhashyams* which are lost for ever).

Understanding Atman

Grief over the death of dear and near ones is genuine. How can one cope with it?

The answer is simple. Once atman and the cycle of birth and death are understood, there will be no need to grieve. Atman is indestructible. It does not kill nor does it get killed. All of us were there before and will remain in the future, even after death. So why should one grieve for the dead? Birth is followed by death and immediately after death one is born again. So, what is there to grieve?

Atman is permanent; it cannot be perceived by human sensory organs or by human intellect. Atman which resides in our hearts is only an observer and is not to be blamed for acts of omission and commission by the body in which it lives. Once one recognizes the atman as the real 'I', the attachment to this world vanishes and one is not touched by pain or pleasure, grief or joy.

To know atman, one should know what is permanent (*nityam*) and what is transient (*anityam*). This world is transient and so are all of us in human form. Everything that we see is like an illusion. To get rid of this illusion one should give up all desires, worldly possessions, control the mind and the body and focus on the ultimate reality, the *Brahman*.

The reason why the *Bhagavad Gita* begins with an explanation of atman and then goes on to *jnana yoga* is that it is the only remedy for genuine grief and genuine doubts about one's actions. Besides, even a little understanding of *jnana yoga* does help to protect one from the fears of life and death. The mere awareness of atman and piecemeal practice of *jnana yoga* have no adverse consequences, as in the case of medication (2-40). Hence Arjuna is told about *jnana yoga* first. At the same time, he is also told firmly that he is not eligible for *jnana yoga* in its true and pure form; his domain is karma; he can, however, do karma with detachment (2-47). In other words, he is entitled to practice *karma yoga.*

Willingness to Endure

Arjuna is told, even at the very outset, that there is no escape from pain and pleasure in life. Once a person is born, the contact with the surroundings will generate pain or pleasure, grief or joy. He must be willing to endure all this (2-14). None of us (in my opinion this includes *sanyasins* as well) can escape from this basic fact of life.

Two Dharmas and Path to Moksha

In his introduction to the *bhashyam*, Adi Shankaracharya makes it clear, that there are two distinct *dharmas*—one for the *sanyasins* and the other for *grihasthas* (belonging to different varnas). The rules that apply to the latter do not apply to the former and vice versa. *Sanyasins* are those who have given up all worldly possessions and their enjoyment and have given up all *karmas* as well, except the ones needed for bare living. They are only entitled to practice *jnana yoga.*

All others belonging to different varnas must follow their *varna dharma*—namely the occupation prescribed for their varna and its moral code of conduct. In addition, they must perform rituals; the prescribed ones belong to two categories: *srautha karmas* and *smartha karmas*.

All *yogas*, other than *jnana yoga* may be practised by all. However, Adi Shankaracharya prescribes *yogas* only for the first three varnas.

It may be noted here that while in the olden times, the first three varnas worshipped *devas* (mentioned in the *Rigveda*), the Shudras and others worshipped only the demons (non-Vedic gods). The method of worship was also different. It may be noted that while the *Manusmriti* mentions only Vedic gods, the *Bhagavad Gita* refers to worship of demons in a very negative way. However, in the contemporary world, this distinction has all but vanished. *Homa* and *yaga* belong to the first group, while pujas belong to the latter. The Rigvedic Gods are no longer worshipped; on the other hand, almost all Gods that we worship today belong to the non-Rigvedic category.

The *grihasthas* belonging to different varnas, following their *varna dharma*, can also become karma *yogis*.

While *jnana yogis* attain *moksha* upon death, the *karma yogis* have necessarily to be reborn, perhaps with a better life. They may also attain the life of a *sanyasin* (from childhood) in the next birth or several births later and attain *moksha* eventually.

Jnana Yoga

Jnana yoga is the most rigorous and most rewarding of all *yogas*. Only one in a million can and does practice this *yoga* in the purest form. *Vairagya* and *karma sanyasa* are essential preconditions for this form of *yoga*. However, almost anyone can try to understand it and practice it in a very small way (2-40). It is still beneficial and hence this *yoga* is taught to Arjuna, although he is not in anyway qualified to become a *jnana yogi.*

How does one, who is not yet actually eligible for this *yoga,* make a beginning? It is definitely not easy. The first step is to try and control one's sensory organs. It is through the perceptions of the sensory organs that the mind is swayed away from the right path. The perceptions create likes and dislikes and induce the mind to desire and dislike. From desires not satisfied anger emerges and anger results in the violation of moral values. This leads to the destruction of the intellect and the person's downfall becomes inevitable (2-58 to 68).

Therefore it is necessary to abandon desires or nip them in the bud. Focus the mind always on the atman. Be composed in grief and be disinterested in pleasures and enjoyment. Discard fear and anger. Do not like or dislike anyone. Be neither happy nor unhappy (2-44 to 49).

Eventually, after several births and deaths, one becomes a *jnana yogi.* Abandoning all desires, the *sanyasi* (*jnana yogi*) walks nonchalantly, untouched by the surroundings, without self consciousness or pride and yet he is not exulted. He attains *moksha* (disappears into the *Brahman*) (2-71, 72). This is the ultimate end achieved only by a *jnana yogi.*

Adi Shankaracharya adds that only those who take *sanyasa* (not formal but real) from *bramhacharya* itself and continue their life in the same way till its end can attain *moksha.*

Karma Yoga

Karma yoga is in fact meant for everyone, although in the *Bhagavad Gita* it is prescribed for the first three varnas only. It is especially recommended for Arjuna who has doubts about the morality of a war against one's kith and kin and also peers. He is asked to fight since it is his *varna dharma* to fight enemies. If in the attempt he dies, he will attain *swarga* and if he wins, he can enjoy the bounty of the kingdom that is won (2-37). He can also fight the war to maintain the social order (here the allusion is to the social order of that time which was a feudal system with a stratified varna society) (3-20). There is, however, a difference between performance of *varna dharma* as one's karma and *karma yoga*. Both may involve the same action, as in this example war, but in *karma yoga* the desire for the end result is absent. One takes success and failure with equanimity. In *karma yoga*, karma should conform to the moral code and it should be done without craving for an end result.

Adi Shankaracharya says *karma yogi* should perform actions only for the sake of God and one should not seek personal favours from God (2-47).

Karma yoga is far inferior to *jnana yoga*, but superior to karma done with a desire for personal gain. Those who do the latter are called mean (2-49).

Srautha and *Smartha Karmas*

In Adi Shankaracharya's days, karma meant primarily the ritual action. These were of two types: *srautha karmas* are those prescribed in the *Brahmanas* and the later Vedic texts (*homa* or *yajna* and *yaga* or sacrifice) and *smartha karmas* are those enshrined in the *Smritis* that includes occupation-based work as well as non-Vedic rites which were borrowed and adapted from local cultures. In Puranic times, these rituals were better known as pujas which in turn may involve idol worship. *Srautha karmas* are more sacrosanct for Brahmanas and also Kshatriyas and Vaishyas, while *smartha karmas* are more or less optional and are practised by all varnas.

From the Upanishadic times, the practitioners of *jnana yoga* were few in number and they lived a secluded life. The concept of *karma yoga* did not exist in Upanishadic times. It finds mention in the *Manusmriti* along with *jnana yoga* and is based on Poorva Mimamsa school. The *Bhagavad Gita* gives a new twist to *karma yoga* and it is assumed that it was probably written to introduce this new concept and to popularize it along with *jnana yoga*. The *Bhagavad Gita* also expands the meaning of *karma yoga* to include a host of other *yogas*. Thus, the *Bhagavad Gita* goes way beyond the *Upanishads* in absorbing new ideas of later times, like the works of Puranic origin. The *Bhagavad Gita* itself is part of a *Purana*—the *Bhagavad Purana*.

However, while *karma yoga*, in the sense it is defined in the *Bhagavad Gita*, was not known, the performance of *srautha* and *smartha karmas* was a very important part of life of all the three varnas. Most priests and scholars who made a living by practising these and helping others to practice them, believed that these karmas are the only important requirement. They ensured welfare in this life and the next. There is nothing more to be achieved beyond that. This stand is diametrically the opposite of the assertions made in the *Bhagavad Gita*. The *Bhagavad Gita* denounces the practitioners of Vedic rituals who deny a role for *jnana* or other *yogas*. It may be noted that Vedic rituals are expounded in Jaimini's *Purva Mimamsa*, while it is criticized by the Vedantic school which is also known as Uttara Mimamsa.

What does the *Gita* say in respect of *srautha-smartha karmas*? The rationale for the *srautha-smartha karmas* is given in *shlokas*

3-10 to 19. These karmas were created along with man by Prajapati so that people could enjoy the fruits of nature. The *devas*, who represent natural phenomena such as rain, sunshine, earth, water and so on, were to be worshipped and offered food and other sacrificial material. The *devas*, pleased by the offerings and praise, produced rain, ensured the bounty of crops and cattle, and made human welfare possible. This symbiotic relationship between men and *devas* (nature) is dependent on karma (rituals). The *Bhagavad Gita* attempts to make the point that such karma should be in the name of *Brahman* and the benefits from it should be shared by all—a Rigvedic value. Nevertheless, the performance of *srautha-smartha karmas* is mandatory for *karma yogis* as well as *jnanis* (only those who are interested in the maintenance of the social order of the times). This is just to encourage people to perform the prescribed karmas according to the *Shastras*. In other words, the *Bhagavad Gita* supports the performance of *srautha-smartha karmas* by all *grihasthas*.

What determines human conduct or karmas? This is governed by the *gunas—satva*, *rajas*, and *tamas*. Every human being at the time of birth inherits the three *gunas* in varying proportions. The *gunas* produce likes and dislikes and man becomes enamoured by these and he performs karma to give vent to his likes and dislikes. *Rajoguna* results in ambition, desire to dominate, aggressiveness, and anger; while *tamoguna* results in irrational behavior, laziness, and ignorance. Ordinarily, people assume that these are their strengths and act accordingly, while in reality they are simply the slaves of nature-induced follies. A *karma yogi* should try and control his likes and dislikes using his intellect to the maximum and should not allow himself to be dictated by the *gunas* (3-27 to 39). He should give up his ego and arrogance. He should control his mind and not allow it to wander at the bidding of the natural instincts. Controlling the sensory organs, the mind, and intellect is the way of the *karma yogi* (3-41 to 43).

Chapter 14 is entirely devoted to the role of *gunas* in karma. This is also known as Sankhya school of thought.

Summary

The *Bhagavad Gita* is meant for the enlightenment of the *grihasthas* belonging to the three varnas. It is not meant for *sanyasins*. Why? Because, it is addressed to Arjuna, a *grihastha,* and it is not addressed to one about to take *sanyasa.* Yet, the emphasis on *jnana* and *jnana yoga* distract the reader and confuse him. At the end of Chapter 2, Arjuna mildly chides Lord Krishna for making mixed up statements and thereby confusing his mind. Mental confusion is natural for the layman and yet for a compelling reason *jnana yoga* had to be explained first. The reason given is that it is the only antidote for genuine grief. While the *jnana yogis* are promised much, the *karma yogi* gets nothing other than encouragement and a better life in the next birth. He has to suffer pain and pleasure, discipline his body and mind and act even ruthlessly. He should expect nothing in return. He must abide by all the rules of conduct prescribed and perform all rituals to perfection. This is a rather harsh prescription; the result is, hardly anyone talks about *karma yoga* today. At the same time, people talk about *bhakti yoga* and even about *jnana yoga* for its promise of *moksha.* Most people want the *yoga* that delivers without much effort, even if it is in the next life. The obvious choices are *bhakti yoga* for its simplicity and *jnana yoga* for its promise of *moksha*; *karma yoga* does not find a place in the hearts and minds of ordinary people.

Jnana yoga is fascinating and the *Bhagavad Gita* continues to dwell on the subject in the following chapters (Chapters 4 to 18). After all, there were many aspects to this fascinating doctrine and there were furious controversies as well. This can be elaborated upon only in another lengthy article. This raises question whether the main purpose was to introduce *jnana yoga* to people even if they are not eligible for it. The answer is yes and the rationale for this is explained in the following chapter.

Arjuna took part in the battle of Kurukshetra and won. He enjoyed the bounty of the kingdom ruled by his elder brother. Ultimately he went to heaven. He did not attain *moksha* nor did any of his brothers, not even the righteous Yudhishtira. Was Arjuna a *karma yogi*? If he was, he was still not entitled to *moksha* and hence, his attainment of heaven at the end.

Eight

The *Bhagavad Gita*: *Karma Yoga*

Introduction

In this section, we focus on Chapters 4 to 6, primarily the concepts of karma and *akarma* and their interface, a fundamental to *karma yoga* as we will see later on.

In his introduction to the fourth chapter and conclusion to the entire study, a broad rationale of the *Bhagavad Gita* is explained by Adi Shankaracharya. The essence of this discussion is explained in my own words below.

What is *Yoga*?

Yoga has to do with the state of the human mind. It is the process by which the mind attains tranquility, peace or a state of bliss. How does this happen? *Tyaga*, or sacrifice of desires, likes, dislikes, etc., is the means. Another interpretation is the application of *jnana* in karma which in turn involves *tyaga* of some kind. When karma is eliminated altogether by *tyaga*, only *jnana* exists, and it is known as *jnana nishta*.

One *Yoga* Two *Nishtas*

Having talked about two *yogas* in Chapters 2 and 3, it may come as a surprise to many that there is actually only one yoga, namely, *jnana yoga*. It is through *jnana* that one practices *yoga*.

Jnana yoga is in fact an all pervasive term and is the operative ingredient in all *yogas*. It exists beyond the domain of karma, while all other *yogas* are subsets of *karma yoga* within the domain of karma. The *jnana yoga* beyond the domain of karma is *jnana nishta*. It is the purest and exists only where there is no karma; *jnana yoga nishta* can exist only in a domain where all other *yogas* have no place. It is because of this unique property of *jnana yoga* that the *Bhagavad Gita* talks about two *nishtas*, one for the born *sanyasins* (*jnana yoga nishta*) and the other for the *grihasthas* (*karma yoga nishta*) (3-3).

Grihasthas can achieve *nishta* only in *karma yoga* after continual practice involving several births since their base is karma as per their *varna ashrama dharma*. The spiritual journey begins when the *grihastha* acquires a bit of *jnana* and his karmas are influenced qualitatively. This is also the start of *karma yoga*, the application of *jnana* in karma. There can be no *yoga* without some *jnana*. *Jnana* is the spiritual ingredient, *yoga* its application, and karma its domain. The immediate result is deliverance from fear and grief.

Jnana nishta requires a very special mental aptitude and this quality must exist at birth. It is genetic in nature, resulting in inborn ascetics or mystics. It is only these one in a million persons who are eligible for *jnana yoga* in its purest form. To my mind the best example is Ramana Maharshi. He left home while he was a school student and took *sanyasa* in Tiruvannamalai temple and lived his whole life in that state. All the rest, including us, have to practice *karma yoga* and, if possible, attain *karma yoga nishta*.

Karma Yoga

In this world, a vast and overwhelming majority of people are rooted to karma in its primordial and human dimensions (3-5). For these people, the *Shastras* have prescribed the *varna ashrama dharma*. Karma here includes both occupational and ritual aspects, besides others. However by using one's intellect, *grihasthas* can still learn about *jnana* and apply it to karma with diligence. When a *grihastha* following *varna dharma* acquires a little bit of *jnana*, he starts a new sojourn in the realm of *karma yoga*. Karma has omniforms and *jnana* has many levels. Chapters 4 to 18 enquire into varied forms of *karma yoga* in practice during 400 AD when the *Bhagawat Gita* was written. Many of those are no longer relevant or in practice.

As one progresses along the path of *karma yoga*, one may start as a keen student wanting to know about *yoga aruruksjhuh* and then pass through the stage of *yoga arudah*, a stage of commitment to *yoga*, and then reach the ultimate *nishta* stage and in a succeeding birth to *jnana nishta*. It is because of this progression to higher levels of yoga that it is emphasized time and again that *karma yoga* is the only path to *jnana yoga*.

Analogy

An analogy (my own) may help to clear doubts that are bound to arise, given the mysticism in any religious discussion.

Karma yoga is like the journey of pilgrims on foot from the down hills of the Himalayas from Rishikesh to Kedarnath.

Beyond Kedarnath one can continue the journey (only a select few will reach this stage) to the top of the snow-covered Himalayan peaks. In my analogy, *karma yoga* begins at Rishikesh and ends in Kedarnath. Beyond that is *jnana yoga* in pure form or more appropriately, *jnana nishta*.

Adi Shankaracharya travelled on foot from Rishikesh and established the temple in Kedarnath. Near the temple is his *samadhi*. According to a legend, Adi Shankaracharya, having high fever, set out on foot alone from Kedarnath on to the glaciers that take one to the top of the mountains. He then disappeared into the *Brahman*. This rather poignant event should be remembered by pilgrims when they go beside the *samadhi* (resting place) of the Acharya near the temple in Kedarnath.

The journey on foot from Rishikesh to Kedarnath is indeed very tough (the allusion here is to the days when there were no roads). Besides the Shivaliks there are two other mountain ranges to be crossed before one reaches the Central Himalayan Range in which Kedarnath is located. The mountains are cut through by rivers and streams. There are numerous spurs separating the streams. The pilgrim has to climb the spurs and come down to the next one and continue this process a hundred times before he reaches Kedarnath.

A pilgrim must carry minimum requirements and put up with all hardship at each stage. The crossing of the streams represents rebirth as well as purification, as the Vedic mantra says:

आपो जनयथा च नः

(*Rigveda*: 10.9.3)

"Oh water! Cause us to be reborn again and again."

This is a later interpretation of the Rigvedic mantra. In the originalcontext, the reference is to bathing, removing dirt and getting refreshed again and again in the very cold waters of the rivers originating from the Himalayas.

After overcoming all the spurs, one reaches the higher level, figuratively of *jnana*. By the time the pilgrim reaches Kedarnath, he is already well set in *karma yoga nishta* and ready for the quantum jump to *jnana nishta*. This will take several births more.

Beyond Kedarnath is ice and snow. The *yogi* who walks over this snow has a heart as pure as the snow. The journey ends here and one attains *moksha*.

The muddy and turbulent waters of the Ganga in Rishikesh and ice and snow beyond Kedarnath allegorically reflect the state of the mind of the pilgrim at the start, a *karma yoga aruruksbuh*, and at the end on reaching the pinnacle, a *jnana nishta*.

A note of caution is appropriate here. Pilgrims who take a bath in the cold waters of the Ganga at Rishikesh would feel that they are already purified and may even think that the journey is over. This feeling appears again and again when one takes bath in the Himalayan streams and rivers. The *Bhagavad Gita* praises the pilgrim's achievement at each stage and the impression is given that the task is already accomplished; however, this is only by way of encouragement. There is indeed a long and difficult way ahead.

Karma and *Akarma*

The first part of the fourth chapter is devoted to an explanation of karma and *akarma*. They are not opposites but one and the same; however, there is a semantic and perceptual problem here. Simply stated, what Arjuna does is karma while what Lord Krishna does is *akarma*. How? Before an answer is given, it is pertinent to ask why this issue is raised at this stage.

The reason is that Lord Krishna has to explain his own presence in human form (He is the Absolute God) and his actions. He has taken a human form to solely maintain the social order of the time and its value system. Hence he has to do all the karmas according to his *varna dharma*. If he flouts it, he will be setting a bad precedent, while his object is to set a good example for people to follow. Second and more significantly, what he does for the benefit of the people, and not for himself, is *akarma*. While *paapa* and *punya* attach to karma, *akarma* has no such luggage since karma is absent here. By this logic, Arjuna earns *paapa* and *punya* from his actions and is reborn again and again. He may go to heaven in case his sins are condoned.

What is *akarma*? How does karma become *akarma*? In Lord Krishna's case, all his actions are *akarma*. In a similar way, all actions performed by those in *jnana nishta* is *akarma*. What *karma yogis* do is mostly karma; however, if they understand *jnana* fully and perform karma only for the sake of *Brahman* without any attachment to results, it would qualify for *akarma*. However, a *karma yogi* will not gain anything by this, neither heaven nor *moksha*. *Akarma* does not earn any *punya* is a point that needs to be well borne in mind.

Karma yogis must know the difference between karma and *akarma*. The awareness of the difference itself is *jnana*. *Karma yogis* can try to perform karmas with no personal gain in mind and or for the welfare of the society as a whole. Besides, one should not perceive oneself as the doer, nor should he claim the result of his actions as his achievement. He should be totally detached. All this will save him from the *paapa* attached to his karma and nothing more. He will not earn any *punya* by this.

Deva Yajna and Jnana Yajna

Karma yogis must perform all the *nitya* and *nimitta karmas*. Besides normally people also perform *deva yajnas*. These have been alluded to in the *Bhagavad Gita* in chapter 3 (*shlokas* 10 to 15). However the *Gita* does not look favourably at these as they are all for obtaining benefits. Nevertheless, a *karma yogi* can perform them if he shares the benefit with all and is satisfied with what is left over. The *Bhagavad Gita* recommends *jnana yajnas* for *karma yogis*. In these *yajnas*, *Agni* represents *Brahman* and the *karma yogi* sacrifices various unwanted things of a personal nature. These sacrifices are of a notional character including sacrifice of one's ego or sacrificing one's *indriyas* to gain their control; similarly one can sacrifice words, and so on. Control of food consumption, *pranayama*, self-learning are other *jnana yajnas*. These are recommended as they pave the way for *yoga nishta*.

There is a suggestion here of sacrificing karma or *karma sanyasa*. This is indirect, to my perception. What it means is sacrificing the normal ritual karmas and perhaps also occupational karmas (not really specified). The point is that this part of the *Bhagavad Gita* seems to be addressed not to the *grihastha* but a person who has already entered *vanaprastha* or even *sanyasa* (this *sanyasa* should not be confused with the *sanyasa* of the *Sankhya* or *tatva jnani*). The term *sanyasa* here means only a formal or ritual *sanyasa* taken by a *grihastha*.

Karma Sanyasa

The fifth chapter is all about *karma sanyasa.* There is an inherent contradiction between *karma yoga* and *karma sanyasa.* Obviously the same person cannot do both. A *grihastha* can be a *karma yogi* but not a *karma sanyasi.*

However, there are other possibilities. Just as some take *sanyasa* from *bramhacharya* itself, others can take *sanyasa* at the early *grihastha* stage. However, the *Shastras* prescribe that a *grihastha* should take up *vanaprastha* when he becomes a grandfather. He should entrust his wife and other children to the care of his eldest son and depart for the forests. After a period of trial, he may enter upon *sanyasa. Karma sanyasa* is an option available to a person in the *vanaprastha* stage. According to the *Manusmriti*, a *vanaprasthin* must perform all karmas (rituals) as before, except occupational karmas.

A *karma yogi* or a *karma sanyasi* are equally *ajnanis.* Why? The reason is that both of them possess *jnana* in an imperfect form. In this less than ideal situation, a definite preference is given to *karma yoga.* The argument is that the *karma yogi* (a *grihastha*) is also a *sanyasi* of sorts. A *karma yogi* has no pretensions of being a *jnani*, while a *karma sanyasi* may entertain that false view. Hence, the preference is for *karma yoga* rather than *karma sanyasa.*

The bulk of Chapter 5 is devoted to an elucidation of the attributes of a true *jnani.* This harping on the ideal may confuse the reader. But this is useful to the *karma yogis* and *karma sanyasins* so that they can try to emulate the ideals set by *jnanis* and reach the level of *karma yoga nishta.*

What are the ideal attributes that deserve emulation? These are very difficult and very hazy propositions. Some of them are:

- One must see *samatvam* or sameness in apparently different things, for example, in a brahmana scholar, a cow, an elephant, a dog, or *chandala*. He must see the *Brahman* in them, and refuse to recognize the outer form.
- One should not get elated by good tidings or get upset by bad tidings.
- One must control desires and anger throughout one's life; for, these two would continue to crop up till death, since they are products of nature.
- One should not feel happy on receiving something liked earlier, nor should one feel unhappy while receiving a disliked object.
- One should know that the *atman* is in no way responsible for one's actions. All karmas are the work of *prakriti* through the *gunas*. One should get out of the influence of *gunas*.
- And there are more, many more.

If anyone feels that all this is too much he may look forward to *dhyana yoga*.

Dhyana Yoga

Dhyana yoga is the subject matter of the sixth chapter, which completes the discussion on the interface between *karma yoga* and *jnana yoga*. Later chapters are less heavy and relate to more down to earthly issues. Moreover, in later chapters, this simplification starts with the acceptance of *Ishwara* in human form as the *Brahman* and suggests *bhakti* or implicit faith in the *Ishwara* as the means of *yoga*.

The interesting thing about *dhyana yoga* is that it directly focuses on the mind rather than on karma. The issue here is to remove the mental distractions and focus on the oneness of atman and *Brahman*. In the process one attains mental peace.

Arjuna, like all of us, points out that the mind is extremely fickle, powerful, dominating and stubborn and as such difficult to control like air and wind. Lord Krishna's answer is equally simple and straight; it can be done through practice and *vairagya* (6-38 and 39). This then is the rationale of *dhyana* or meditation.

The advanced *dhyana yoga* is described in detail in *shlokas* 6-10 to 32. This is meant for a *brahmacharin* and by inference in an ashram under a guru's guidance. He should select a secluded place which is clean and be seated comfortably in any *aasana* of his choice and concentrate on the *Brahman* by focussing his eye on the tip of his nose. There are several other such prescriptions; these follow pattern of the *asthanga raja yoga* of Patanjali more or less. This will eventually lead to *samadhi*, the state of lasting happiness while still in this life.

Arjuna's question about the fickle mind and the difficulty of controlling it reflect the layman's problem rather than the professional's. The answer is that he should emulate or try to emulate the professional as much as he can. Arjuna then worries about the adverse consequences of imperfect meditation and the answer is that there is no adverse effect on anything done in a *bona fide* spirit and with sincerity keeping the Absolute God in mind.

Dhyana yoga does not call for any elaborate rituals; it is simple and it can be done in seclusion at home whenever you find the time. Remember the rules prescribed and follow them as much as you can. But you must not seek benefit or try to measure it. It is perhaps the best method for a learner to acquire *jnana* and cultivate it. One should supplement this by self learning using texts of one's choice. The experience will get deeper with practice. Do not expect too much, better still expect nothing.

Summary

There is much that distracts the reader of the *Bhagavad Gita* in Chapters 4 to 6. The tedious and often repetitive exposition of *jnana yoga* in its various forms does more often kill rather than generate interest; after all, this level of *yoga* is definitely not meant for *karma yogis* like us. *Jnana yoga* is meant purely for the *Sankhya* (*sanyasi* from childhood). The arguments on karma and *akarma*, like its counterparts on day and night in Chapter 2, lean heavily on mysticism. However, unlike a *Sankhya*, a *karma yogi* is not a mystic. There are clearly limits to his ability to adopt the ways of the mystic, who practices yoga so easily and naturally.

So what is there for us who aspire to become karma yogis? We are not entitled to anything else, except perhaps *karma sanyasa*. My own view is that there are many things that we can gain from. Nevertheless, each person has to read the *Bhagavad Gita* and identify the things that he can actually adopt and practice. Here is a tentative list:

- Do not aspire for *moksha* (this is not meant for us).
- Do not aspire for a better life; it will come on its own.
- Do not perform rituals for self-benefit; it has a negative effect on your next life.
- Perform rituals only for self-purification (*atma shudhi*).

- Meditate daily for 10 to 15 minutes. Focus on the atman. Relax.
- Give up as many desires as you can. Ask what among the things that you have or want you can give up.
- Do not get angry or get worked up on any account. Always go to a secluded place and meditate when you get angry.
- Accept failures and disappointments.
- Do not celebrate success; if you must do it quietly.
- Examine why you like or dislike persons whom you know. Eliminate likes and dislikes equally.
- There are neither friends nor any enemies.
- Do introspect and examine your weak points, mistakes, wrongs done to others, honestly.

For a *karma yogi*, karma is the world. Take care of your mental health and live happily. Leave the rest to God.

Nine

The *Bhagavad Gita: Bhakti Yoga*

Introduction

Chapters 7 to 12 of the *Bhagavad Gita* focus on *bhakti yoga.* However, *jnana* appears time and again, since it is a vital ingredient.

What is *bhakti*? It is faith in a specified God and it exists in all religions. There are many religions and many Gods; in Hinduism itself we have pantheon of Gods. In the *Bhagavad Gita*, *bhakti* means absolute faith in Lord Krishna, to the exclusion of all other Gods.

All religions recognize *bhakti* or faith as a potent agent of mental peace and ultimate happiness. Consequently, *bhakti yoga* can exist without *jnana*. However, the *Bhagavad Gita* suggests a combination of both; unlike *bhakti*, *jnana* is unique to Hinduism and *jnana yoga* stands on a higher pedestal than *bhakti yoga.* The very concept of *bhakti* poses tricky questions. *Jnana* involves atman and *Brahman*, both very abstract beyond the cognitive ability of man. *Bhakti,* on the other hand, is an emotive down to earth concept which focuses on an objective God, Lord Krishna. How can *Brahman* and Lord Krishna be one and the same? A possible explanation is given in Chapter 7 which deals with *jnana* and *vijnana*. In a nutshell, *Brahman* is the deductive Absolute God while Lord Krishna is his empirical counterpart. The problem then is to know the attributes and powers of the Absolute God . This requires a detailed description of the empirical God and his vast powers. To the uninitiated, he is just a person; to others he is an extraordinary one; to still others he is a God in human form; and finally to a few he is the Absolute. The *Bhagavad Gita* explores some of these shades of perception. Significantly, it lays a sound theoretical basis for practising *bhakti* with *jnana*. The two contrasting concepts are harmoniously integrated.

Jnana and *Vijnana*

The concept of *jnana* has already been explained. Chapter 7 of the *Bhagavad Gita* introduces the concept of *vijnana*. What is this new term? Like karma and *akarma*, *jnana* and *vijnana* are same as well as different. They are the same because they represent two facets of *Brahman* and different because *vijnana* can be seen or heard, while *jnana* is not cognizable.

At this stage, two other sets of terms in this chapter are introduced. They are *para* and *apara*, and *kshetrajna* and *kshetra*. Intrinsically, these terms are synonymous with *jnana* and *vijnana*, with some nuances in their actual use. This will become clear as one reads the *Bhagavad Gita* or this write-up.

Apara is the phenomenal world that we see and experience around us. This includes not only the earth but the whole universe, all the human body and Lord Krishna. The scale of this concept is wide. What is *para* then? *Para* is *Brahman*, in other words, atman that resides in our hearts. The notion here is that *para* and *apara* are the same representing two aspects of *Brahman*. Lord Krishna says that "I am *Brahman* and *Prakriti*, at the same time. Further, that my person, seen as *Ishwara* in human form is *apara*; but I am hence *Brahman*." Para 7 to 5, *shlokas* 6 to 13 amplifies this concept further.

Ishwara

The *Ishwara*, namely, Lord Krishna, ought to be seen not as a human being but as the creator of all the objects, living and otherwise, visible and non-visible attributes of the universe including the stars, the sun, moon, earth and their phenomena of all sorts. Furthermore, He is simply not the creator alone; he embodies both the five *bhutas* (elements) and the three *gunas*. Also, He represents all tenses of time and he knows everything that happens to the living things as they are simply his doings. It means that the *Ishwara* can be perceived by people and identified. However, the *bhaktas* should realize these phenomena including the *Ishwara* in human form as *maya* and the reality beyond that. A *bhakta* should see the *Brahman* in the *Ishwara* and the *para* in the *apara*, the *kshetrajna* in the *kshetra*. This is *jnana*, whereas what the ordinary *bhakta* sees or hears is *vijnana*.

Bhaktas

While some recognize the *Ishwara* in Lord Krishna, others do not. Those who have faith in Lord Krishna are called his *bhaktas*. They belong to four categories:

- Those who seek the *Ishwara* for protection from disease, thieves, tigers, etc. (*aartha*).
- Those who desire to know more about the *Ishwara*, especially the aspects not revealed to human perception (*jijnasu*).
- Those who desire wealth (*artharthi*).
- Those who already know the truth about the *Ishwara* (*jnanis*).

The first three categories are ordinary *bhaktas* and the fourth is aptly described as *jnanis* and not *bhaktas*. In the first and third, there is desire for personal gain; they are *ajnanis*. The *bhatkas* of second category are in quest for *jnana* and hence are *yogis*, a kind of *karma yogis*. Here *bhakti yoga* becomes another form of *karma yoga*.

Bhajan

Bhakti and *bhajan* go together. A *bhakta* must offer prayers (*bhajan*) to his Lord and remember him constantly. The *Bhagavad Gita* suggests addition of *jnana* within the milieu of *bhakti*. This is done by understanding the duality of *jnana* and *vijnana* that may appear as antithesis but actually are one and the same. Of course *jnana* means *tyaga* especially of the fruits of karma. Converting *vijnana* into *jnana* is not easy. Do not be carried away by its simplicity and praise showered on the true *bhaktas*. These are only meant for such *bhaktas* as they understand and practice *jnana* in some measure.

A *bhakta* must remember the Lord always. Why? The undisputed fact is that those who remember the Lord and recite his name at the time of death, attain the Lord. This is a very tricky proposition. Hence there is the need to practice the art of *bhajan* and *japa*. One would not then fail to remember the Lord at the time of death (8-5 to 10).

Furthermore, karma either in terms of rituals or occupational activities should not be neglected by the *bhakta* (8-7). *Bhakti* must and does coexist with karma. *Bhakti* as seen earlier is always associated with an objective God, while in *jnana,* one relates it exclusively with the *Brahman*, the Absolute God.

Vibhuti

The greatness of Lord Krishna may be understood by *bhaktas* through the prism of His own manifest-self in all living things in this world. One should try and practice to understand this fully. And if one fails, the Lord Himself provides a detailed description of His greatness in Chapters 9 and 10. Even this, admittedly is only a small selection of His infinite presence. Examples mentioned in these two chapters are cognizable objects and attributes and as such are *apara*. However, the *bhakta* should understand that outward appearances are unimportant, while the inner self is real. *Apara* is to be understood as an outward form, which is subject to destruction and renewal, while *para* is permanent and indestructible.

Many examples are in the first person singular. Thus Lord Krishna says that "I am Brihaspathi among the *purohits*, *gayatri* among the Vedic meters, *Sama* among the *Vedas*, the sun among the bright objects in the sky", and so on. This means that while the Lord exists in everything, His greatness is best represented in the leading objects and their attributes. He is simply not just the object but the thing that makes them great. This subtle message could easily be lost on the ordinary *bhakta* and hence repeatedly stressed. This may sound rather laborious to an intellectual, but to the *bhakta* it is the nectar.

There is, however, a lingering doubt about what is actually understood—the form or the substance (*apara* or *para*). There are several hints that urge the *bhakta* to focus on the *para* and through that attain *moksha*; but to me the repetitiveness only reinforces the outward form rather than the inner self. This is the real problem with *bhakti* and *bhaktas*. *Vijnana* does not necessarily lead to *jnana*; on the other hand, it might obscure it.

Vishwadharshan

The description of *Ishwara*'s true nature and powers in verbal form is inadequate to quench the thirst of *bhaktas* to experience *Ishwara* (*vijnana*). The *bhakta* would like to personally see the *Ishwara*. Lord Krishna willingly provides Arjuna (and through him to all of us) a special spectrum of His creations and His powers. Moreover, the past, present and future are shown. In particular, Arjuna was shown the destruction of his enemies thus clearing his doubts about the outcome of the war. He is then fully satisfied (Chapter 11).

The presentation of *Ishwara* here is in stark contrast with that of the *Upanishads*. The reason is simple. *Bhakti* appeals to ordinary people but *jnanis*. But then *bhakti* is for the masses or *karma yogis* and those below the level of *jnana*.

Even those who understand the nuances of *jnana* and *yoga* practice *bhakti* through *bhajan* in its plagiarized versions. This is a matter of practical expediency. It is admitted in the *Shastras* that *jnanis* and *yogis* depend on the *grihastha* for food and basic survival. They are, therefore, obliged to the devoted *bhakta,* like Lord Krishna who was obligated to Arjuna, his devoted *bhakta.*

Bhakti Yoga Versus *Jnana Yoga*

In Chapter 12, the question is asked as to which among the two, *bhakti yoga* or *jnana yoga,* is better. This question is then answered diplomatically by first praising *bhakti yoga* and then pointing out the unique qualities of *jnana yoga* and its superiority.

The above is a typical example of the *Bhagavad Gita* style; praise the underdog before pointing out the superiority of the front runner which is always *jnana yoga.* This style might create some confusion when out of context quotations are given. In the concluding part of his *bhashyam,* Adi Shnkaracharya starts by asking "where is the doubt?"; ruling out scope for any doubt. Of course, the Acharya is right, as he always is. However, many *bhaktas* still remain confused.

Why is *jnana yoga* better than *bhakti yoga*? The reason is that the *jnani* identifies himself with the Absolute God (atman/ *Brahman*). He is thus God himself. The *bhakta* is the obedient servant of his master. He surrenders himself at the feet of his *Ishwara.* He has total faith in the *Ishwara* and he is overjoyed at the mention of his attributes and powers. Yet, all these and the *Ishwara* himself are products of *maya* and this illusion is the work of *Brahman.* Only those who traverse beyond become *jnanis* and to them only *Brahman* remains.

It is true that *bhakti* can exist without any *jnana* at all and in this situation, the *bhakta* may be compared to the householder who worships *devas* for self-benefit. With a little bit of *jnana, bhakti* becomes *bhakti yoga* and at this stage it is comparable to the initial phase of *karma yoga*. As *bhakti* and *jnana* deepen, one may attain a *nishta* stage and this may lead to *jnana nishta* in another birth.

There is no conflict between *bhakti*, karma, and *jnana* in the initial stages; in the final stage, both karma and *bhakti* disappear and only *jnana* remains.

Summary

Bhakti is the most popular form of religious practice among Hindus today. However, Lord Krishna as the Supreme God is accepted only by a few; there are other choices, the prominent ones among them being Shiva, Shakti, Sri Ram, Muruga, and so on. This has been the case throughout historical times. The relative importance of various supreme gods varied from time to time, place to place, and person to person. In today's liberalized and even global (many Hindus are abroad) religious values, there is intense competition for religious space. Recently, we have seen the popularity of Ayyappa and other modern day gods; besides, some individuals are revered as God's incarnation. Mention may be made of Satya Sai Baba of Puttaparthi, who has a large following. He himself, I believe, has never made such a claim.

Today *bhaktas* belong to two categories: *Aartha* (meaning frightened), and *Artharthi* (seeker of wealth). The latter tend to change gods when their purpose is not served. Many others look upon faith as an insurance against future exigencies. There are some who are genuine seekers of God without self-benefit in view (*Jijnasu*).

The rise of *bhakti* in recent times, in my opinion, is largely due to the decline of the value attached to rituals (karmas) in daily life. In the past, *Manusmriti* was taken seriously and the average Hindu's daily life was dominated by rituals advocated by *Manusmriti*. There was no time or need for *bhajan* as a ritual or in an organized form. In fact, at this time, Vedic rituals and concepts of *paap* and *punya* effectively negated even *jnana yoga*. *Jnana yoga* has always remained as an unseen undercurrent; it was neither victorious nor vanquished at any time.

Modern day *bhaktas* take religion rather lightly. *Bhakti* is preferred over Vedic rituals which are rarely understood. *Bhajans* today emphasize form rather content, but they are adequate for the emotional needs of the lay. Hence, we see the popularity of *bhakti*. I would not call this *bhakti yoga*, since it hardly involves any *jnana*. Besides, *yoga* means, to most people, physical exercise and meditation (*dhyana*).

Ten

The *Bhagavad Gita: Tatva Jnana*

Introduction

Tatva jnana is the subject matter of Chapters 13 to 18. The elements of *tatva jnana* have been dealt time and again earlier, but these six chapters elaborate the concepts and principles with special focus on individual character and conduct rather than on *jnana nishta*.

What is *tatva jnana*? It is actually Sankhya—one of the six branches of Hindu philosophy. Another branch, Vedanta, is closely related to Sankhya with two substantive points of disagreement. The *Bhagavad Gita* has borrowed ideas from several schools of thought, and puts greater weight on these two branches. The word Sankhya appears in several places in the *Bhagavad Gita* (*Vedanta* is also mentioned, but it is the basis of the whole work), starting from Chapter 3 (3-3). Later, in Chapter 10, Lord Krishna Himself says that "I am Kapila among the *siddhas*" (Kapila *Muni* is the founder of the Sankhya school of thought). However, the *Bhagavad Gita* does often deviate from the formulations of Kapila

Muni; this is justified since Lord Krishna was himself Kapila *Muni* and hence no contradiction is involved—a rather clever justification by the author of the *Bhagavad Gita*.

Sankhya literally means numbers. The Sankhya school outlines 24 *tatvas* in addition to *Purusha*, the soul (which constitutes the 25th *tatva*). The 24 *tatvas* are—*prakriti* which includes five *bhutas* and three *gunas*; *Jnanendriyas* and *karmendriyas* have five *tatvas* each; the five *vishayas* or subject matter of the *indriyas*; and finally the mind. The understanding of *tatvas* and their inter-relationships is the subject matter of Sankhya philosophy. The object of this philosophy is to free *purusha* from the milieu of the 24 *tatvas* that constitute the *apara*. The Sankhya school does not recognize a creator nor does it recognize a maintainer of the *apara* world order. In their opinion, the 24 *tatvas* can sustain themselves. The *vedantins* recognize *Brahman* as the creator of the world, while *Ishwara* as the maintainer of the world is a Puranic concept, central to the thesis of the *Bhagavad Gita*.

In this section, the discussion begins with the concepts of *kshetra* and *kshetrajna* and then the three *gunas* and continues with the application of *gunas* to the social order. The concluding chapter of the *Gita* looks at the *guna* system within the framework of *varnas* and reviews the whole subject matter with an appropriate benediction.

Kshetra and Kshetrajna

The human body is the *kshetra* and the atman that resides in it is *kshetrajna*. The *kshetra* comprises of the 24 *tatvas* already mentioned and *kshetrajna* is the *Purusha*, the 25th *tatva*. Those who understand *kshetra* as the *apara* and *kshetrajna* as the *para* of *Brahman* have *jnana*; others do not.

What is perhaps unique is that *kshetrajna* or *Purusha* is described as *jiva*. The difference is that the *Purusha* in this framework is not only an observer over karmas done by the body but is also a *bhokta* (enjoyer) of the fruits of karma or he appears to be that. The result is that the *Purusha* is enslaved in the *jiva* and he cannot escape from the cycle of birth and death resulting from karmas. The object then is to free *Purusha* from this slavery to the *jiva*.

A series of character traits are mentioned as the means by which *jnana* may be achieved (3-6 to 18). The examples of the same are as follows: absence of exaggerated self-esteem, non-display of pride, non-violence, respect for guru, detachment from pleasurable things, etc. This may described as self-purification or *adhyatmam*.

Jnana may be obtained in one of at least three ways already described in earlier chapters. These are meditation, other forms of *karma yoga*, and through *tatva jnana*. Most of the things mentioned here constitute old wine in a new bottle.

Three *Gunas*

What binds *kshetra* and *kshetrajna* together are the three *gunas* of *Prakriti*. *Gunas* create desires, likes and dislikes in one's mind and thus cause action by the body. In this process, both the *kshetra* and *kshetrajna* get involved in the enjoyment of pain and pleasure and get further entangled in the mesh of likes and dislikes. *Gunas*, therefore, have a basic role in life in this world; in turn, they also influence the nature of next life. *Gunas* constitute the operating mechanism of life.

The three *gunas* of *Prakriti* are *satva*, *rajas* and *tamas*. *Satva guna* is pure, enlightening and bright, and non-harming and it is associated with *jnana* and happiness. *Rajas*, on the other hand, propels the desire for objects not presently possessed and a longing for things which have in the past produced pleasure. *Rajas* binds man to karma to satisfy his desires; he then craves for the pleasurable fruits of his action. *Tamas* induces indifference and nonchalance, laziness, and the tendency to sleep. It gravitates towards *ajnana* or the denial of *jnana* and further unrealistic desires in man (*moha*) (*shlokas* 14-5 to 9).

The three *gunas* are always present in varying degrees in each person. At any given point in time, one *guna* may dominate and the consequence becomes evident in one's behaviour. Precisely, the relative strength of the three *gunas* can vary from time to time. Admittedly, everyone inherits a certain quantum of each of the *gunas* varied in measure at birth. The permutations and combinations of *gunas* are indeed infinite and hence no two individuals are alike. The dominant *guna* in the person at the time of death will determine the mix of *gunas* in the next birth (14-14 and 15). The consequences of the three *gunas* in the next birth are explained in *shlokas* 16 to 18.

During one's life time it is possible to overcome the influence of all *gunas*, *satva guna* included. This is accomplished by disengagement of self from the results of *satvic*, *rajasic* and *tamsic* karmas. This karma *phala tyaga* alone will lead to *jnana*. A *jnani* is devoid of all the three *gunas*.

Inverted Tree

The symbolism of the inverted tree originates from the Upanishadic times, when questions almost invariably focussed on the 'root of the problem' or alternately on the support of whatever is in question. Trees are supported by their roots and these nourish them as well. These roots are invisible and what they do is also not in the realm of visibility or let us say human perception.

The inverted tree is the subject matter of Chapter 15 of the *Gita*. The roots of the inverted tree represent the *Brahman* and these spread over the sky in outer space, where *Brahman* is supposed to reside. The trunk and branches, leaves, fruits etc., represent this world or *samsara*. Hence this tree is called the *samsara vriksha*.

The three *gunas* are like the sap of the tree that nourishes its branches, leaves, fruits, etc., and make them function the way they do. In short, life in this tree is controlled by the *gunas*.

The creator of the inverted tree of *samsara* is *Brahman* himself and he is also present in all the living things in this world as *Purusha*, the soul. Thus, *Brahman* may be described as *Purushothama*. He is not only the sum total of all the *Purushas* or souls and much more and he is pure and hence this title.

Sura and *Asura*

Prajapati, the mythological creator of this world, categorized people as the good and the bad; or the godlike and demonlike. Their roots are traced to pre-Rigvedic times and perhaps mentioned here for that reason alone. The classification is against the grain of Sankhya which invariably classified everything into three.

Chapter 16 gives detailed characteristics of good men (*shlokas* 1 to 5) and bad men (*shlokas* 7 to 24), marking the end of the very short chapter.

One may notice that there are only five *shlokas* on the good qualities, but as many as eighteen deal with the bad qualities. The reason for this is that while the good qualities have been highlighted even earlier, the bad ones have not been touched upon to the same extent before. Besides, the thrust here is to give up the bad qualities. For this, in the first instance, one should know what the bad qualities are. Hence one should always remember *shlokas* 7 to 24.

The good and bad qualities described in this chapter are widely well known and hence do not need to be recited here. One can read the *Bhagavad Gita* for full picture.

A very interesting sidelight here is that Arjuna did entertain doubt about his category. The Lord assures him that he belongs to the category of good men. Nowadays such people will be few and hence Lord Krishna need not descend on earth to clarify doubt. Every one of us belongs to the good category, since everyone has only good qualities, where is the need to read this chapter? To pin down the people they dislike in the asura category?

Triads

Three tier classification, *thriams* or triads, is a characteristic of Sankhya school. They are based on the three *gunas*. In Chapter 17, we have an elaboration of this idea with respect to faith, food, *yajna*, penance, and gifts. This methodology is continued into Chapter 18 and the final chapter as well.

Those who have never seen or read the *Shastras* or have only a poor understanding of the same are often most steadfast in their religious beliefs and practices. This is genuine faith. Such persons are of three types: those who worship *devas*, those who worship *yakshas* and *rakshasas*, and those who worship demons and ghosts. The *bhashyam* says that the latter are more common than the former; true then and now as well.

Food that enhances longevity of life, improves the intellect, gives strength, health and is pleasing, is *satvic*; sour, hot, bitter or salty food is *rajasic*—these cause sickness and pain; and food that stinks, is prepared days before or otherwise stale, and leftovers is *tamasic*.

Yajna performed without the desire for benefit or merit and which is performed as a matter of duty alone and in accordance with the *Shastras* is *satvic*; *yajna* done with the hope of getting desired results or merit and *yajna* performed for show and for enhancing one's status in society is *rajasic*; while *yajnas* done not in accordance with the *Shastras* and without mantras and gifts to *Brahmanas* is *tamasic*.

Penance or *tapas* involves the body, speech or mind. There is a variety of these, commonly performed by people. Here again *tapas* not done for personal gain or merit is *satvic*; *tapas* done for show is *rajasic* while *tapas* involving hurt or pain to oneself or others is *tamasic*.

Gifts in the nature of *non quid pro quo* are *satvic* and *quid pro quo* are *rajasic* and those with the object of insulting or hurting a person is *tamasic*.

The words, *om*, *tat*, and *sat* (individually) shall be invoked only in *yajnas* that are of *satvic*, *rajasic*, and *tamasic* nature.

Further elaboration of the *tatvas* continues in the final chapter (18) with the focus on *tyaga* and *sanyasa* which takes one ultimately to *jnana nishta*. Several three-fold typologies are used as paradigms to drive home the point of distinction between *satvic* and other paths (*shlokas* 18 to 40). The important ones relate to *jnana* (in the sense of the means to *jnana*), karma, *kartha*, intellect, self-command, happiness, and so on. *Tatva jnana* involves the correct understanding of all these and their right use towards *jnana nishta*. This process obviously involves *tyaga* and *sanyasa*, which means the same thing (18–24). Ultimately the *jnani* gives up everything—all worldly possessions, all karmas including rituals, all three *gunas* and their concomitant behavioural attributes. Give up everything under the sun and be happy for ever, that then is the essence of *jnana nishta*.

Four Varnas

The neat and simple rule of threes does not fit in when it comes to the social system of *Bhagavad Gita* time. Nevertheless, the four varnas were the basis of the social system then. How is it then accommodated in the Sankhya method?

Rather ingeniously, the four varnas are divided into two categories: the first three varnas or the twice born, which fits into the system, and secondly, the Shudras (though constituting 90 per cent of the population then) reduced to the status of servitude to the upper three varnas. According to Adi Shankaracharya (see Chapter 8), the Shudras are entitled neither to *yogas* of any kind, nor to study the *Vedas* as well (18–41). Thus the rule of threes is restored more or less. The fourth category is left out as it has no independent status.

Varnas are a product of *gunas* according to the Sankhya school. While Brahmanas possess *satva guna* predominantly, the Kshatriyas have *satva* and *rajasa guna* in equal measure. The Vaishyas have a bit of *tamas* along with *rajas*, while Shudras have predominantly *tamas* and a little bit of *rajas*. Thus the four-fold social system is fitted into the three-fold *gunas* (18–41).

The *gunas* determine character and conduct of men. The Brahmanas have several good qualities such as self-command, calmness, cleanliness, knowledge and experience; while Kshatriyas are courageous and valourous and possess a good personality, are steadfast in whatever they do and have an inclination to shower gifts on others. The Vaishyas are well-versed in agriculture, animal husbandry and trade. Shudras by nature are born to serve the other three varnas (18–44). This is a very convenient framework that suits the Brahmanas and Kshatriyas, the former more than the latter. It is obviously clear as to who framed the rules. The four-fold division of people into varnas suited the feudal system very well and hence it is held to be sacrosanct.

By following the *varna dharma,* one can attain *jnana nishta* eventually. By accepting one's *varna dharma* and performing one's duties willingly and thoroughly one attains self purity, which will qualify him for a better birth the next time. By this process—after several births—persons belonging to all varnas can attain full *jnana* and eventually *moksha* (18–45 to 55).

It is absolutely important that one adheres to one's own *varna dharma*. Departure from this will have serious negative consequences. Lord Krishna, after mentioning this point, tells Arjuna bluntly that he must fight. There is no other choice.

Finally, Lord Krishna gives his benediction to Arjuna:

"Dedicate all your actions to me and in me alone you trust. I shall absolve you of all your sins."

This benediction does not promise *moksha* to Arjuna. He is promised relief from sins arising from his actions in the war for justice. As a result, Arjuna attains heaven after death.

Summary

Tatva jnana is meant for those who are intellectually inclined and the *Bhagavad Gita* treats it as if there is no difference between the Vedantic school of thought and the concept of *tatva jnana.* However, Vedanta, as outlined in the *Upanishads,* is highly individualistic and is not concerned with the social milieu. On the contrary, *tatva jnana* is more or less integrated with the varna-based social system. The *Bhagavad Gita* also attempts to integrate Vedanta with the social system of 400 AD. This probably explains the inclusion of *tatva jnana* in the *Bhagavad Gita*. It may be noted here that the *Upanishads* were composed centuries before Kapila *Muni* created the Sankhya school of philosophy.

The social value system in present day India is directly in conflict with *tatva jnana*. Some people oppose the *Bhagavad Gita* for this reason; however, the social aspect is not central to the main thesis of the text.

Among the four conceptual frames outlined in the *Bhagavad Gita*, namely, *jnana yoga*, *karma yoga*, *bhakti yoga* and *tatva jnana*, the last is perhaps the least understood by the public. It is generally ignored by intellectuals today.

Eleven

Time Perspective in Hinduism

Introduction

It is now commonly recognized that time or *kaalam* in Sanskrit is a central concept in understanding the various spiritual paths or *yogas* as recommended in the *Bhagavad Gita*. In the ultimate analysis, time has no beginning or end; it is *nityam*. *Brahman* is *nityam* and *nityam* is *Brahman*. Time, therefore, is the ultimate reality and by its realization one is released from this world characterized by repeated births and deaths.

Time in the phenomenal world (*prakriti*) has many perceptual scales, of which two are important. They are *janma–marana* and *prabhava-pralaya* time scale. It is important to note that time, in the phenomenal world, always has a beginning and an end. As such, it is *anityam*—transient or ephemeral. The phenomenal world itself is *anityam*.

Time Scale

Any unit of time has a beginning and an end. Thus we have day, night, week, month, year, etc., on which foundations of both science and religion are built. The intervals of these time scales are measurable and are more or less constant. They are important to human life on earth. However, in terms of Hindu religious doctrines, the units of time are the life span of the human body and the existence of the soul or atman. Both the scales have variable intervals and are themselves *anityam*. These are examined in some detail below:

Janma–Marana Time Scale

The time that elapses from birth to death is life span. The expectation of life at birth is over 60 years now in India which was only 30 throughout the historical period and until about 70 years ago. In recent decades, modern medicines have pushed it to higher levels.

A child may die within the age of five. This is known as infant mortality, which is now around 10 to 12 per cent in India. The survivors can expect to live several decades more than the average expectation of life at birth. This explains the presence of older people even in ancient times.

The maximum liveable age is still around 115 years now, as it was throughout. Old age normally begins at 60 years. The average expectation of life at birth or at other age levels is of little value to an individual who would like to know how long he would live. Unfortunately, this is not predictable.

In general, everyone wants to live long. People have always been fascinated by the concept of immortality and they have tried all methods towards it, but in vain and dreaded death at every stage. All religions essentially draw strength from this human weakness.

In the *Rigveda* and other *Vedas* as well, people wanted longevity of life. This is true today as it was in the past.

***Prabhava–Pralaya* Time Scale**

The soul or atman is distinct from the body although it is a resident of it. The life span of the atman begins from creation or *prabhava* and in most cases it ends with *pralaya* or total destruction of *prakriti*. This is more popularly known as a *yuga*. In Hindu mythology, there are four *yugas* but in the *Bhagavad Gita* there are vague allusions to many more *yugas*.

What is the duration of a *yuga*? This is not clearly mentioned anywhere, definitely not in realistic terms. During a *yuga,* an atman goes through hundreds or even thousands of births and deaths. Given the life span of 30 years, 100 birth-death cycles would mean 3,000 years from Rigvedic times to the present. This is somewhat incomprehensible.

While the lowest forms of life may have emanated about 500 million years ago on earth, Homo sapiens came into existence only about 50,000 years ago. The world's earliest civilizations date back to about 7,000 years at best. To put it in other words, from the days of Angiras, the father of the *Rigveda*, to the present, we have no more than 100 generations. Adi Shankaracharya would be about 40 generations before us.

As a result, wherever there is an allusion to the number of generations before and after a given point in time in the *Bhagavad Gita*, one has to understand the element of hyperbole so replete in Hindu mythology.

The life of the atman can, however, be shorter than the span of a *yuga*, for it is possible for a person to attain *moksha* during the course of a *yuga* itself and thus get released from the cycle of births and deaths.

It is ironical that while people want to prolong their life as long as possible, they would also like to reduce the life span of the atman and get it released sooner from the cycle of births and deaths. Most people do not want to go through another life cycle. In general, people are interested in explaining the present life cycle in terms of past cycle or cycles, but are never keen on discussing the future.

Where is the contradiction? An ordinary person and a spiritual person or *jnani* have altogether different perceptions. The *jnani* desiring *moksha* attains timelessness or he becomes ever-present or *nityam*. For him time and existence have different connotations.

Yogas

The *Bhagavad Gita* deals with *yogas* within the two time frames already mentioned. For the sake of brevity we shall use the term JM for *janana-marana* time scale and PP for the *prabhava-pralaya* time scale. The objective of *yoga* is to exit from the time scales that are *anityam* to the time scale that is *nityam*.

The practice of *yoga* is the substantive subject matter of the *Bhagavad Gita*. It has multiple connotations and definitions. Religion is not science and definitions have no sanctity. In the *Bhagavad Gita*, the word *yoga* appears in the headings of all 18 chapters and throughout it is used both in its liberal and restricted contextual meanings. Contextual definitions of *yoga* appear in several parts of the *Bhagavad Gita*.

For purposes of this analysis, *yoga* may be defined as a process by which the *jivatman* is purified. In other words, by *yoga* a person attains *atma shudhi*. This process is slow; several *janmas* (hundreds would be an exaggeration) are needed to achieve complete purification and it cannot be achieved in one life time, unless one has already achieved a very high level of purification from previous births. When the *jivatman* is completely purified, only atman remains, and it disappears into the *Brahman* when the person attains *moksha*.

Adi Shankaracharya's explanation of *Bhagavad Gita* and his own well known work, the *Bhaja Govindam,* are the foundation for my interpretation of *yogas* and in particular for the study of their interrelationship with time scales.

Yoga in the JM Time Scale

Human beings are uniquely endowed with mind and intellect. In other respects, they are similar to animals and like them, man is always engaged in various activities to satisfy his basic needs and in addition, man has desires which often work in an uncontrolled fashion. However, man has the ability to control his mind using his intellect. *Yoga*, in a nutshell, refers to the very process. This implies that only those who have a developed intellect can practice *yoga*. To practice *yoga* one requires training and knowledge about the nature of *prakriti* and its creator. One learns these from a guru during the early stage of his life and acquires proficiency.

Ashramas

The time from birth to death is divided into four stages in the *Smritis* as *brahmacharya*, *grihasthya*, *vanaprastha* and *sanyasa*. This deliberately excludes infanthood. The duration of various stages is flexible. The initiation into *brahmacharya* begins at age

7–11 depending on varna and *brahmacharya*—learning under a guru—which may last for over a decade. Puberty is the starting point for *grihasthya*. Most stay in this stage until death, but venture for *vanaprastha* and even fewer for *sanyasa*. This may occur in most cases at age 50 or above barring exceptions.

Yogas in Practice

Although a very large number of *yogas* are mentioned in the *Bhagavad Gita*, for the purposes of this analysis only four principal *yogas* are selected. They are: *karma, bhakti, dhyana* and *jnana yoga*. Although *bhakti yoga* and *dhyana yoga* are strictly subsets of *karma yoga*, I have treated *karma yoga* here as the primal stage, while the others as more advanced. These are progressive in nature and *jnana yoga* on high note being the ultimate stage leading to *moksha*. Everyone begins from *karma yoga* and finally attains *jnana yoga* and *moksha*. The *yoga* scale with four stages (all of flexible duration) may operate within a JM period as well as in the PP scale involving a number of life cycles.

The reason why the progress in *yoga* spans both the time scales is because one life time is totally inadequate to attain full *jnana* and the complete purification of *jivatman*. The level of *jnana* and the degree of purification of the *jivatman* are synonymous.

Yogas and Ashramas

As a student or *brahmacharin*, a person may become aware and get enlightened with the concepts of atman and *Brahman* and the workings of *prakriti* from his guru. He would also come to know about *yogas* which involve control of the mind, and therefore of actions by the intellect using various methods.

As a *grihastha* and as an adult, one is responsible for his own actions. A small percentage of them would actually practice *karma yoga*; some from the very beginning of *grihasthya* stage or later at random.

Some would advance to *vanaprastha* and experience *bhakti yoga* and still later take *sanyasa* and become a *dhyana yogi* on the lines prescribed by the *Pantanjali Sutra. Bhakti yoga* signifies a higher level since karmas assume a minor role while karmas are the main focus of life in the *karma yoga*. The attributes of *karma yogi* need no reiteration as they have already been well said.

Dhyana yoga is still at a higher plane and it can be attained only through *sanyasa*. It requires a very high state of *jnana* and concomitantly a higher level of purity of the *jivatman*.

The mere practice of karma, *bhakti* and *dhyana yoga* in succession during *grihasthya*, *vanaprastha* and *sanyasa* would not make one automatically eligible for *moksha* at the end of the *janma*, according to Adi Shankaracharya.

Jnana yoga is prescribed solely for those who become *sanyasins* from *brahmacharya* stage itself as *vairagis* and *sarva karma sanyasins*, and continue in that state for their entire life. In order to be eligible to reach this stage, they must have practised all other *yogas* in their previous births and attained a very high level of purity or *atma shudhi*.

***Yoga* in the PP Time Scale**

When does *yoga* begin in the PP scale? In the JM scale, *yoga* begins in *grihasthya* stage and rarely in the *brahmacharya* stage as well. In the PP scale, at the time of creation, all *jivatmans* are not of equal purity although they originate from the *Brahman*. There are two possibilities. First, the disparities arise from random allocation of the three *gunas* in each body, and second, the *jivas* are actually carried over from the previous *yuga* and their purity would vary, according to their previous karmas.

Furthermore, as the *jivas* with their new bodies are reborn, their association with *prakriti* and *gunas* would make them impure. In almost all cases, this impurity will increase with successive births. One could assume that in the cases of humans it will take some time for the mind and the intellect to mature. Such a period of maturity is not uniform to all either. More over, a certain level of intellect is also necessary for *yoga*. This explains the presence of some early birds at the time when many still struggle intellectually to mature to this point.

We may say that Hinduism's early preceptors were the first to practice *yogas* to attain *moksha*. Starting from Angiras, we may include some 20 generations of Rigvedic *rishis* and then the authors of the *Upanishads* and *Bhagavad Gita* to Adi Shankaracharya and up to Ramana Maharshi in the contemporary world. These are of course only the well-known names; there may also be a few thousand unsung more in this category. It must be noted here that the concepts of *yoga* did not exist in Rigvedic times and even in the earlier stages of the *Upanishads* and thus including in our list the Rigvedic *rishis* is not strictly justified.

There may be a few *jnana yogis* even at the present time. However a thousand is minuscule in relation to nearly a billion Hindus. What is their position today?

All the intellectuals of today were present during the days of Angiras but they were not intellectuals then. Among the intellectuals of today, some are more advanced than others. In doctrinal terms, some have purer *jivatmans*. The question of the level of purity of the *jivatman* already attained is of some significance but it is extremely difficult to scale it.

Purity of the *Jivatman*

Can we leave the measurement of the purity of the *jivatman* to each individual? While everyone would rate it fairly high, others may have an opposite view point. Can we use any objective criteria to measure the purity of the *jivatman*? Perhaps, it has to remain necessarily and exclusively subjective.

In practice, those who take to *sanyasa* from bachelorhood and continue in that state have a high rank in the purity scale. The number of years spent as *sanyasin* does carry some weight, especially if the person has a better reputation. Those who have not taken to *sanyasa* is ranked lower in the purity scale. All *grihasthas* fall in this category. Among *grihasthas* some might have a greater degree of purity or *atma shudhi*, but I have not found a way this could be objectively measured. Performance of rituals, participation in *bhajans* and related social functions do not count according to the *Bhagavad Gita*. Social service would qualify for *atma shudhi*; *Bhagavad Gita* says this is *akarma* capable of giving *atma shudhi*. Beyond this one has to make subjective assessments.

Prognosis

The *Bhagavad Gita* does not offer much to *grihasthas* and *yogis* in general. *Yogis* can look forward to *atma shudhi* and perhaps a better life in the next birth, that is, a life with a higher level of *jnana*.

The rest of us, who have not entered the *yoga* stage, need patience and the desire to sharpen our intellect; only then we shall be eligible to imbibe *jnana*. There is plenty of time ahead of us to think and to use our intellect in the right direction.

Epilogue

In Hinduism, time is an enigmatic concept. For those who are not aware of the doctrines of the *Bhagavad Gita,* 'time' is the 'present' and they expect and want much from gods now. They focus on rituals, both Vedic and non-Vedic and even primitive religious practices. The present and the immediate future are all that matters. Here time is *anityam* and ephemeral.

The intellectuals, who know the doctrine, worry about the next birth and they focus on atma sudhi. They practice *yogas* at any one of the appropriate levels. The distinction between *nityam* and *anityam*, however, may not be fully understood.

For a few, one in a million, time is timeless. It is *nityam* or ever lasting. They spend hours contemplating it. Some achieve happiness, lasting happiness, in this contemplation.

Twelve

Bhaja Govindam: A Review

Introduction

Bhaja Govindam is a well-known collection of verses in Sanskrit composed by Adi Shankaracharya in 800 AD. Its original title was *Moha Mudgara* and it consists of 31 *shlokas*. Rajaji made it known in Tamil Nadu by his commentary which was later translated into English and published by Bharatiya Vidya Bhavan. MS Subbulakshmi's superb rendering of the verses in musical form has endeared it to people in South India.

This work is well known to students of Sanskrit; many *shlokas* from this work have found their way into textbooks. RG Bhandarkar has used this work widely in his classic books on Sanskrit grammar. Bhandarkar's books published in the latter half of the 19th Century are still used as textbooks in schools and colleges all over India.

Adi Shankaracharya is acclaimed for his critical analysis of the *Upanishads*, the *Bhagavad Gita* and the *Brahma Sutra*, in Sanskrit prose.

They constitute the *prasthana thriam* or the foundation of the Vedanta school as defined by the Acharya. He has also composed many verses or collection of verses which are well-known. The *Bhaja Govindam* stands apart as it represents an overview of his thinking that can be easily understood by ordinary people. This work is not about what the scriptures say or prescribe; it is all about what the Acharya thinks that ordinary householders should or should not do. He tries to guide them to the spiritual path leading to salvation pointing out human follies and the resulting life of miseries.

In the 8th Century, Buddhism was already a spent force in India; it could not make headway in a society bound by *jati* and varna. Buddhism expounded a casteless society. Yet, for all its idealism, the social system in India was too deep-rooted to change the situation. Furthermore, the *Puranas* and epics were more attractive, requiring little by way of intellect or self discipline. They also provided ample entertainment.

Adi Shankaracharya travelled on foot to different regions in India and established four *mutts* in the four corners of the country, namely, at Jyotirmutt near Badrinath, at Dwaraka in Gujarat, at Puri in Orissa, and at Sringeri in Karnataka. He is widely credited with the cultural integration of India by the unification of thousands of local gods into the three-fold system of gods of the Indian pantheon. To what extent this claim is true, I am not sure. Anyway, he made a great impact all over India during his life time and he is well-known to all Hindus from Srinagar to Kanyakumari and Gujarat to Assam. Most Brahmanas and others in India accept him as the supreme teacher or *paramacharya*.

Bhakti* and *Jnana

Shankaracharya opens his advocacy by asking us to worship the supreme God Govinda, who teaches *dharma* to humanity in the *Bhagavad Gita*. Worship the God Govinda, for faith is far more important than bookish knowledge.

Coming as this does from a scholar par eminence, known for his advocacy of *jnana yoga*, it does take one by surprise. However, as we go along, it becomes clear that *bhakti* is only the starting point and *jnana* is the ultimate goal. The last two *shlokas* of this work make this absolutely clear. We shall come back to this point later.

The *Bhagavad Gita* is directly mentioned in *shloka* 20 and is alluded to in several others. This is the only scriptural text mentioned by the Acharya in this work and he recommends reading of this text in unequivocal terms. In the *Bhagavad Gita*, the *bhakti*, *karma*, *dhyana* and *jnana yogas* are examined in detail, while *jnana yoga* occupies higher pedestal as the ultimate goal.

While there is no conflict between the different *yogas* or spiritual paths, all of us at a given time follow only one of the paths. *Karma yoga* is the path of the ordinary householder focussing on earning a living; as he progresses in life, he becomes closer to the *bhakti marga* and at a later stage, giving up family and possessions, he enters the *dhyana marga*. A *grihastha* is not entitled to *jnana marga* in the present life, but he could do so in the next life if he has, by that time, attained a high level of *atma shudhi*.

Perhaps the most important function of *bhakti* is to eliminate fear—fear of future events and in particular death. *Bhakti* without *jnana* will not take one beyond this stage. Alone, it will not result in *moksha*. This was stressed even earlier.

It is important to note that the Bhakti Movement originated in Tamil Nadu and spread to the North and attained a climax in 1200 AD in the South. Adi Shankaracharya started his career in the South and went to the nook and corners of India in 800 AD. At this time, the Bhakti Movement was in its early stages. *Kamba Ramayanam*, in Tamil, belongs to 900 AD, and *Tulsi Ramayan*, in Hindi, was written in 1600 AD. There was no Rama cult in the North or South during the time of Adi Shankaracharya. The Krishna cult, as we know it today, also did not exist then. The Krishna cult belongs to 1600 AD and this is based on the *Brahmavaivarta Purana*.

Futility of Rituals

Shankaracharya says that taking a bath in the Ganga or the sea, following austerities and penance, or giving donations or gifts will not result in *moksha* if unaccompanied by *jnana*. A *jnani* will, however, do none of these things since he is by definition a *karma sanyasi*—one who has forsaken all karmas or rituals. Shankaracharya strongly recommends *japa* or recitation and *dhyana*. He says that one should recite the name of the God (*japa*) and constantly remember his form, namely that of Govinda (Verse 27). He would like one to read the *Bhagavad Gita*, even if this is done in the form of a recitation. There is nothing wrong in giving gifts so long as nothing is expected in return. Rituals performed for the sake of family or self is not recommended, since it will invite rebirth and preclude *moksha*. Performing rituals for common good or to God, without expecting reward, is justified.

Wrong Conduct

Personal conduct receives much attention, although the focus here is more on wrong conduct rather than right conduct. There are many forms of wrong conduct resulting from desires. *Kama* (lust), *krodha* (anger), *lobha* (greed), *moha* (craving) must be discarded (Verse 26). Self pride and the emphasis on prestige result in misery. These are like diseases that cause suffering in the world (Verse 4). One has to eliminate these desires. People pride themselves on their youth, wealth, and their mastery over other people (Verse 11). These are ephemeral and are swept away by time.

Children are engrossed in play, youth is attracted towards maiden, and the old are a worried lot. No one is interested in religion and God. It is interesting that even in the 8th Century AD, majority of people did not care for religion. They were interested in enjoyment of life.

Rebirth

The cycle of birth and death is mentioned in Verse 21, and faith in God is recommended as a remedy, but only casually. Again this subject is retouched in Verse 17, wherein it is stated that without *jnana* one will not get salvation even after hundred births. Rebirth is often considered as the most important concept in Hinduism. However, for a *jnani* this is irrelevant.

Mystics

Several verses are devoted to mystics in society; not all the mystics were genuine. In Verse 14, the Acharya describes these fake mystics as persons putting on different appearances, while all this is only for filling one's stomach. It is a way of living as a parasite. He calls them fools. Verse 16 is in the same mould. Verses 18, 19 and 22 describe true mystics. These mystics have given up all possessions and are dressed only in torn pieces of cloth. They are not bothered about people's opinion. They constantly contemplate on the Absolute God. They are happy, no matter what their physical appearance or condition is. A mystic is a true *vairagi* who has given up the enjoyment of all worldly possessions and yet is very happy.

Family Relations

The family as the basic unit of society in 800 AD is seen in several verses. Wife and son are frequently mentioned (Verses 8, 13, 25, and 29) while father and mother figure in Verse 23, the family is mentioned directly in verse 10 and indirectly in Verses 5 and 6. Often the family is the cause for worry or unhappiness; when there is no money, the family becomes indifferent. When there is money, there is fear that the son would make his demands. Nowhere the family is seen as a positivity. There is no happy family in Acharya's eyes.

Economics

A major element of surprise is that Adi Shankaracharya mentions wealth and income in as many as five verses. It says do not crave after money, be satisfied with whatever you get by your own effort. He goes on to say in Verse 5 that when a person is no longer able to earn, his family is no longer interested in him or does not even care to ask him about his wellbeing. A person without money has no family (Verse 10). People are worried about loss of wealth (Verse 13). Wealth generates daily worries; there is fear even from sons who may claim a share of father's wealth (Verse 29).

These insights into home economics are as true today as they were in 800 AD.

Social System Ignored

There is no mention of varna or *jati* in *Bhaja Govindam*. There are references to the *Bhagavad Gita* and not *Manusmriti*. Shankaracharya was essentially a unifier of society and not a divider. Ignoring varna and *jati* perhaps was very obvious that his advice applied to all.

There is also no mention of kings or the 'State' which enforces the *dharma*. For him it was unimportant. It should be noted here that Adi Shankaracharya never ever mentions the name of any king who was a contemporary to him despite the fact that he visited all parts of the country and met many kings. Is this arrogance or total disinterest in contemporary affairs? However, he gives us a clear idea of contemporary life—an example of subaltern history as opposed to dynastic history.

Bhakti—Prelude To *Jnana*

While *bhakti* is recommended, the Acharya never suggests that it is the end. *Bhakti* can only overcome the fear of death and rebirth but *jnana* takes one beyond.

On the other hand, the Acharya is conscious that *jnana* is not for all, particularly to a person involved in worldly life. For this person, *bhakti* is the only solace. He must continue to cultivate it (Verses 20, 21, and 27).

Dhyana Yoga

The Acharya's final advice is contained in Verses 30 and 31. These verses summarize the *ashtanga raja yoga* of *Pantanjali Sutra*. The first three stages in this yoga, viz., *yama*, *niyama* and *asana* are not mentioned. The assumption is that since these have already been followed, only the later steps which require withdrawal from society needed to be emphasized. This is because the advice is primarily intended for the person about to enter *vanaprastha*. *Pranayama*, *pratyahara*, *dharana*, *dhyana* and *samadhi* are the last five steps. *Samadhi* is the ultimate stage.

In order to attain this, there is a need to seek and follow the advice of a guru. Also, one must withdraw from worldly life (become a *vairagi* and a *sanyasin*). Thereafter, by practice and guidance from the guru, one attains control over one's actions and mind. This would enable him to see the God residing in his own heart.

The 29 verses preceding these are to be thought of only as an advice to the *grihastha* or householder to see life in its true colours and prepare himself for the final destination, *sanyasa*.

Conclusion

The *Bhaja Govindam* is an outstanding work and it should be read again and again by all who have an interest in Hinduism. By totally ignoring divisive aspects like *jati* and *varna*, this work has universal appeal and acceptability. It does not offend any group, nor does it place any group on high on scale. True, there is a slight gender bias. The work is addressed to the householder, who by implication is a male. In Verse 8 the Acharya says: "Oh brother, think of the principles of life." However, there are no harsh comments on the role of women, in contrast with the *Manusmriti* which is harsh on women and their role in society.

To begin with, there is a little bit of gentle but good advice for the middle-aged householder. He says please live and be happy with the money that you earn and do not aspire for too much. The obsession of men with sex, anger, and excessive desires are to be avoided or eliminated altogether. Self discipline is a must. The Acharya comes down heavily on self pride and the craving for status. He equates these with diseases leading to misery.

Simple *bhakti*, with no elaborate rituals, focussing only on reading of the *Bhagavad Gita*, *japa* and *dhyana* are more than adequate. They will definitely save one from mental tension and fear of the future.

At the fag end of one's life, the Acharya would like one to enter the spiritual path knowing fully the difficulties (Verse 11). The Acharya does not compromise with his basic principles of *jnana* and the path towards *moksha*. *Vairagya*, which means giving up all worldly possessions and their enjoyment, and *sanyasa*, that is giving up of family and the world around us, are prescribed basics. One must also seek out a guru and be totally dedicated to him. This prescription is put into practice only by the rarest of rare individuals.

However, if one is not seeking *moksha*, then the path is simpler to tread. One can focus on *japa* and *dhyana* without *vairagya* and *sanyasa*. This is what most people actually do. *Bhakti*, supported by *japa* and *dhyana* of the *ishta devta*, is adequate. This is what the *Bhagavad Gita* finally prescribes for everyone.

PART II

Hindu Society

Thirteen

Land and People

The Indo-Gangetic Plain is the home of Hinduism based on Sanskrit texts; it is also the home of Buddhism, Jainism and Sikhism. When did this plain originate? When did people first settle down here? The answer to these and several other similar questions are the subject matter of this rather technical chapter. It should certainly interest those who are keen in the history and origin of these religions and their social systems. The Hindu religion itself focusses on the origin of earth and life. The viewpoint here is purely scientific and has nothing to do with their validity or otherwise.

Geological Past

The Indian Subcontinent consists of three parts—the Himalayan mountain chain, Peninsular India and the vast Indo-Gangetic Plain. Peninsular India is by far the oldest and it dates back to Pre-Cambrian times (over 500 million years ago). At that time it formed part of a continent called Gondwanaland, which included Africa, South America, Australia and Antarctica. The word 'Gondwanaland' literally means forests of the Gonds; Gonds are a well-known tribe of Central India. In the Northern Hemisphere, we had another continent—the Angaraland—that covered all of Asia, Europe and North America. Between the two, that is, Gondwanaland and Angaraland, was an open ocean known as the Tethys Sea. Around 300 million years ago, the continents of Africa, Australia, South America, as well as Peninsular India broke away from Antarctica and started moving north towards Angaraland. Today, these landmasses are known as 'plates' and the theory that deals with their movements is known as plate tectonics. This process took a long time and in fact continues even into the present.

Origin of Himalayas

As Peninsular India moved towards Angaraland, more specifically the Tibetan Plateau region, the sedimentary rocks laid under the Tethys Sea were pushed against the hard rocks of the Tibetan plateau, giving rise to the folded mountains of the Great Himalayas. The Himalayas are a series of mountain ranges, each representing a fold; the Shivaliks represent the newest addition. As the Himalayas rose, the Tethys Sea became narrower and shallower and concentrated in the south at the fringe of Peninsular India. Rivers emerged from the folded mountains of the Himalayas and flowed south into the Tethys Sea, depositing huge quantities of rich alluvium. Eventually, the Tethys Sea vanished, exposing the vast alluvial plains extending east to west. This plain forms an intermediate zone between the Himalayas and Peninsular India, now called Indo-Gangetic Plain.

When did the Himalayas originate? The answer is that it took some time to happen. It is believed that the Himalayas attained their current height around 50 million years ago and they are still growing.

Origin of Indo-Gangetic Plain

The Indo-Gangetic Plain is of still later origin as it took a lot of time for the Tethys Sea to vanish and for the intervening space to be filled up with several layers of clay and sand. In the Middle Ganga Plains, these alluvial deposits are about 20,000 feet deep; one will have to dig below that level to find solid rock. These sand beds have huge water reservoirs, as old as millions of years. Even the water nowadays pumped out from bore wells could be several thousand years of age. The question then is at what time did the Indo-Gangetic Plain assume its present profile? This is indeed very recent, only about 10,000 years ago.

How do we know that the Indo-Gangetic Plains originated around 10,000 years ago? The clue lies in the four glacial and three inter-glacial periods that occurred in the Pleistocene time all over the world. This four-fold glacial phase extends over about one million years and it ended only around 10,000 years ago. The period after this, namely the present, is known as Holocene. After every glacial phase, the glaciers in the Himalayas melted and receded. This melting of ice resulted in large quantities of water flooding the rivers. It carried enormous quantities of sand and alluvium to the plains. These deposits altered the configuration of the plains and channels along which the rivers flowed. Thus we may conclude that the present configuration of the river channels of the Indo-Gangetic Plain is only about 10,000 years old.

Two other aspects of the recent history of the plains and the mountains are relevant. One aspect is the two major river systems that flowed into the sea at the two ends of the Peninsular block. While the Indus flowed directly to the south into the Arabian Sea, the Ganga flowed as far south as possible until it reached the Peninsular block and then turned eastwards to reach the Bay of Bengal. Likewise, the southward flow of the Brahmaputra is blocked by an outlier of Peninsular India, the Shillong plateau. Guwahati is on the peninsular block, although it is on the banks of the Brahmaputra. The Ganga Plain slopes north-south and west to east, and its northern margins are better drained and it is this belt where people established their first settlement. Subsequently, such settlements extended to south and east of the Ganga Plain, since the southern and eastern belts were more heavily forested and were also subject to flooding.

The glacial periods have left their footmarks in the Himalayas and it is possible to study the fauna and flora at the time of glacial and interglacial periods from fossil remains in the glacial deposits of those times. The landscape of the Himalayan river valleys tells us a lot about the past. The habitable land which stretches along the rivers are the river terraces; there are a whole series of such terraces in all Himalayan rivers; the notable ones are along the Alakananda River. At the origins of these rivers are the holy places of Badrinath, Kedarnath, and Gomukh. It is neither possible nor necessary to go into the very interesting details of what we know and what we can learn from the geological history of the Himalayas; we may just note that we have learnt quite a bit and that there is much more to learn in the future.

The most important finding so far is that there is no evidence about the presence of humans in the Himalayas during the

Pleistocene glacial periods. This contrasts strongly with the situation in the Alps, where we have considerable evidence of pre-human and even human life during the Pleistocene period. Anthropologists have described the evolution of Paleolithic (Old Stone Age) cultures in the Alps and surrounding areas in great detail. There were in all six stages of cultural evolution during this period; three in the lower Paleolithic and three in Upper Paleolithic periods. There is no evidence of any Paleolithic cultures in either the Himalayas or elsewhere in the Indian Subcontinent. The earliest human settlements in India belong to the Neolithic period, for which we have archaeological evidence.

Prehistorical and Historical Past

When did man first appear in the subcontinent? This is not a very difficult question and the answer is that man appeared about 10,000 years ago. The study of the evolution of man and the original home of man has been studied with great vigour during the past 100 years or so. The current opinion is that man, or Homo sapiens, originated in Africa around 60,000 years ago and later migrated to various parts of the world. It may be noted that there are considerable evidences of pre-humans in Europe, Africa, China and elsewhere, but not in India. The pre-human people in Europe and elsewhere were replaced by humans coming out of Africa. Major streams of mankind went to Europe, Central Asia and from there to China and Southeast Asia and even North and South America. The people who settled in these newer lands developed distinct racial characteristics, in terms of skin colour, hair form, and so on over a period of time and thus we have today three major racial types—Caucasoid, Mongoloid and Negroid.

These primary racial groups evolved in Central Asia, China and South Africa respectively. The Indian Subcontinent was inhabited at a later point in time when the above racial types were already fully developed. No racial type evolved in India because the history of human habitation in the Subcontinent is too short—only about 10,000 years. There is a gap of 50,000 years between the time when humans first appeared in Africa and the time they arrived in the Indian Subcontinent. On the other hand, China and Europe have a much longer history of human habitations. The people now inhabiting these lands developed distinct racial characteristics as a result of long years of habitation there.

Early Migrations

Migrations of people into the Indian Subcontinent occurred not at one go but in several streams at different points in time. As indicated before, the earliest migrations of people into India took place around 10,000 years ago. The early migrants used the Makran coast in Iran and Baluchisthan in Pakistan while the later migrants used the Khyber and other passes in northwest of the subcontinent. Migrations also took place across the Himalayas to the south from Tibet and from Burma towards the north. It is even more important to note that the Indian Subcontinent, in particular, continued to receive new streams of people, especially from Central Asia even during medieval times (1000 AD to 1800 AD). Thus, migrations of people into India have been an important feature of both pre-historical and historical periods.

The aspect of recurrent migrations is especially important from the point of view of the composition of the population of the Indian Subcontinent. As a result, the Indian population has a mixture of racial elements. Perhaps the earliest people to arrive in India were Negroids; the Andaman Islands still have people with true Negroid features. They were followed by the Australoids, who are distinguished from Negroids by their wavy hair form; in the north and northeastern parts of the country, we have people with Mongoloid characteristics and still later we have a very large scale influx of Paleo-Mediterranean racial type; this is followed by several waves of migration of other racial types. The predominant racial type in India, both in north and south, are the Paleo-Mediterranean. This is actually a sub-division of the Caucasoid racial type.

This brings us back to the first question—how do we know that man appeared in the subcontinent about 10,000 years ago? We have excavations of Neolithic settlements in various parts of India. These date back to 10,000 years as determined by the radio carbon method. Apart from Neolithic settlements, we also have cave and rock paintings in the southern and central parts of India. Nevertheless, we do not know much about the culture of these people. In general terms, the Neolithic people practised agriculture and animal husbandry but were not aware of metals and hence all their tools were made of stone. Neolithic people had their own religions; this is clearly indicated by the urns in which they buried their dead.

The more significant developments that occurred in later time periods are described below. One should note that there is a big gap of about 5,000 years between the first appearance of Neolithic settlements and the subcontinent's oldest civilization. During this period, the entire subcontinent witnessed the spread of human settlements to all parts. The population of the Subcontinent also increased from zero level to about three to four million at the start of the third millennium BC.

Harappan Civilization

The pre-historical and historical periods have been dealt with in this book in context of the evolution of Hinduism. Here the focus is on aspects that have not been touched upon earlier. The subcontinent's first civilization emerged on the banks of the Indus River around 2500 BC, and it is known today as the Harappan civilization.

The Harappan civilization was first discovered in 1921 and later excavations were carried out on sites which are now in Pakistan. However, much of our recent knowledge about this civilization comes from excavations on Harappan sites on the Indian side and we now have a wealth of information. The Harappan sites on the Pakistan side are rather neglected, as there is no interest in that country in ancient Indian history.

What these excavations reveal is that a very advanced urban civilization existed in the Indian Subcontinent covering the whole of Pakistan from Punjab to Sind and the entire western part of India extending to Gujarat, Rajasthan and western Uttar Pradesh. This advanced civilization was comparable to those of Mesopotamia, with whom it had trade relations. Nevertheless, the inability to decipher the Harappan script has made it impossible to know how this civilization disappeared by 1800 BC. The most probable reason is that it declined slowly due to persistent drought and pestilence.

Even more important is our inability to relate this civilization to the one that emerged gradually at a later point in time. This new emerging civilization was based on two languages—Sanskrit and Pali. While the texts relating to Hinduism are in Sanskrit, those relating to Buddhism and Jainism are in Pali. Pali was the spoken language of common people of this time in the Middle Ganga Plains, while Sanskrit was the language of the Hindu priestly class.

The religion of the Harappan people can be inferred from the terracotta figurines. They indicate worship of what appears to be Shiva lingam; there are also evidences of the worship of mother goddesses, spirits of various kinds, trees and animals. All these play an important role in Hinduism today. It is important to note that the influence of the Harappan civilization was not confined to North India; the South was equally influenced by it. We may even postulate that the degree of influence declined inversely with distance from the core region of Harappan civilization. There is no doubt that the Harappan culture continued to have a very wide influence even after its decline in the Indus region, in both North and South of India.

Urbanization of Ganga Plain

Archaeological excavations in the Ganga Plain have revealed two major phases of human settlements. The first is located around Jamuna River. In this phase, the settlements are of a rural nature and they belong to the period between 1200 BC and 800 BC. This culture is known to archaeologists as the Painted Grey Ware culture. This culture corresponds to the society of the later Vedic period.

The second discovery is that of settlements having a few urban places. This culture is centred on eastern Uttar Pradesh and Bihar. It dates back to around 600 BC to 300 BC. This cluster of several hundred settlements was discovered by archaeologists and represents the second urban civilization of India. From this time onwards, we have a continuous history of urbanization and culture. In all these cases, the radiocarbon dating method is used to pinpoint the exact time periods involved. The religious developments of this time period have been explained in the context of the evolution of Hinduism and the same need not be gone into again.

What is important to note are the factors that led to the emergence of an urban civilization in the Middle Ganga Plains. The explanations focus on two aspects—ecological setting and technology. As the Rigvedic people moved eastwards from the Jamuna-Ganga interfluve, the climatic conditions changed for the better. These lands received more rain and could support rice cultivation. While near Jamuna they cultivated wheat and barley, in the Middle Ganga Plains it was rice. In the Nile Valley and in Mesopotamia, surplus agricultural production resulted from irrigation but since Ganga Plains depended solely on rainfall it is the technology that contributed to the surplus. This technology of farming belongs to the pre-Rigvedic people.

Further, the ecological condition and the advanced technology as revealed by the use of iron tools supported a more productive agriculture. The present day Jharkhand was the source for iron; the tribals of the region had mastered the art of steel production from the local iron, using wood as fuel. Had it not been for their contributions, the urban culture of the Middle Ganga Plains may not have emerged at this time.

The art of writing came as a boon in the middle of 500 BC; how or who contributed to the invention of writing is still a mystery. The ability to record information is considered as a pre-requisite for urbanization. Its utility in three situations needs extraordinary stress—traders for keeping transaction records especially when the volume of trade is very large; the king's treasurer for accounting of tax collections and expenses on various items; and finally, the priestly class for making manuscripts of sacred verses as their volume increased.

All the developments described above set the stage for the emergence of kingdoms and their capital cities. There is no doubt that the urban culture of the Middle Ganga Plains is a result of combined efforts of both the Rigvedic and pre-Rigvedic people.

Peninsular India

There are evidences of several settlements in peninsular region from Neolithic times. However, notable settlement sites belong to the long span of Chalcolithic age, part of which is contemporaneous with the Harappan period. These settlements were located on high ground and the people practised hunting, fishing and rudimentary agriculture. Copper was widely used. Peninsular India is rich in its mineral resources while the Ganga Plains had none. Jharkhand and Rajasthan are mineral-rich beds from where people of Ganga Plains drew copper and iron for making tools and weapons.

The urban centres of the South probably date back to 300 BC. Kanchipuram and Nagarjunakonda were important urban centres of Buddhist and Jaina religions; the old kingdoms of the South, namely those of the Pandya and Chola dynasties existed around 200 BC. Madurai and Korkai were the twin capitals of the Pandyas while Uraiyur and Puhar were Chola capitals. From this point, South India has a continuous cultural history. The South is also rich in terms of temple architecture, but these belong to the periods from 500 AD. The most distinctive feature of the culture of South is the role played by the Tamil language which has a rich and ancient literary tradition.

The Sanskritic texts, especially, the *Manusmriti* talks of *Aryavarta*. This land is defined as covering all areas between the Himalayas in the north and the Vindhyas in the south and the seas to the east and west. The Vindhyas and Satpura mountains extend east to west, starting from the west coast and extending close to the east coast. This region still has extensive forests and is inhabited by tribal people, some of whom still speak Dravidian language. The tribal belt of India, which coincides with this mountainous region, covers significant portions of Orissa, Jharkhand, Chattisgarh, Madhya Pradesh, Rajasthan and Gujarat which is traditionally accepted as the divide between the North and the South. There was however, close contact between the Indo-Gangetic Plain and the far South despite this somewhat inhospitable terrain and forests.

North-South Pathways

There are three migratory routes that link the North with the South. The first is the east coast route from Bengal and Orissa through Andhra to the delta of the Kaveri River. A well-known Chola king of 1000 AD used this route to take his army as far as the Ganga River. The Buddhist and Jaina monks were perhaps the first to use this route to explore the South in early 300 BC. They were followed by groups of Brahmanas at later points in time. The Smartha Brahmanas of the South came from Magadha and they carried with them the Poorva Mimamsa tradition of Hinduism with its emphasis on the *Yajurveda* and *Manusmriti*. They also brought with them the concept of land-grant villages.

The Srivaishnava Brahmanas of the South probably came from Bengal. They carried with them the tradition of Vaishnavaism with emphasis on the *Samaveda*. Among this group, the Chakravarti Brahmanas claim superiority over the others; a tradition that they probably brought from Bengal where the Chakraborty Brahmanas hold the same view.

The second was the west coast route, starting from Gujarat along the Konkan coast to Kerala, but it was never used by invading armies. It is through this route that Brahmana communities from North, especially Kashmir, migrated to Konkan, Goa and Kerala. The Chitpavan and Saraswat Brahmanas trace their origins to Kashmir. The Namboodiri Brahmanas of Kerala do not make any special claims, but they are very well-versed in Sanskrit and the Hindu traditions flowing from it. They can rightly claim to have given us Adi Shankaracharya who is recognized as a supreme teacher of all Hindus.

The central Indian trade routes generally followed Malwa-Khandesh route (from Ujjain through Indore and Burhanpur) through parts of Madhya Pradesh and Maharashtra. It was used by the kings belonging to the Rashtrakuta, Vakataka, and Satavahana dynasties and by the medieval Muslim rulers. Probably the earliest Brahmana migrations followed this route, since all the dynasties mentioned above and many more were themselves Brahmanas. An alternate one used in ancient times is the Jabalpur-Balaghat route.

The Brahmana groups, who came from North, are responsible for the Sankritization of the South. This process started from 300 BC and continued well into the medieval period. The Brahmana groups in the South did not, however, forget their roots and they did make periodic visits to North and in particular to Varanasi, the holiest place for all Hindus.

During historical times, pilgrims went from South to Varanasi, Hardwar and other places in the North mainly using the coastal routes. Adi Shankaracharchya walked on foot to the four corners of India and established religious Mutts in Badrinath in the Himalayas, Dwaraka in Gujarat, Puri in Orissa, and finally Sringeri in Karnataka in 800 AD. The temple priests at Badrinath in the Himalayas come from Kerala every year in spring and return in late autumn. This two-way journey was carried on foot during most of the period from 800 AD to the recent past. The priests coming from closely related families of Brahmanas in Kerala continue to enjoy their right to perform their functions in Badrinath even today. The point is that the whole of India was interlinked with pathways frequented by traders and others. The people used these pathways not only to visit places of pilgrimage but also to migrate from troubled areas to comfortable lands from pre-historic times to the present.

The study of pre-history and history of India highlight the pathways of connectivity rather than emphasize the oft-repeated cliché of impenetrable mountains and forests. The North and South of India were always united by these pathways. Even the Himalayas did not prevent close cultural contact between China and India. The Vindhya and Satpura mountains are much smaller in relation to the Himalayas. They did not inhibit the flow of people from North to South or in the opposite direction at any time.

Fourteen

Manusmriti: Varna Ashrama Dharma

Introduction

The *Manusmriti* is a classic treatise on the Hindu social laws written in 3rd Century. It preceded the *Bhagavad Gita* by several centuries. It specifies Vedic Gods and emphasizes Vedic rituals. The mention of Yavanas (Greeks) and Shudra kings imparts a feeling that it is post-Mauryan era.

The introductory verses describe how a group of *rishis* led by *Maharishi* Brighu approached Manu and requested him to explain to them the social laws for people belonging to the four varnas. However, after explaining the creation of the worlds, both real and astral, and the cyclic nature of creation, he hands over the charge to his son and student, *Maharishi* Brighu, to explain the actual laws. The *Manusmriti* is, therefore, a series of well-organized lectures by *Maharishi* Brighu to a group of *rishis*. *Rishis* mentioned in the *Smritis* and *Puranas* are of a legendary and astral character and they are distinct from the poets of the Rigvedic age.

The *Manusmriti* consists of 12 chapters made up from 2,694 *shlokas*. These verses are easy to understand and are very straightforward and totally devoid of symbolism, metaphors and other paraphernalia generally associated with poetry. The verses deal with practical issues of life. Platitudinous or even general statements rarely appear when spiritual matter is touched upon.

The *Manusmriti* is about *karma yoga* and this is stated in Chapter 2 and the concluding chapter. Nevertheless, the *karma yoga* in the *Manusmriti* is different from that of the *Bhagavad Gita*. In the *Manusmriti, karma yoga* is defined as performing karmas according to *varna ashrama dharma*. When diligently completed, it leads to *moksha*.

The *Manusmriti,* by and large, follows the Poorva Mimamsa school. According to this school of Jaimini, performing Vedic rituals is all that is needed. Vedanta harps on *moksha* in which giving up of Vedic rituals and *vairagya* are essential. The *Manusmriti* tries to cement the differences and accepts both as legitimate ways of achieving *moksha*.

Another conflict which the *Manusmriti* attempts to resolve is the offering and eating of meat in connection with Vedic rituals. It justifies the eating and offering of meat to Gods in several contexts, while at the same time showing definite preference for vegetarianism at the end.

On the whole, the *Manusmriti* is not dogmatic. It recognizes the complexities of society and allows for flexibility in social laws. This may come as a surprise to many. In this chapter, we will focus on the first six chapters of the *Manusmriti* that deal with *varna ashrama dharma*.

Creation

The first chapter of the *Manusmriti*, consisting of 119 verses, deals with the creation of the world, the cyclic nature of creation, the basis of the varna system, praise of Brahmanas and rationale, and organization of the treatise.

To begin with, there was total darkness. Only *Brahman*, the Absolute God who cannot be seen or heard, existed. Desiring to create the world of living objects, *Brahman* first created water and into that he laid his seed. A golden egg (*hiranya garbha*) emerged out of water. The egg split into two and the cosmic man, better known as *Purusha* or *Prajapati*, emerged. The two halves became earth and heaven respectively and the space in between became the sky. (*Prajapati* is also known as Brahma; *Purusha* is also known as Vishnu and both are equated with *Brahman*).

Prajapati created all life on earth step by step, distinguishing them by their appearance, mode of reproduction, and by other attributes. Thus plants of various types, worms and insects, a great variety of animals, fish and birds appeared on earth. The process of creation starts with the lowest forms and gradually moves upwards.

Finally, from the different parts of his own body, *Prajapati* created four classes (varnas) of men (and also women). These were Brahmanas, Kshatriyas, Vaishyas, and Shudras. He assigned them different roles in society. He also created Manu to frame social laws appropriate to each of these varnas. The term varna in the *Manusmriti* strictly means classes; it has no racial connotation whatsoever. In theory at least, the three upper varnas belong to the same Rigvedic society; how can they lead to new races or have different skin colour?

The Brahmanas are permitted the following duties—learning and teaching, performing *yajnas* and helping others to perform it, and giving and receiving of gifts. The Kshatriya was authorized to look after the people's welfare, give gifts, perform *yajnas*, and study the *Vedas* (if he wants). He should not overindulge in music, dance and other leisurely activities. Vaishya may take care of cattle, give gifts, perform *yajnas*, study the *Vedas*, practice trade or usury or engage in agriculture. The Shudra should assist all the other varnas in their respective tasks.

What is the rationale for introducing the varna system? The breakup of the tribal society, to my understanding, is not relevant but the role of the priestly class in the emerging feudal system with the warrior classes in the commanding position of kingship and army is indeed important. In reality, the Kshatriyas had wielded more power, privileges, and wealth. In a compromise arrangement between the two top classes of society—the priests and warriors—the Brahmanas put themselves at the top slot to perpetuate their relevance and placed the Kshatriyas next. The farmers and traders, who were economically pivotal, came third, while the artisans, servants, and agricultural workers were relegated to in the last place. The four-fold social system was not unique to India; these four classes existed in all other feudal societies. The difference is that in Hinduism it is of divine origin. The maintenance of the varna system was essential to the very survival of the Hindu feudal society and hence the importance given to it in the *Manusmriti* and later in the *Bhagavad Gita*.

Cyclic Nature of Creation

The creation of the world and its eventual destruction occurred periodically. Each time a new world was created, a new Manu was also created to frame social laws. These laws varied with every cycle since there were significant changes in the appearance and qualities of people from one cycle to another. The overall moral order declined gradually. In the *Kali Yuga* of the current cycle, the moral order is at its lowest. In simple words, the past was always better than the present. The Manu of the present *yuga* is known as *Vivaswata,* son of the Sun God. He created a number of learned *rishis* headed by the legendary *Maharishi* Brighu and it is to him that we owe the *Manusmriti.*

In all religions, historical persons are later transformed into legendary figures and all kinds of supernatural virtues and miracles are ascribed to them. It is necessary to distinguish between fact and fiction. The *Manusmriti* is, fortunately, 99 per cent factual. The author of the *Manusmriti* was, obviously, a human and a Brahmana. The name Manu will hereafter be used to connote that sense. The true name of the author of this work is not known.

Praise of Brahmanas

In Manu's scheme of social laws, the Brahmanas have the primary duty to study, understand, and interpret social laws. Brahmanas are praised by Manu as being worthy of the trust and respect of all the other varnas.

Among Brahmanas, those who have studied the *Vedas* are superior to all others; those, in addition to the above, practice all the Vedic karmas dutifully are better and the most superior are those who are *brahma jnanis.* Practice of dharma is even more important than mere learning and knowledge. Brahmanas must set an example to others by strictly following the Manu dharma.

The first chapter of the *Manusmriti* concludes with a very brief overview of the succeeding chapters.

Brahmacharya

In 249 verses, Chapter 2 of the *Manusmriti* frames rules for the ritual and non-ritual practices from conception to the end of *brahmacharya* period. The treatment follows a chronological order.

What is Dharma?

Dharma is defined in many ways. Here the *Smritis* constitute dharma and more specifically, *Manusmriti* is the authority on what constitutes dharma.

In *brahmacharya* one learns the *Vedas* and the *Smritis.* The former gives spiritual knowledge and the latter teaches dharma.

The *acharya* should teach the student the rules for the performance of *srautha* and *smartha* karmas which constitute dharma.

Srautha-smartha karmas are all *kamya* karmas and hence are looked down upon by Vedantins. The *Manusmriti,* however, endorses the view of the Poorva Mimamsikas which affirm that *purushartha* is the sole objective of life and that all of them are attained by following dharma. The four *purusharthas* are: dharma, *artha, kama,* and *moksha.*

Interestingly, in the *Manusmriti,* the term *karma yoga* appears from start to end and there is a full discussion on this subject in the last chapter. However, the *karma yoga* of the *Manusmriti* is different from that of the *Bhagavad Gita.* In *Manusmriti, karma yoga* means the joining together of karma and dharma. The term *yoga* literally means joining together. In *varna dharma,* it is very legitimate to aspire for results of one's actions; as mentioned earlier, all karmas are *kamya* karmas.

Aryavarta

The *Manusmriti* confines the territorial limits of the first three varnas to the land between the Himalayas and the Vindhyas and the seas toward the east and the west. The Shudras lived within and outside *Aryavarta*. However, the continued invasions into the *Aryavarta* since the *Manusmriti* was written resulted in large scale migrations of Brahmanas to different regions of South India. This explains the presence of Brahmanas in the south, beyond the *Aryavarta*. The Smartha Brahmanas or Iyers of the south are well-known for their expertise in the *Smritis* and also the *Vedas* which they brought along from the north. To be recognized as a Brahmana, a person must have thorough knowledge of the *Vedas* and *Smritis*, he must know Sanskrit and he should be able to recite mantras well. It is not easy for those not born into Brahmana families to acquire these skills. However, the possibility of talented boys, even from among Shudras, acquiring these skills from a learned Brahmana cannot be ruled out.

Childhood to *Brahmacharya*

Rituals for the welfare of child and mother are to be done during pregnancy. The child has to be given a name within ten days of birth, followed by exposure to the sun and *anna prasam* in four months. Tonsuring ceremony is to be done within a year. All these vary according to the varnas and there is provision for extending the time limits. Children are to be named after their grandparents, unless their number is too large.

The *upanayana* ceremony is to be held during the eighth year (from conception) for Brahmanas, 11th year for Kshatriyas, and 12th year for Vaishyas. This can be extended to 16 years and thereafter the child is considered to be a Shudra. The *upanayana* rules are elaborated for the three varnas. The type of upper and lower garments, the *yajnopavitham* (the sacred thread) and its raw material, the stick or *dandam*, and so on, are also specified.

After *upanayana*, a *brahmacharin* should seek *bhiksha* on a daily basis and hand over the collections to his teacher. Rules are framed about the persons from whom he may seek *bhiksha* and other connected etiquettes. Again, these vary according to the varna. The *brahmacharin* may eat only specified food and this should be of a quality and quantity lower than his teacher's. The rituals before and after eating are specified. A reference to *grihya sutras* is to be made in cases of variation.

A *brahmacharin* should not sleep during the day. He should rise before his teacher and go to bed after the teacher has fallen asleep. For girls, the rituals to be performed during birth, death, etc., are same but mantras should not be uttered during these ceremonies.

Teacher and Gurukula

Upon *upanayana*, a *brahmacharin* may go to the house of a chosen teacher. However, this is not a must. He may study under his own father (a very common situation) or take instruction from a teacher in his neighbourhood as a daytime student.

In the olden days, parents had the problem of choosing a teacher as the teacher could accept or also reject a student. The grounds for such a rejection are specified clearly.

Curriculum

The curriculum taught at the *gurukula* includes personal cleanliness, the *Vedas* (memorization of mantras) and grammar.

Sandhya vandana is a must; it should be performed three times a day. *Gayatri mantra japa* is another important daily ritual. It is to be recited in silence. Silent prayers are far more effective. The student learns the rules of all rituals.

Later, the student may be secretly initiated into the *Upanishads*. Still later, a student is taught to practice *yama* and *niyama*. Simultaneously, he must learn to control his *indriyas*—both *jnanendriyas* and *karmendriyas*. The student is then initiated into the concept of *jnana*. *Tyaga* and detachment are pre-requisites for *jnana*. There is a close resemblance here to the *Bhagavad Gita*.

The *Manusmriti* mentions only *karma yoga* and *jnana yoga* and not other *yogas*; even here, *karma yoga* means practice of *varna ashrama dharma*.

Prelude to *Grihastha* Stage

Once the substantive part of the education is over, the student has to choose between *grihastha* and *sanyasa,* or continue education under an appropriate teacher.

Those inclined towards the metaphysical may opt for *sanyasa*; others will move to the *grihastha* stage. However, the second course is the preferred option. The stress is on *purushartha* and makes the point that following dharma is a legitimate path for *moksha*.

The *Manusmriti* emphasizes that students should continue to respect their teachers even after passing on to the *grihastha* stage; treat the teacher on par with parents until their death; often give gifts to his teacher personally or through someone; always obey his parent's instructions and should not make independent decisions.

The stage of the *brahmacharya* ends with giving the teacher an appropriate gift. There are no hard and fast rules as regards the kind of gift. The right gift is what the student can afford and pleases the teacher.

Grihasthashrama I

Chapters 3, 4 and 5 of the *Manusmriti* deal with *grihasthasrama*. The third chapter deals with marriage and the basic ritual duties of a *grihastha*. This chapter has a total of 286 verses. More than half of these are devoted to *pitr karmas* which was considered to be the most important as this affects his next life (and also that of his ancestors and progenies). *Deva karmas* are for the welfare of the family in this life and if any, it has a negative effect on his next life.

The discussion in these chapters includes all three varnas and varna specific characteristics are mentioned as and when needed. On the whole, the emphasis is on Brahmanas while others are mentioned incidentally.

Marriage

When does one enter into marriage? Obviously, this would depend on the completion of studies. There is no fixed rule as to when does one's studies end. To master a *Veda* it takes at least a minimum of three to nine years and it may take one as many as 18 years to study all the *Vedas*. The student in fact has to decide when to stop his education and enter into marriage. Parents' and the teacher's consent is also a must in this case.

Marriages should take place within the varna; the bride should not be either from the groom's father's or mother's *gotra*.

Cross cousin marriages are not permitted. *Jatis* are neither mentioned in the context of marriages nor in any other context. One's varna alone matters in life.

Bride's family background and not wealth is important. She should be healthy, good looking, and so also her parents and siblings. One interesting condition is that the girl's parents must have at least one son. This condition stems from the belief that a bride belonging to a family that has only girls may not produce a male offspring. The theory is that male child is born when the father's seed is stronger than the mother's egg and vice versa.

Marriage from lower varnas are permissible for second or third marriages. Men indulged in polygamy and rich people had several wives. However, only the wife belonging to the same varna is allowed to participate in rituals. In case, if there are more than one belonging to the same varna, then the first among them alone can participate.

Types of Marriages

The educated Brahmana is invited with due respect and the bride (usually one's own daughter) is offered as *kanyadan*. This is called *brahmya* marriage and it is done only for the first varna. When a boy and a girl mutually agree to marry, it is *gandharva* marriage. A marriage in which a boy takes a girl by force is *rakshasa* marriage. A girl offered as a gift to a priest in a *yajna* is *daivikam;* it is considered an offering to God. A *kanyadan* involving some gifts from the bridegroom, but not amounting to bride-money is called *arsha*. Marrying a bride by offering lots of money or gifts to the bride's family is called *asura*. *Prajapatya* marriage is between a groom who is not educated and a bride who is offered as *kanyadan*. A marriage that involves seduction and rape of a helpless girl is called *paisacha*.

Giving bride-money was fairly common in the olden times even among Brahmanas. This is true even today among some communities in India. Possibly, there was scarcity of eligible women for the following reasons—the rich taking several wives; the poor marrying over and over again due to death of wives in labour or sickness; and the neglect of the female infants.

The types of permissible and non-permissible marriages for each *varna* is explained, so also the punishment for non-permissible marriages. Punishments are always God-given—dreaded hell or a lower order in the next birth.

Conjugal Relations

Sex in marriage is permitted only on specified days of the month, taking into account the onset of menses. In effect, sex is possible only less than 10 days in a month. Sex on the sixth, eighth and tenth day from the start of menses will result in the birth of male child. Conversely, sex on other odd days will produce a female child.

Wife should be treated well in the household. An unhappy wife will not be able to make *aditi* or *shrardha* Brahmanas happy and hence all *yajnas* performed in the house will go futile or may even have negative effects. Gifts of ornaments and dress should be given to the wife to make her happy.

Pancha Yajnas

A *grihastha*, in addition to the *sandhyavandana karma*, should perform the prescribed five *yajnas* on a daily basis. These five *yajnas* are teaching of the *Vedas* or *brahma yajnam*, *pitr tarpanam* or *pitr yajnam*, *daiva yajnam* or *homam*, *bhuta yajnam* or offering of food for birds and animals, and *nriyajna* or *aditi poojanam*. It is not clear whether *aditi poojanam* is a daily affair, since the conditions set for it may not occur daily (see later section).

A *grihastha* is supposed to be well-versed in at least one of the *Vedas* and hence it is his duty to teach the *Veda* to anyone on a daily basis. If he has no students, he must recite the *Veda* as *swaadhyayam* (self-learning).

Tarpanam is to be done daily. This is followed by feeding at least one Brahmana as *pitr yajna*. That Brahmana should also be well-versed in the *Vedas*—a requirement that seems not very practical, since he cannot be a friend or even a known person. Daily *tarpanam* and *pitr yajnam* probably ceased to exist long ago.

Daiva yajnam is the daily *homa*. The *grihastha* is supposed to keep five *agnis* (originally three in Vedic times) and *havis* is to be offered to the *devagni* on a daily basis. The gods mentioned here are the 10 *vishwedevas*. These are Rigvedic Gods.

Bhuta yajnam is actually food offered to birds and animals generally by the wife of the householder. This is done in the morning and in the evening.

Aditi poojanam is meant for an unexpected guest and this may happen only on some days, except perhaps in the case of very rich persons, where itinerant guests come daily; not the same guest but different ones. *Brahma yajna* is by far the most important, followed by *daiva yajna*.

Aditi Yajna

The performance of *pitr yajna* (160 verses) and *aditi yajna* (40 verses) receive a lot of attention. Let us look at *aditi yajna* first.

Hospitality to an uninvited guest is an important value, but there are conditions and the treatment of the guest also differs according to his status.

Hospitality is not meant for making new friends or reciprocity. The guest must be an outsider and unknown. Serving such a person alone will bring credit to the host. Conversely, a guest cannot present himself repeatedly and he must not stay with the host for more than a night (*aditi* means one *thithi* or day). Besides, a person presenting himself as a guest in different homes day after day has to be rejected; he will attract demerit and will be punished by God.

An *aditi* is treated according to his status in relation to the host; rich and costly food is served to dignitaries. Here status is measured by knowledge, wealth and position in society. Special drinks made of ghee, milk, honey, and sugar may be offered to high ranking guests.

There is a long list of persons of doubtful character who should not be accepted as *aditi*. Hence, it is important to enquire subtly about the guest's past. Entertaining bad guests involves demerit. The list of bad characters, which occurs time and again in the *Manusmriti*, mirrors a true picture of the society of that time.

Ordinarily, a guest must be provided with a mat, a place to sleep, water to drink and wash legs, and food. The host and his wife should eat whatever is left over. Above all, the guests should be treated with courtesy and good words. A Brahmana need not accept a person of lower varna as a guest. Children, sick members of the family and pregnant women should be fed before the guest.

Shrardha

Apart from the daily *tarpanam* and *pitr yajnam*, the *grihastha* must perform an elaborate monthly *shrardha*. Presently, this is reduced to a monthly *tarpanam* and annual *shrardha*. There is no reference to annual *shrardha* in the *Manusmriti*.

The above *pitr yajnas* are extremely important for the welfare of the family. It has maximum religious merit, especially when Brahmanas have given up *brahma yajnam* and *nitya karmam*.

The most difficult part of performing a *shrardha* is finding the right persons to represent the three generations of *pitr* in both male and female lines. Besides, one should also find one or more persons to represent the *vishwedevas*. The objective is to please the *pitr* and *devas*. The *pitr* are not easily pleased. They would insist on several prerequisites.

The number of Brahmanas to be invited for *shrardha* may be a minimum of one each for *pitr* and *devas* to a maximum of six for *pitr* and three for *devas*. The number depends on availability and the capacity of *grihastha* to host them. The point is made that it is better to have fewer Brahmanas—the more the number will lead to greater difficulty to please them all and elaborate preparations will increase the chances of mistakes of all kinds.

It is the duty of the *grihastha* to verify the antecedents of the Brahmanas he invites. He must ensure that they are well-read in the *Vedas*. Knowledge of the *Veda* is always a pre-requisite since every Brahmana is expected to reveal his *pravara* (*gotra*) and *charana* (*Veda* studied by him). Gentle enquiry on his *charana* is, however, generally customary. Nowadays, most Brahmanas do not even know their *gotras*, leave alone the *pravara* and *charana*. He must also verify his character and occupation if any. Most Brahmanas always had some lucrative occupations such as money lending, trading, etc., in addition to the normal Vedic duties.

The kind of person who should not be invited has been elaborated in detail and it is long indeed and raises several doubts in my mind. Anyway, character defects, physical defects, behavioural defects and unacceptable occupations are mentioned. For example, a one-eyed man or a man with squint should not be invited. Likewise, a butcher should not be invited. The fact is that there were Brahmana butchers at that time. It is naïve to think of the past as glorious; the reality is that it was as mundane as it is today.

Another important aspect is the kind of food served to the Brahmanas. The objective is to please them with food. Dal, curry, ghee, curd, rice, and honey are mentioned. Variety of fruits is to be offered. But by far the most amazing thing is the inclusion of meat and they are considered to be the most important part. Varieties of meat from different animals are mentioned in increasing order of their merit: fish of various types, sheep and goats of various types, a great many types of deer, birds, wild boar, buffaloes, rhino, rabbits, and tortoise. Meat is also mentioned on earlier occasions when food is mentioned as in daily rituals. Meat as a legitimate offering in rituals is mentioned throughout the *Manusmriti*.

There are detailed rules for preparation of the area in which food is to be served, the formalities involved in serving, courtesy of the server, description of the quality of food served to Brahmanas and the rituals involved after the meal is eaten. The leftovers are to be shared by the servants—something not permitted in recent years. My experience is that the leftover is buried.

I would think that the detailed prescriptions in the *Manusmriti* apply only to rich Brahmanas, and that the vast majority of Brahmanas then were indeed very poor and they lived on *bhiksha* or food served free in the houses of feudal chiefs and kings. They could hardly afford to feed other Brahmanas and that too with specially made dishes.

Brahmanas had very limited opportunities for earning a decent living in those days. The *Puranas* give a truer picture of the majority of Brahmanas in those days. By all accounts, they were poor indeed.

Grihasthashrama II

Normally *brahmacharya* ends by age 25 and the person becomes a *grihastha;* he continues in that state until age 50. *Grihastha* is the foundation of Hindu social life and all others are dependent on him. Thus, the other ashramas such as *brahmacharya, vanaprastha* and *sanyasa* are not possible without the *grihastha.* Therefore, he deserves respect.

In his role as the sole supporter of society, a *grihastha* must store grain for at least three years. If he cannot do that, he must store grain for at least one year. At the other end, a poor *grihastha* may store grain for three days, and poorest will have nothing for next day. They will live on a day-to-day basis.

However, it is the adherence to dharma that is important and not wealth or resources. Further, a wealthy man would often find it impossible to adhere to dharma and a poor man can be more meritorious than a rich man. The *Manusmriti* acknowledges *brahma jnani*, who is apparently very poor, as the most meritorious human being dearest to God. There are obvious contradictions here, but that is normal for any religious text.

How Brahmanas make a Living

For Brahmanas, teaching the *Vedas* is the ideal profession. Very few are qualified to do this and even they have to subsist on meager incomes. Other legitimate ways of making a living are by *bhiksha* and receiving gifts. The latter is often undependable and even small (there are occasional exceptions) while the former means a hand-to-mouth subsistence and leaves little time and resources for daily *yajnas*.

What then should a *Brahmana grihastha* do? He is allowed to practice agriculture or trade, not directly but indirectly. However, he should never physically serve another man but the state or practice priesthood and perform *yajnas* for others for a fee. This practice for livelihood is looked down upon in the *Manusmriti*. According to *Manusmriti*, only *homa* is recognized for *deva yajna* in which the *devas* are of Rigvedic origin. One should remember that the present day gods did not exist when the *Manusmriti* was written. However, the Shudras worshipped non-Vedic gods and had temples for these Gods in their hamlets or outside the main village. The Brahmanas practising as temple priests and a Brahmana priest helping another Brahmana to perform a Vedic ritual are of recent origin.

A Brahmana should not accept music or dance as a profession. It may be noted that dancing came to be accepted by Brahmana girls in the South only at the beginning of the 20th Century, while music and dance existed several centuries earlier. Saint Tyagaraja, the doyen of the musical world in the South, did not earn a living by music. He practised *uccha vritti* for a living. Music as a career is of recent origin among Brahmanas.

There were rich Brahmanas in the past too. In the olden times, it is the land grants that made them rich. They stored grains for years. The Namboodiri Illams in Kerala owned thousands of acres of land.

The Pallava and Chola kings gave entire villages to groups of Brahmanas whom they invited to their kingdom. These land-grant villages are known as *agraharams*. There are hundreds of such *agraharams* in the South. This practice was started in the north during the Gupta period (4th Century AD). When the *Manusmriti* was written, such villages did not exist but Brahmanas at that time did own land in the same way as others (Kshatriyas) did, that is, by occupying it. There was plenty of land. They used Shudras to cultivate the land.

The landowning Brahmanas are a formidable force in Bihar and in all parts of India. In the South, the lands were taken out of their hands only after Independence as a result of land reforms. These reforms abolished the old and well-established system of landlords getting their land cultivated by tenant farmers. The majority of Brahmanas were poor both in the North and the South. This holds true of the past as well as recent times.

Upakarma and Study of *Vedas*

Each year the study of *Vedas* begins with an initiating and a concluding ceremony. The first one is called *upakarma* while the latter is called *veda visarjana*. The intervening period of four and a half months starts from the full moon day of *Shravana* and the first day after new moon in the month of *Magha*.

During these months one can teach or learn the *Vedas*. In the other months, *Vedas* are read by both students and teachers during the *shukla paksha*, while other *Shastras* including grammar, Vedanta etc., are studied in the *krishna paksha*. Teaching goes on through out the year with small breaks.

For over a century now Brahmanas perform the initiating ceremony but do not learn or teach the *Vedas*. Nor do they do any Vedic or Shastric studies at any time.

Vedic studies and reading are not allowed during rains, dust storms or any other kinds of disturbances. Similarly, new moon and full moon days are avoided as also a few other days.

Only one *Veda* should be taught in any day. One can learn one Veda or all three at different times; the study of each Veda will take at least three years.

The *Rigveda* is meant for the *devas*, the *Yajurveda* for humans, and the *Samaveda* for *pitr* or ancestors. The *Samaveda* is considered to be impure because of its association with *pitr* and hence, it should not be mixed with the other two. There is a prohibition on reciting the other two *Vedas* along with the *Samaveda*. As a result, it is necessary to hire a specialist priest to recite the mantras from the *Samaveda* in any household ritual.

The study or reciting of *Vedas* should always start with *Om Bhur Bhuva Swaha*, and the *gayatri mantra* and it should also end with these. The three words following *Om* represent the three worlds of gods, men and ancestors; thus they refer to the three *Vedas* as well.

Personal Conduct

A person's conduct should reflect his age, occupation, wealth, learning, and family status as well as in his dress, speech, and general appearance.

He should shave and dress his hair regularly. He should take bath thrice a day and apply cosmetics. He may wear gold ornaments, carry the appropriate *dandam*, a pot of water, and a collection of *darba* grass for ritual purposes.

It is the duty of a Brahmana of standing to be well-versed in a number of *Shastras*, in addition to the three *Vedas*, *Upanishads*, and *Smritis*, some of which may help him to make money while others will widen his knowledge, enhance his reputation, and thus increase his income.

When the new crop of grains comes, a Brahmana should perform a *yaga* at the end of each of the four seasons. During the two solstices he should perform a *yaga* involving the sacrifice of a male calf. Without performing this sacrifice, he should not eat meat in the following months.

Acceptance of Gifts

Learned Brahmanas were in great demand for bestowing gifts as this earned merit and even prestige. The Shudra kings and chieftains were very keen to bestow lands to the Brahmanas to give respectability and legitimacy to their positions in society. Receiving gifts, even though allowed for Brahmanas, earned demerits, especially when it is accepted from the wrong type of person. The *Manusmriti* lists the kinds of persons from whom gifts should not be accepted. For example, gifts are prohibited from Shudras (even if they happen to be kings or chieftains), traders in oil, spirits and meat, middle men in trade and from agents of prostitutes. Gifts from Kshatriya kings should not be accepted if they have deviated from their dharma. Those who accept gifts may go to any one of the 21 different types of hells. These are listed. Similarly, acceptance of gifts by Brahmanas not well-versed in the *Vedas* will attract punishment in one of the 21 hells. Gifts from all those who observe dharma and offer gifts with due respect may be accepted.

Brahmanas with adequate means should give gifts of rice, cows, land, clothes, gold and various other articles.

Finally, the *Manusmriti* recommends that learned Brahmanas should not accept gifts from anyone but may give gifts to deserving people.

It may be noted that Brahmanas in the South did accept land grants from Shudra kings and chieftains. After getting these lands and establishing *agraharams*, the Brahmanas became independent. They continued to practice Vedic religion with diligence and they were well known for their expertise in the performance of Vedic rituals. The Palakkad Iyers—a branch of Iyers to which I belong—accepted land grants from a local chieftain and established 18 *agraharams* in the latter part of the 18th Century in and around the modern day city of Palakkad in Kerala. They came from the Kaveri delta of Tamil Nadu.

General Prescriptions

A Brahmana should not live in a kingdom ruled by a king who does not believe in *dharma*. They should also abandon a village if it gets under the sway of vagabonds. It is this prescription that made many Brahmana families leave *Aryavarta* and seek newer pastures in the South. A Brahmana should never engage in games of chance or in betting.

One should tell the truth, but only the truth that is pleasing to the other person; he should not tell a truth which is unpleasant. One should always respond by the word '*subham*'. One should never enter into an argument with anyone and this includes wife and other relations.

One should not look down upon disabled or ugly persons and likewise the poor, the old, the uneducated, and the lower varnas. One should not envy others who are better placed in life.

One should avoid doing things that require assistance from others and focus on things that one can do alone. Seeking assistance from others may later be regretted. What a gospel utterance! One should enjoy doing whatever one is doing.

A Brahmana should avoid criticizing others. He should not criticize the *Vedas* or gods; he should not engage in self-praise, or have excessive self-pride. He should not get angry with anyone and he should not try to punish others, especially using violent means. This applies to his conduct towards his wife, children and even servants.

Persons belonging to other varnas should not hurt a Brahmana. On the contrary, they should treat him with respect under all circumstances. A person who is pure in speech and mind and keeps it that way throughout his life will attain everything that there is to attain. Following dharma alone will help one in the next birth.

Yama and Niyama

The *Manusmriti* recommends the middle-aged *grihastha* to follow *yama* and *niyama*. *Yama* stands for ahimsa, truth, *brahmacharya*, straightforwardness, and non-greed. Not getting angry, service to guru, cleanliness, moderation in food, and devotion to dharma constitute *niyama*. *Yamas* are more important than *niyama* as they must be observed daily. In addition to the above, a *grihastha* may also practise *dhyana* early in the morning in a secluded place. These measures will help him to enter into the *vanaprastha* stage later. These observances are common to both Hinduism and Jainism.

Grihasthashrama III

The third and the concluding chapter on *grihasthashrama* is very short (169 *shlokas*) and it focusses on death-related issues. The causes of death are identified but the focus is on food. The author of the *Manusmriti* goes out of the way to justify the sanctity of eating the flesh of all kinds of fish, birds and animals. The *Vedas* legitimize the use of meat in rituals and as food, and hence Manu could not oppose it. At the end, however, he leans towards a vegetarian diet—a clear indication of the influence of Jainism on Hinduism. Vegetarianism appears clearly as an escape.

Births and deaths among relations cause pollution among relatives. The duration of the pollution period and related rituals are elaborated in detail.

Thereafter, cleanliness and the lack of it are discussed. In ritual terms, this is known as *saucham* and *asaucham*. Body cleanliness is discussed first followed by the polluting effect of food and other materials.

The concluding part of this chapter deals with women—young, married and widowed. Almost everything said here is not only unacceptable, but clearly objectionable today.

Causes of Death

Why do people die? The main reason is that they are not following dharma; the second factor is polluted and prohibited food consumption. Only the latter aspect is explored here.

Food that should be excluded is onions, both white and red, which are very commonly consumed today in India. Meat from various animals, fish and birds are mentioned as contributing to death. These include the common pig which eats human excreta. Birds such as woodpecker, stork, ducks, swans, owl, parrots, and certain varieties of fish, monkeys, and snakes are forbidden. There is a more exhaustive list in the text. Interestingly, it does not mention about not eating beef. In fact, male calves and bulls were sacrificed and eaten in *yaga* ceremonies.

Apart from vegetables such as onions, all other vegetables may be eaten; there is only one condition that they should not be grown using human excreta as fertilizer or with the use of dirty water.

Rice, pulses, wheat and barley are the common food items and they are recommended. In fact, rice is the main food and it is used in rituals. It symbolizes well-being.

Several verses justify eating meat of those animals which are not in the banned list. The most important argument is that meat is the natural food of many animals and man as well. There is nothing wrong in what is natural and made by God. The second argument is that animals killed for *yajna* are meant to please Gods and therefore do not involve any sin. Likewise, eating meat that is left over from the ritual is sacred and good and should be eaten. A Brahmana who refuses to eat meat as part of the *shrardha* ceremony will go to hell. Animal sacrifice and the eating of beef are sanctioned in the *Vedas* and therefore are permissible.

This elaborate justification for meat eating in the *Manusmriti* itself is a reaction to the criticism of meat eating by Jainas who object to violence against all, including animals. Jainas are very strict vegetarians.

The *Manusmriti*, at the end of this section, makes a *volte-face* and recommends ahimsa. It says that a person who does not want to sacrifice animals in a *yajna* is a better person. Finally, it says that vegetarianism is better than meat eating. The author of the *Manusmriti* being in a dilemma could not go against the *Vedas* that permit and even sanctify meat eating, while he was personally in agreement with the Jainas on ahimsa.

Today, the Brahmanas of India are equally divided between those who eat meat and those who are, like the Jainas, total vegetarians. The Brahmanas of Bengal, Bihar and eastern Uttar Pradesh eat meat and fish. The Kashmiri Pandits and the Saraswat Brahmanas of the Konkan are also meat eaters. Elsewhere, and in South India in particular, Brahmanas are pure vegetarians.

Death and Pollution

Births and deaths are polluting events to the *sapindis,* that is, those from the same *gotra* up to six generations. The duration of pollution is 10 days but this is reduced to three or four days if a person is well-versed in the *Vedas*. The rationale is that there should be least breaks for the study of the *Vedas* and Vedic karmas.

Birth causes pollution only to the parents and even here the mother alone has 10 days of pollution while the father gets purified after a bath. During the menstrual cycle, a woman is untouchable for three days and she can participate in rituals only after five days.

The death of a child who is less than two years old causes no pollution to anyone and it should be buried and not cremated. All others should be cremated on death. This applies to all varnas. For relations living far away, pollution begins only on hearing the news and it lasts for the remainder of the 10-day period. If the news is received after 10 days, a simple bath is enough to remove the pollution. A death on the mother's side will cause pollution for three days alone.

The death of a king causes pollution to all his subjects and for his relations for the remainder of the daytime or nighttime as the case may be. The shortening of the pollution period is to enable a new king to take over reign.

Purity and Pollution

The concepts of purity and pollution are very important in Hindu social life. Social anthropologists have studied this in great detail in respect of Indian village life. However, the actual practice of these concepts differs considerably from the prescriptions mentioned in the *Manusmriti*. In rural India, these concepts are applied to social relations between *jatis*. However, the *Manusmriti* does not recognize the concept of *jati* and it certainly does not mention it in the discussion on this subject.

Here we examine the views of the *Manusmriti*. There are two aspects—the purity of the human body and the purity of materials and objects.

The objective here is to remove the pollution and restore purity. The objects used for purifying mind, body and materials are *brahma jnana*, *tapas*, water, fire, wind, earth, intellect, karmas, food in the form of *prasada*, and finally time.

A person may purify himself by accepting his guilt; by not responding to insults and abuse; by forgiving his opponents; by *japa* for sins committed secretly, and by taking *sanyasa* if the sins are too many.

Physical impurities of the body may be removed with water and earth, as in the case of impurities caused during urination and defecation. For other kinds of bodily dirt (12 types are mentioned) washing with water is sufficient.

Gold, silver, and gems are purified by ash and water; copper, iron, bronze, brass, and lead (articles made from these) are purified by acidic water. In some cases, the polluted part may be removed and water sprinkled over it to purify. For example, butter polluted by a fly requires the removal of that part where it is found and a little sprinkling of water. Various articles used in rituals are purified with cow's urine and water.

The house and the land around it may be purified with cow dung mixed with water. Sometimes land is purified by removing the top soil and applying cow dung on it. Sweeping is another mode for cleaning floors and land used for ritual purposes.

Women

Educated women will be most upset by reading this section and I do share their anguish. Remember that the *Manusmriti* is now no longer accepted by all as a sacred text.

According to the *Manusmriti*, women of all ages must not do anything independently. They should seek permission from their father, husband, brother or whoever is the male head of the household. She should not even think of living alone and away from her male guardian.

Despite this, a woman is always expected to bear a satisfied and pleasing look. She should be well-versed in household duties. She should take good care of everything in the house. She must be thrifty and very responsible. Her only objective in life is to please her husband or guardian. A woman should not feel bad at any circumstance.

A woman must accept a husband chosen by her father or brother and should serve him throughout life. If her husband dies, she should not remarry and should stay with her husband's relatives. Serving her husband entitles her to heaven.

Even if her husband has another wife or he does not follow the normal rules of conduct, or if he has no good qualities at all, even then a wife should respect him like a God.

A widow should lead a simple life with minimum food; she should not even think about men. She is equated with *vanaprastha* life. By doing this she can aspire to attain heaven.

If a woman seeks another man for the sake of having a child, she discredits herself in this life as well as the next. Her child has no legitimacy. She will be born as a fox in her next life (this is, however, contradicted in a later chapter). The fact is that many contradictions of this kind are most common.

A woman who follows the dharma attains heaven or whatever fate her husband attains. In fact, she gets a share of his punishment. If a woman dies before her husband and if he is less than 50 years of age, he should remarry to continue the performance of daily rituals of a *grihastha*. In fact, the *Manusmriti* recommends an immediate (soon after cremation) replacement for the dead wife. He can also give up *grihasthashrama* if he has a married son and a soft heart. This applies only to Brahmanas. The rationale is that the performance of daily rituals should not suffer.

Vanaprastha and *Sanyasa*

The sixth chapter of the *Manusmriti* deals with the third and fourth stages in the life cycle. It is rather short, only 97 verses long, as opposed to *grihasthashrama* which has over 700 verses. The reason is that life is highly individualistic here; a person's varna has no meaning at this stage, although the *Manusmriti* looks at it primarily from the Brahmana point of view. Senior citizens should be interested in this chapter. However, these two stages of the life cycle are to be spent in the fringes of the forests, taking advantage of food provided by the natural vegetation. Today it is impossible to do such a thing—first, there is hardly any natural vegetation left, and secondly, it is illegal to do so. Further, there are far too many encroachments in forest areas and there is severe competition for forest produce.

Vanaprastha

When old age symptoms appear, such as grey hair and wrinkled skin, and when one becomes a grandfather, it is time to enter the *vanaprastha* stage of life.

A person must decide for himself whether or not he wants to enter the *vanaprastha* stage. On deciding, he must leave his home with the barest minimum needed for performing the daily *yajnas*. If his wife is willing, she may accompany her husband.

Vanaprastha life described in the *Manusmriti* is very tough; a *vanaprastin* has to lead a lonely life in the forests; adopt *brahmacharya* and perform all the daily *yajnas*. He must collect his own food from forest, which usually includes wild grains, fruits, roots, and leaves. He must wear clothing made of skin or the bark of trees or leaves or grass. He must sleep on earth. He is allowed to accept gifts from other forest dwellers, but he must not depend on them.

Apart from the daily rituals, a *vanaprastin* must also perform seasonal rituals as on the solstices. For *yajnas* and for his own use, he may collect and store forest produce, but he should not accept produce from agriculture, that is, grains or vegetables produced by tilling land.

He should eat only once a day. He can choose the time—morning, evening, or night. He must bathe thrice a day. During his spare time, he must devote to *japa* or any other form of *tapas*. He may read the *Upanishads* or *Smritis* and contemplate on the atman or the *Brahman*.

When his mind is fully focussed on the *Brahman* and is under complete control, he may take *sanyasa*, which is a lot tougher as we will see presently.

Mahaprasthanam

Vanaprastha life is harsh and the life of a *sanyasin* is harsher. There is a shortcut which is not easy either. This is called *mahaprasthanam* which means the great departure. This alternate route is taken by those who for reasons of poor health want to end their life sooner than later. They go to the forest alone taking nothing with them, give up all *yajnas* and focus only on *japa* and *dhyana*. They take only water and no food. They get *moksha* when they die. This does not mean that they will not be reborn; they will in fact be reborn, but in the next life they may by instinct take *sanyasa* from *brahmacharya* itself, and continue in that state till the end and then attain true *moksha*.

In Kalidasa's *Raghuvamsam*, taking one's life in old age was known as *prayopavesa*. Instances of such a practice are given in both the epics and their associated legends. *Prayopavesa* may also involve drowning or getting engulfed by fire.

Sanyasa

A *vanaprastin*, used to a lonely forest life with contemplation of the *Brahman* as his sole preoccupation, may opt for *sanyasa*. This will relieve him from all rituals. He must travel alone and stay in a very secluded place at night without the company of other men. During the day, he may go out in the afternoons and seek *bhiksha* from *grihasthas*. He must not accept ceremonial offering of *bhiksha* and he should not accept *bhiksha* from the same person more than once. He must keep moving and not develop any attachment to anyone or any place. He should not take part in feasts or join assemblies of other *sanyasins* or *vanaprastins*.

A *sanyasin* can have very meager possessions, such as a vessel made of wood, gourd, or bamboo, a stick, and worn out clothes. He should not use anything made of metal.

A true *sanyasin* does not fear anything or anyone. He sees himself in all things. He is fully focussed on the *Brahman* and he does not bother about what other people say. He keeps his eye on the ground and does not hurt any living thing while walking.

He does not look forward to death nor does he look forward to living. He whiles away time nonchalantly.

Kuticharan

Those who feel that forest life is too harsh may opt to stay with their own son in a small hut nearby and seek daily *bhiksha* from the son. They should take only one meal a day. At all times, he should remain cut off from the family. He should devote all his time to the study of the *Upanishads*. He should practice *dhyana*. He need not practice any rituals. A *kuticharan* is also a *sanyasi*.

Ten Indicators of Dharma

The *Manusmriti* is all about dharma. The following are the indicators of dharma—contentment, forgiveness, mental control, absence of greed, cleanliness, control over desires, knowledge of *Shastras*, *atma jnanam*, truthfulness, and calmness. Those who possess all the above attributes attain *moksha*.

Summary

The *Manusmriti* deals with life as it existed some 2,000 years ago. This was before the age of the *Puranas*. The *Manusmriti* does not mention about any of the gods of the *Puranas* or about the epics. There were no temples (except the ones used by Shudras) and Gods in human form did not exist. There is no mention of holy places or even of pilgrimages. Even Brahmanas ate meat of all kinds, as the detailed descriptions of these in the text illustrate.

However, *Manusmriti* talks about kings and in particular about Shudra kings. The first Shudra kings were the Mauryas of 300 BC. Thereafter, we have had many Shudra kings. In fact, according to one historian, the last truly Kshatriya kings were the Nandas (the predecessors of the Mauryas). All the kings of the South were either Shudras or Brahmanas.

When *Manusmriti* was written it had already become partly irrelevant. Kshatriya kings were eliminated by invasions of the Greeks and by local intrigue. Still later, other communities from Central Asia came to India. These included the Scythians, Parthians, Hunas, and Kushans. While most Brahmanas survived this troublesome period by accepting the new reality, other Brahmanas opted to become kings themselves both in the North and in the South; others who moved to the South were welcomed by Shudra kings. Here they lived a relatively quiet life and preserved the *Vedas* and the *Smritis*. The *Smartha Brahmanas* of South India were so named since they were well-versed in the *Smritis*. This movement started from around 300 BC and continued for over 2,000 years.

In North India, the new invaders became rulers from around 300 BC. Most of the early newcomers converted to Hinduism, but the later ones, namely, Muslims did not. They, however, had little influence in remote rural areas where the Brahmanas carried considerable influence and power.

The creation of the British Empire in 1800 changed everything. Brahmanas and the upper varnas took to Western education and jobs under the British. The Brahmanas, in most parts of India, were in the forefront of this westernization process. Gradually, the rituals and values enshrined in *Manusmriti* lost its relevance.

The *varna ashrama dharma* propounded in the *Manusmriti* is no longer followed by Hindus; not even by Brahmanas who, however, did practice it until recently.

Fifteen

Manusmriti: Raja Dharma

Introduction

This chapter on the *Manusmriti* deals with the laws of a Hindu State. Human societies evolved from tribal to a peasant society, and later into small kingdoms. The Rigvedic society was tribal in nature and during the Upanishadic period the society consisted of peasants. Later, around 600 BC, the oldest kingdom Kasi with its capital at Varanasi, emerged in India. By 300 BC, also known as the *Manusmriti* period, there were a hundred or more kingdoms, then known as *Janapadas*. The Buddhist and Jaina literature as well as Kautilya's *Arthashastra* give the names and other details of them. Kautilya discusses statecraft in great detail in his classic work.

A kingdom, or a State, must have seven attributes—a king or a head of the State, a capital city, an army, a treasury, civil administrative staff, a system of taxation, and a judicial system. The main focus in the *Manusmriti* is on the last aspect. It does deal with the other aspects, but briefly.

Three chapters (7, 8 and 9) deal with *raja dharma* under normal times and they focus on how a king should conduct himself with respect to his subject and with regard to his relationship with his neighbours and enemies. Chapter 8 deals with disputes among people within the State and the modalities of dealing with them including the punishments to guilty. Chapter 9 relates to property rights, succession, adoption and various related issues.

Raja Dharma I

A king's conduct is dealt with as the daily routine of a king, starting from early morning till late evening. Various issues crop up during the hypothetical day and they are dealt with in terms of the principles that should govern his decisions. Unlike *Arthashastra*, the *Manusmriti* is basically a religious text and hence it begins with an assertion of the king's moral rights arising from his divine origins. This may be considered as a *quid pro quo* to Kshatriya kings for giving the Brahmanas important advisory roles and other favours.

In all feudal societies, religion and religious leaders played an important role and their relationship with the ruling class was for mutual benefit. This was true the world over. In some rare cases, the king was also the supreme religious leader. The association of religion with State is as old as civilization. The queen of England is still the notional head of the Church of England and she appoints the Archbishop of Canterbury.

Divine Origin of Kings

Prajapati created kings in order that people may live in peace and their life is not made difficult by disorder, absence of security of life, or even anarchy. The first kings were created by taking various attributes of Gods, namely, *Indra*, *Varuna*, *Agni*, *Surya*, *Vayu*, etc. Thus the kings possessed divine qualities and were therefore respected and feared by the people. Fear and punishment are essential pre-requisites for maintaining law and order.

While the first kings possessed divine qualities, they were not considered as Gods in the *Manusmriti*. Also it does give the impression that only the original kings had divine qualities but not all. This implies that these qualities eroded with time.

A king will always be expected to follow *raja dharma*; in its absence, he will be reduced to an ordinary being and he will be destroyed. What constitutes *raja dharma* will be interpreted by Brahmanas, giving them a slight advantage.

To ensure that dharma is followed, the king should always consult a learned Brahmana and he should treat all Brahmanas in his kingdom with respect. A king should invariably be from the Kshatriya varna and he should follow the dharma prescribed.

A king should be well-versed in *dharma shastras* and he should always act neither cruelly nor with too much leniency. However, Brahmanas who violate the laws should be treated leniently or their punishment should be left to a learned Brahmana only.

A king must have humility and he should be composed at all times. He should face both success and failures with grace and try to take necessary steps to regain power. A king should avoid the following bad habits—hunting wild animals, play games of chance, sleep during the day time, indulge in women, ridicule others, sing, dance or drink alcoholic beverages.

He should avoid unnecessary travel; he should not envy the successes of others, engage in empty talk, award cruel punishments, try to attach other's property, or refuse to give money where it is owed.

Capital

A king should rule over a land that is well-watered, with flourishing agriculture, trade, and transport routes, and where the people follow dharma and are not afflicted by serious health problems.

Once the above conditions are met, the king should build a capital city. This city should be well-fortified against attack from enemies and should be easy to defend. A fortified city on hilly terrain is recommended as the ideal. However, in the Ganga Plains hills are absent; the *Manusmriti* was probably written keeping in mind Rajagriha, the capital of Magadha, which is on hilly terrain. This city in ruins lies far to the south of the Ganga River. It was an important capital city at the time of Buddha and later.

Within the walled city, the king should build several concentric zones with their own walls and fortifications. Servants should be housed in the outermost zone, followed by administrative staff, and the army. The palace complex should be in the centre. This spatial ordering is mentioned in the Buddhist texts as well.

The fortified capital city must have access to reliable water supply, adequate storage of grains and fodder, and it must have a stockpile of weapons of warfare. All these and more are needed to protect the city in case of protracted siege.

The king should marry a bride from the Kshatriya varna and must have secure quarters for his harem. This should be separate from the assembly where he would conduct his royal duties.

Administration

The king should appoint a court *purohit* who will supervise over all religious functions in the palace. At a different level, he should appoint a very learned Brahmana as his advisor in all matters concerning dharma and also matters of State policy.

At the next level, he should appoint a number of ministers and heads of departments like the treasury, taxation, justice, security, army, and so on. The ministers should meet the king daily and confer on matters of State.

At the territorial level, outside the capital city, the king should appoint a hierarchy of officers starting from the village level. Each village will have a head, two villages will have a supervisory head; in a similar fashion 20, 100 and 1,000 villages will have higher level functionaries in charge. Taxes are collected at all levels and sent to the king's treasury. The officers outside the capital city are paid indirectly through land grants for their private use. The concept of land grants, mentioned in the *Manusmriti*, was expanded upon by the Guptas (4th Century AD) and it forms the basis for *agraharams* and temples in the South.

The king, in addition to the above, must appoint as many envoys as necessary to maintain communication with other kingdoms; he should have a secret service to provide him information on things happening within his kingdom and outside.

The lower-end employees must be paid daily wages in cash and they should be given two dhotis every six months and a certain quantity of grain every month.

Taxes

Taxes should be levied on goods and services and this income is the basis for the strength of the king. He cannot be lenient on this aspect.

For agricultural and other forms of production, one-sixth of the produce may be collected. This proportion may be varied according to the situation. For items of trade, two per cent of value is legitimate. Service tax on goldsmiths, carpenters and others may be in the form of one day's service to the king in a month. Learned Brahmanas will go tax-free.

In all cases, a proper evaluation must be made regarding the fairness of taxation; taxes should help the king and at the same time it should not hamper production or trade.

Some tax collectors under the king may collect more from the people while remitting less to the treasury. Such officials should be strictly punished. Some officers of the king may engage in wrong acts, such as attaching properties of others and so on; the king has the duty to protect the people from such persons.

When people suffer from the abuse of power, it indicates that the king is indolent. Such kings will be destroyed in course of time.

Army and Waging of Wars

A substantial part of this chapter deals with various aspects of war and ways of dealing with internal and external enemies. The king should discuss such issues daily with his ministers.

A king should consider a neighbouring king as an enemy and the neighbor of an enemy as a potential friend. Those beyond are to be considered as neutrals.

A king may establish six types of relationships with other kings: having a treaty, preparing for war, moving towards war, wage war, seeking help from friends. Each of these has at least two sub-categories, for example, treaties may be for co-operation or for neutrality.

War should be considered when all conditions are favourable. Most important among these is internal stability and the willingness of people to co-operate. The army should be well-prepared and there should be adequate stock of grains and other stores for waging war.

Also, the formation of the armed forces and various strategies in war are discussed.

War should be fought in a fair manner—non-combatants, women, children, old, and disabled people should not be killed. Soldiers wounded in battle should not be killed. The king should not use weapons using poison or nails and other secret tools.

After victory, the people of the conquered land should be treated well and the land itself should be handed over to a new king selected from the lineage of the past king.

While foot soldiers may keep all animals and metal objects captured during the war, gold and silver objects should be handed over to the king.

King's Daily Chores

A king's daily chores are discussed in various sections of this chapter. They are put in a nutshell here. A king should wake up long before sunrise; he should bathe and perform the *nitya karma* and *homa*. He should then proceed to the assembly to meet his subjects and listen to their petitions and grievances patiently.

Thereafter, he should meet his ministers, heads of various departments, and discuss matters of the State with his advisors, especially those dealing with issues of war and peace. He must also discuss certain family matters, such as marriage of daughters or education of sons, with his personal advisor, a Brahmana.

In all matters of the State, utmost secrecy should be maintained and he must see to it that disgruntled and dissatisfied servants are not around at any time. He should always be alert about internal security in the royal house.

After these meetings, he should retire to his harem, take bath and lunch. Care should be taken to see that the food is not poisoned. He may then relax for some time.

In the afternoon, he should inspect his armed forces and ensure their preparedness, and check on the upkeep of war equipment and the horses and elephants used in warfare.

At sunset, he should perform the *sandhya vandana,* thereafter, meet his specially appointed spies in a secluded place.

He may then retire to his harem, have dinner and entertain himself in the company of musicians and dancers.

He should retire for sleep and get up early next morning.

Raja Dharma II

This chapter deals with disputes among the subjects and how it should be settled by the king. The chapter has the largest number of verses; a total of 420. Every morning, the king attends an assembly where these disputes are settled and the guilty punished.

The king is the supreme judge and he hears cases daily in the company of his advisors, who are mostly drawn from the

Brahmana varna. Shudras are prohibited from being members of any such council. The king can delegate his powers to a very learned Brahmana if he is not in a position to attend the assembly for any reason.

Types of Cases

The *Manusmriti* lists 18 primary categories of common disputes that come up before the king. They are—non-payment of loans; refusal to return goods given for safe custody; selling of goods or properties of others; partnership disputes between traders; refusal to part with gifts; non-payment of wages; breach of contract; withdrawal from sale agreement; disputes between owner and caretaker; boundary disputes; brawls and fights; rioting; stealing; robbery; adultery; marriage disputes; division of properties, and betting on cock and bull fights.

Basics

- No one should tell a lie in court. It is punishable by the king, and if he failed to detect it, God will punish the king eventually.
- No sin attaches to the king, or his advisors, if the guilty person is punished, even with death.
- Failure to punish the guilty or remaining as a mute spectator will entail sin for the king and his advisors and they will be punished by God.
- The king and his advisors should detect the truth from the tone of speech, change of skin colour, eye contact, sweating, trembling, or other movements of limbs.

- The king has the duty to protect the rights of women, minors, widows, sick persons, and the old.
- Properties, where there are no rightful owners, can be attached by the king. Lost properties when returned would entail a deduction of one-sixth for costs to the king.
- A Brahmana, who discovers a lost property, can retain it.
- Valuables dug from under the earth have to be shared equally by the king and Brahmanas.
- Stolen properties for which the rightful owner cannot be identified must be given to people. It is wrong for Brahmanas or the king to use stolen property.
- The king should respect the traditional values of people that are of a local or regional character and are specific to a community. This prescription, which is repeated in other contexts, show that the society then was not homogenous, similar to what we have in Indian villages even today.

Examination of Witnesses

Most cases are decided by evidence given by witnesses cited by either party to a dispute.

- It is the duty of the witnesses to come to court and give evidence and thereby help the king to establish the truth. Willful absenteeism is punishable. Giving false evidence is also punishable, especially if it is based on monetary inducements.
- The king cannot be mentioned as a witness in any case.
- Old, deaf, blind, disabled persons, women, children, and sick people cannot be cited as witnesses to a case. In criminal cases, the above rule will not apply.

- Witnesses not cited by anyone, but who have valuable information, should present themselves in court and give evidence. Helping the king to uncover the truth is the duty of his subjects.
- The king may require the witness to take an oath appropriate to his varna and occupation. Oath is in the name of *Yama* (God of Death) or the present Manu—Vivaswata.
- For those who give false evidence, there is an elaborate enumeration of punishments by God. This is necessary because often witnesses succeed in giving false evidence.
- If a witness falls sick within seven days of testifying, it will be assumed that he has given false evidence and he will be punished by the king.
- A witness who refuses to testify may be punished by the king.
- It appears that it was difficult to get witnesses to tell the truth in those days for fear of reprisal by locally powerful men.
- Brahmanas who make a living by tending cattle, trade, or services like carpentry, or are in the service of other persons, will be treated as Shudras, in case they appear as witnesses. One should note the great variety of occupations actually practised by Brahmanas while they are clearly the ones prescribed for Shudras. Theory and practice are altogether different, then and now.
- Telling a lie to save the life of anyone will not amount to a lie in the eyes of God. However, such a person should do penance later.

- Physical punishment may be inflicted on the following parts of the body—back, waist, tongue, hands, and feet. However, Brahmanas cannot be punished physically.
- Punishments must be progressive in nature for minor offences. A first offence may be punished by severe warning; a second one by fine, a third by physical punishment, and finally by cutting away a body part.

Disputes about Loans

As this involves money, there is an elaborate description of money used at that time. There were coins made of copper, silver and gold. In each case there were coins with increasing weights. All weights were measured in terms of seeds of mustard or other non-edible seeds. There were complex ratios of weights from the lowest to the heaviest. The multiplicative numbers were: 3, 4, 6, 8, 10, 12, 16, and even 100 or at the most 1,000 units.

- *Panam* was the common term used for money and perhaps the most popular coin of that time.
- In most disputes the number of *panams* owed or charged as fine is mentioned.
- Manu recommends the rates of interest on loans based on an authority on the subject at that time, Vashiṣht. Accordingly, the lowest interest rate per month is 1.25 per cent but this can go up to 5 per cent depending on the circumstances. Loans are given on the basis of mortgage. It may be written down or it may be oral in nature.
- If a loan is not returned, nor the interest, the mortgaged property will become the absolute property of the lender.

- When interest on loans is not paid on time, the interest may be added on to the capital. Thereafter, interest can be charged on the new capital. This is called the compounding principle.
- Heirs are not responsible for loans taken for betting, drinking or other social evils.
- The head of the household is not responsible for loans taken by his dependents, if such loans are taken without his permission. However, debts incurred by the head for the family for legitimate reasons, has to be paid by his heirs.

Safekeeping

- When a person denies that he has received something for safekeeping, the king may verify the same through secret agents.
- Things entrusted for safekeeping should not be returned to the heirs, even one's own sons, so long as the owner is alive. Experience shows that even sons are not reliable. Goods given for safekeeping may be sealed or unsealed. Goods given for safekeeping if destroyed by fire, floods or by theft need not be returned. The owner has to bear the risk.
- Those who make false claims should be punished.

Selling Other's Property

- Those who cheat and take possession of other's property shall be publicly killed along with their accomplices.

- A person who sells property or goods not owned by him is guilty and shall be punished with fine.
- A person buying property, not knowing that it belongs to another, is not guilty. However, if the rightful owner wants to repossess it, he should give it to him at the half the price that he paid for it.
- Property owned without proof does not amount to ownership.

Bride Money

- Accepting bride money by promising a girl and then giving another in her place is wrong. The groom can then take both the girls.
- While marrying off a girl, her disabilities or abnormalities should be disclosed to the groom, otherwise it is punishable.
- *Panigrahanan* followed by *saptapati* with Vedic mantras alone constitute legal marriage for Brahmanas.
- False accusations made against a girl's character, for reasons of enmity, is punishable. The accuser, besides paying fines will also have to do penance.
- Mixing water, stone, etc., with milk, or goods is punishable with fines.

Wages

- Detailed rules are prescribed for sharing of fees for performing rituals jointly by several priests. The categories of priests mentioned are *Ritwik*, *Adwaryu*, *Hotri*, *Udgadha*, and Brahman.

- Wages need not be paid if a worker is absent without reason. Delays in work execution may be condoned if it is completed later and if there are proper reasons for it.
- A person agreeing to transport goods fails to do so on time, without any justification, need not be paid the transport fee.
- Those who enter into a contract with traders must abide by it. Goods purchased may be returned within 10 days if they are found to be of lower quality.

Cattle, sheep and goats

- Cattle, sheep, or goats entrusted to a herder for grazing should be protected by the herder. However, he is not responsible for any attack from wild animals or stealing by gangs.
- The herder can take the milk of one out of 10 cows as wages.
- Cattle lost or injured in anyway due to negligence is punishable by fine.
- There should be adequate common grazing lands around every village and town. The agricultural lands of the village, bordering this should be fenced by their owners. Herders are not responsible if cattle stray into unfenced agricultural land.

Boundary Issues

- The boundary between villages should be clearly demarcated during the summer months. After delineation of the boundaries between villages, the king should mark them off by planting trees or by other methods. Other possibilities are growing of bamboo clusters, thorny trees and creepers. Walls may also be built, if warranted. Other ways of marking boundaries, especially between agricultural fields are by stone markers, pots buried with bones, stones or pebbles. Streams and rivers serve are natural boundaries.

- In the peripheral areas of the village, consisting of common grazing grounds, ponds, wells and even temples (reference is to local tribal Gods) may be built.
- Boundary disputes between villages were common, especially regarding the common grazing lands.
- Boundary disputes between villages and between landowners (and also house owners) must be settled by the king on the basis of evidence or testimony of witnesses.
- In the case of village boundaries, elders of the concerned villages and even those engaged in collection of forest produce, hunters etc may be consulted.
- Disputes over houses, wells, ponds, agricultural land, gardens, etc., between people must be settled by the king after examining all evidence and the witnesses.
- When a dispute remains indeterminate, the king may award his verdict in favour of the weaker party.

Verbal Abuse

- If a Brahmana is verbally attacked by a Kshatriya, the latter may be fined hundred *panams*, and the fine increases if it is a Vaishya. A Shudra should be beaten up for the same offence, in addition to the fine.

- Verbal abuse by persons of the same varna should be fined 12 *panams*. This can be increased depending on the circumstances.
- The tongue of a Shudra may be cut off for uttering words of abuse against other varnas.
- Those who insult a one-eyed or one-legged man or a person with any disability, should be fined.
- Those who insult father, mother, brother, or son or accuse them of bad conduct should be fined hundred *panams*.

Physical Attack

- A person who attacks another of a higher varna should be punished by breaking his hands or legs.
- A Shudra wanting to sit beside a person of a higher varna should be punished by placing hot iron rods on his waist.
- For spitting at a Brahmana, the attacker's lips should be cut off.
- For causing wounds, the attacker should not only be punished physically, but he must also be sent out of the country.
- Wife, son, servants, and younger brothers can be punished for misconduct by beating with a stick or rope on his or her back.
- Causing destruction of plants or animals through negligence or as a willful act must be punished severely.
- Physical injury caused by a horse driven vehicle will entail responsibility on the owner. He will have to pay damages and cost of medication. The owner is responsible for the

driver's negligence. However, in case of accidents (10 types are mentioned) no one is responsible. It is an act of God.

Theft

- A king who protects his people from thieves gets one-sixth of their dharma; a king who fails to protect his people gets one-fourth share of their sins and also a share of the thieves' sins. A king is not entitled to collect taxes from his people if he fails to protect them. There is a *quid pro quo* to this transaction.
- Punishments for theft vary from fines to capital punishment; for petty thefts a fine is enough, for theft of valuables physical punishment is necessary.
- Stealing articles meant for *yaga* or *yajna* attract maximum punishment.

Robbery

- While theft involves taking away of goods without the knowledge of the owner, robbery involves force and it is often done in the presence of the owner. Punishment for robbery is very severe and the minimum is cutting away of body parts of all members of the gang, so that they cannot do any such thing in the future.
- Punishments for theft and robbery are increased when it is performed by the higher varnas. A Brahmana robber gets maximum punishment. It may be noted here that some of the leading dacoits of North India, in the past decades, were Bhumihar Brahmanas. All communities have produced robbers and thieves both in the past and at the present time.

- When law and order breaks down, people of all varnas can take to arms to protect themselves. Killing in self-defense and for the protection of women, children, the aged, and especially Brahmanas, will not amount to murder.
- One can kill anyone who comes to his house with the intention of killing or setting fire to his house or property, or stealing valuables.

Sex-related Offences

- Punishment for most sexual offences indicates excessive fear of mixing of varnas. Men who cohabit with other men's wives should be banished from the kingdom after cutting their lips.
- For valid reasons, and in public, men can converse with wives of other men. However, this should not be done in an isolated place, likes the banks of a river, a thorn forest, and so on.
- Exchanging perfumes, embracing, touching hands and other parts of the body, or sitting together, constitute sufficient evidence for adultery. Hands and or legs of the man may be cut off for this offence.
- Beggars, priests, cooks, and male servants can talk to women.
- Rape of a girl of higher varna is punishable by death. A girl of a lower varna may cohabit with a man of a higher varna. A girl of a higher varna cohabiting with a man of lower varna has to be physically confined to the house and the man punished. Raping a girl of the same varna involves a fine and payment of bride money and marriage.

Failure to pay fine must be punished with cutting away of the man's fingers or his hand.

- Women insulting unmarried girls must be fined. In severe cases, the woman may be tonsured, her fingers cut, or she is made to ride an ass in public view.
- A woman having relations with another man due to pride in her beauty should be punished by allowing female dogs to bite her in a public place.
- A Shudra having sex with a woman of higher varna should be fried on a hot iron plate.
- A man of higher varna having sex with an outcast girl must be fined 1,000 *panams*.
- Detailed punishments of lesser cruelty are prescribed for sex relations between men and women of the three higher varnas.
- A Brahmana raping a Brahmana girl should be fined 1,000 *panams*.

General Rules

- A king may assume the title of a *samrat* if in his kingdom there are no thieves or robbers, or men of violent and bad character.
- A person who abandons his wife, son, or parents must be punished. However, this is not applicable if there is a valid reason.
- If a feast is given for 20 or more persons, all Brahmanas in the surrounding areas should be invited.
- No tax should be collected from the blind or disabled, old people, women, and children.

- The king should welcome educated Brahmanas and give them gifts. He should also give gifts to the old, the young students, the poor men of good family.
- Smugglers of goods that are prohibited should be punished by confiscating all their properties.
- Providing wrong information to custom officials is punishable; such information includes undervaluation, mention of wrong origins or destinations, under or overstatement of quality of products.
- The king should review prices of goods periodically with a group of merchants to determine customs duties and taxes.
- Weights and measures should have the king's seal. They should be inspected periodically.
- At the point of entry into the country, an entry tax should be levied on individuals, animals and carts without load.
- Travel through boats in rivers should be regulated and taxed.
- The king should enforce work from Vaishyas and Shudras. The king also has the responsibility to see that the people belonging to different varnas are able to make a living by the occupations prescribed for them.

Raja Dharma III

This chapter, containing 330 verses, focusses on rights to property based on succession. All heirs are born out of man-woman relations and this can be complex as we will see. Deaths of father or sons, existence of multiple wives, adoption by male and female members, and even remarriage of women receive due attention. This chapter gives insight into the social life of people around 300 BC. It is down-to-earth and constitutes excellent subaltern history.

Stree Dharma

The subject matter of the chapter is introduced by explaining *stree dharma*. It is women who produce sons who become heirs to the father's property. However, a woman has no rights and this is explained in terms of certain analogies.

- Since a woman is necessary for performing karmas, for producing a successor, and doing all household chores including the feeding of guests, she should be respected and protected. She is first protected by her father and he gets bride money for that service, and then by her husband for the services mentioned above, and then by her son. The last one has no selfish motive. She should never be left alone to fend for herself; this may lead to immoral acts and the intermixing of varnas.
- It is the duty of a woman to protect all valuables in the house, keep the house clean, cook food, look after the children, and feed her husband as well as guests. However, a woman cannot be compelled to do all the above without any co-operation. For that reason her husband should try to please her by presents.
- No matter what bad qualities her husband has, a woman should put up with all those things. Age and the ugliness of her husband should not matter to her.
- Women and girls are not entitled to birth cycle rituals.

- Women may have bad qualities; some of these are fickleness of mind, too many desires, tendency to get angry, desire for personal ornamentation, given to too much talking and using bad language, beating servants, and so on.
- Like a river that merges into the ocean, a woman becomes part of her husband. If her husband is meritorious, she gets merit as well. Hence parents should try to find meritorious grooms for their daughters.

Children

In the *Manusmriti,* a woman is compared to an agricultural plot of land. A man sows his seeds in her and she produces a child just the same way a plot of land would behave when seeds are sown. The children, according to the *Manusmriti,* take father's qualities and they are in fact a part of him.

However, children born to a wedded wife alone are his; the wife or mother has no ownership rights over the children. If a man has children by a woman to whom he is not married then that child (or children) belong to their mother; he has no rights over these children; even though they are from his seed.

In a farm land, the produce belongs to owner of the land and not to the cultivator who may have supplied the seeds as well. Similarly, if a cow owned by a person is impregnated by a bull owned by another, the resulting calf belongs to the owner of the cow. The argument is that a wife is owned by her husband and hence the children are his. Women cannot own anything under Manu's law.

While the ownership angle is at least rational and consistent, the analogy of land and seed is faulty if not nauseating. Firstly, land cannot be compared with a woman, since she is a living thing while land is not. Secondly, the seed sown in land has already been fertilized in the flowering stage, while man's seed needs to combine with the woman's egg; this aspect was not known to Manu and hence the wrong analogy.

Women in Distress

The rules mentioned below apply to all varnas other than Brahmanas.

- When a man dies and he does not have even one child, then his widowed wife can cohabit with her brother-in-law or any agnate of her husband and bear a child; she cannot have more than two children in this way. Cohabitation should be strictly for producing a child, otherwise the normal relationships continue.
- If a groom dies before formal marriage, his brother can marry the bride in the normal way. He need not pay additional bride money.
- After marriage, if it is found that the bride has disabilities which were not disclosed earlier, she can be returned to her parents and the bride money taken back as well.
- A husband can demand bride money if his wife goes back to her parents and does not return for a year.
- A man can marry again if his wife has certain disabilities or if she fails to bear a child, or more specifically a son.
- A girl is to be married off at the age of 8 to a man who is 24 years of age; or at 12 years to a man of 30 years. The rationale is not explained. Probably, the higher age

specification for men is to enable them to complete their education in a gurukula.

Division of Property

In a joint family situation, where brothers live together, the eldest son manages the properties after the father's death; in other words he assumes the role of the father. However, the more common practice was to divide the property among the sons equally. There are several variations from this arithmetic rule.

First, the eldest son gets a slightly higher share and he is entitled to choose the best cows, the best plot of land and so on. This is to compensate him for his responsibility to the surviving mother and other family burdens.

Where there are unmarried girls, there is a provision for them as well, but the married girls get nothing.

In the event certain properties are not divisible, the excess part cannot be sold, but it can be taken by the eldest brother.

Problems arise when there are many wives, and some of whom are from lower varnas. The problem in those days was so complex, even though in a very small number of cases, that Manu was compelled to make elaborate rules in this regard. The reason is that the few cases that occurred pertain to rich and important people.

The problem is further compounded by the fact that sons may be adopted or an orphan taken in.

Further, upon the death of her husband, a childless woman is allowed to have two children by her brother-in-law or in his absence by an agnate. These sons can inherit the property share of her original husband.

For sons born of lower varna wives, the shares of properties are reduced progressively in the case of Kshatriya, Vaishya, and Shudra wives. Generally, sons born to Shudra wives are not entitled to property rights. They can accept whatever is given. The *Manusmriti* defines 12 types of sons of whom only the first six are eligible for inheriting properties.

There is the problem of deciding the seniority among sons when many wives are involved; earlier birth, mother's varna, and her seniority are all to be taken into account.

At the other extreme, a person may leave his properties without an heir. Excepting Brahmana properties, those left by other varnas may be taken by the king. In the case of a Brahmana, the same has to be given as gift to another Brahmana by the king.

Adoption of a son is allowed only when there is no natural son in the family, that is, among all the same varna wives. There is no mention of adoption of daughters.

Upon the death of husband, a wife inherits the property (if there are no children) and then she can beget a son by another person of the same *gotra* and then eventually the properties will go to that son.

In the absence of a son, the properties can go to the daughter(s). If a father marries his daughter with the stated object of giving his wealth to his grandson, his wishes should be respected.

A woman is entitled to property—*stree dhanam*—in the form of ornaments that are given to her by her father, brothers and even husband. These properties will go to her daughters. If she dies without children, they will go to her husband.

Properties of wives without children will go to the children of the first same varna wife.

Sons with various disabilities such as blindness, mental disability, deaf, mute, physically disabled, etc., are not entitled to a share of the property but those who take a share will have to feed them and take care of them.

If any son has self-earned property, he need not share it with others at the time of partition. A father can discharge a son with his own income by giving him a token gift.

If the eldest son cheats and deprives the younger ones of their share of property, the king can punish him.

When partition takes place while father is alive, father gets a larger share of the property and the rest is distributed among the sons. Sons born after partition will get only a share of the father's share of property. Both assets and liabilities should be shared equally at the time of partition. Clothes, ornaments, servants are not part of divisible assets.

Property of an unmarried son will go to his mother.

Property-related Crimes

Most of the offences mentioned here relate to the 18 offences described in Chapter 8. Perhaps the repetition here is to show its relevance to property rights and duties.

Betting as a crime has already been discussed in Chapter 8. The point perhaps is that betting involves property, particularly valuables like gold and silver, as well as land. Secondly, betting was a major vice in those days when there was little scope for entertainment at home. The king should punish all parties involved in betting by heavy fines.

Bribery, cheating and blackmail were other common crimes involving property. Bribery involved employees of the king and it calls for very strict punishment. All these crimes should be detected by engaging spies and the officers who are lax in dealing with such cases should also be punished.

The king could not possibly handle all the disputes himself and he had to appoint judges at the local level. The king should not accept appeals from these courts unless he has reason to believe that injustice has been done. In that case, he should fine the judges as well.

Well-known criminals were branded by stamping signs, like a palm tree, on their forehead. People then could boycott them and be vigilant.

Thieves and robbers were a big menace. Thieves had a tendency to frequent certain places where people gather such as assemblies, eating places, brothels, and wine shops. Robbers preferred isolated places for hiding themselves and stolen materials. The king should send his troops to such places and look for the places of their hide-out. Spies should also be engaged for this purpose.

Anti-social elements try to destroy or poison common facilities such as wells, tanks, river embankments and so on. They should be apprehended and killed.

Those who defecate on roads or make it unclean should be asked to clean the road and they should be fined as well.

Statecraft

All the seven pillars of the State are should function effectively. It is the duty of the king to keep a close watch on all aspects. He should make all his subjects engage in constructive activities. Agriculture, animal husbandry and trade should receive particular attention. The Vaishyas have the primary duty to oversee these sectors and inform the king.

Trade and relations with other countries require knowledge of other languages and the king's agents should be fully trained in these; the multiplicity of languages and dialects was very relevant to statecraft even in 300 BC.

Above all, the Brahmanas in the kingdom should be kept happy. Their knowledge of dharma is important to the king in maintaining peace.

Summary

The three chapters in the *Manusmriti* dealing with *raja dharma* give us an idea about the origins of our legal system. There were other *Smritis*, perhaps of later origin, but the *Manusmriti* is accepted as the most important work of this genre.

The legal-judicial system of early kingdoms was indeed very basic and rudimentary. The *Manusmriti* is meant for a society where very small kingdoms dominated and where the king could have direct contact with his people. As kingdoms matured and became larger, this was no longer possible. In such a situation, the authority of the king was exercised by his functionaries at lower levels. Nevertheless, the *Manusmriti* as a source book of law survived centuries of political turmoil by its local applicability in a feudal milieu.

The *Manusmriti* should be read along with Kautilya's *Arthashastra*; the latter deals with a more complex and territorially-larger State. Yet, both have a lot in common. While the *Arthashastra* is basically secular, the *Manusmriti* is indeed a religious text. The laws prescribed in the *Manusmriti*, therefore, have divine sanction. Observance of the *raja dharma* is the duty of the king as much as it is the duty of the citizen. Failure in this respect will attract divine punishment for the king as well as his subjects.

Sixteen

Manusmriti: Varna Samkara

Introduction

The last three chapters of the *Manusmriti* deal with aspects of social disruption, self-punishment, and divine punishment for deviation from the dharma.

Even at the very outset, the *Manusmriti* asserts that there are only four varnas and not five. This assertion has to be viewed in the context of inter-varna marriages, formal and informal, which tend to destroy the very basics of varna system of a society deeply rooted in *Manusmriti* and *Bhagavad Gita* in the long run. On the other hand, the *Manusmriti* takes note of inter-varna marriages at that time. Again, the ideal and the actual are at variance.

The varna differentiation is the foundation of the Hindu feudal system. With the elimination of Hindu kings after Independence, the Hindu feudal system no longer exists in India. It has been abolished in Nepal, which represents the very last bastion of Hindu feudalism. The Brahmanas in India no longer study Sanskrit and 99 per cent of Brahmanas have never seen any of the four *Vedas* and those who have read it are even fewer in number. The *Manusmriti* says that Brahmanas, Kshatriyas, and Vaishyas should be considered as Shudras if they do not follow the dharma prescribed for them. Those who have not studied at least one *Veda* cannot claim to be a Brahmana, Kshatriya or Vaishya. As a result, hardly anyone can claim to be following the dharma prescribed in the *Manusmriti*.

The reality is that there is only one varna among Hindus today and that is the fourth varna; the alternative is to deny or reject the varna system in its entirety. There is no other choice. Rejection of the varna system would still leave the *jati* or *jatis* intact as this concept is outside the framework of religion. Most *jatis* in India today, accounting for over 80 per cent of Hindus, are followers of an oral tradition. To them *varna ashrama dharma* never had any real relevance.

It is oft-repeated that the *Manusmriti* does not mention anywhere the term *jati* as it is known today. *Jati* is a social phenomenon and we have many religions that are specific to one or more *jatis*, although these religions also go by the name of Hinduism. The concept of *jati* extends beyond the frontiers of Hinduism and it exists among Christians and Muslims in India. We shall explore this aspect in a later chapter. One should not mix up the two entirely different concepts of *jati* and varna. Varna is central to Hindu religion as defined in the *Manusmriti* and *Bhagavad Gita*, while *jati* is not. *Jati* existed and still exists outside the framework of varna.

The discussion on inter-varna marriages and their consequences is followed by a set of alternate prescriptions for occupations for the three varnas in times of difficulty. The fact was that in 300 BC there were Shudra kings at one extreme and Brahmana butchers at the other. The reality was very complex and the occupations prescribed by Manu for the three varnas were far too few and basic. As a result, we find that even in 300 BC, the upper three varnas practised a great many occupations than was actually permitted. This reality is acknowledged in various contexts in the *Manusmriti*. In this chapter, the *Manusmriti* grudgingly allows Brahmanas and Kshatriyas to practice agriculture and trade—the two principal occupations of mankind until the industrial revolution.

Varna Mixture

In Chapter 10, the *Manusmriti* discusses inter-varna marriages and the origin of *samkara varnas*. It does not use the term *jati*, however, some traditional scholars have interpreted the inter-varna marriages as the cause for the formation of numerous *jatis* in India. This is not really true. The word *samkara* literally means unification; the unification of varnas would destroy the feudal system with the king at its apex and hence it is seen as a major threat to the feudal society. Prajapati created four varnas from his body and that is the foundation on which both the *Manusmriti* and *Bhagavad Gita* are based. The four varnas formed the four pillars of Hindu feudal order.

Mixture through Marriage

It is clear that the *Manusmriti* looks down on inter-varna marriages. Marriage between a man and woman of the same varna is the ideal and perhaps the most common type. Marriage between a man of a higher varna and a woman of a lower varna is called *anuloma* marriage and is grudgingly allowed. But the marriage of a man of a lower varna with a woman of a higher varna—*pratiloma* marriage—is condemned in no uncertain terms. Children born out of the second type of marriages constitute *samkara varnas*. They are the outcasts of society. They are to be treated a shade lower than the Shudras. The children of the *anuloma* marriages merge into their mother's varna and do not form a new category. In actual practice, the children born out of *pratiloma* marriages merged into the father's varna, however, the *Manusmriti* puts them on a lower level (lower than the Shudra varna).

The *Manusmriti* holds the view that man or the seed is more important than the woman or the field and the child's purity is determined by the male seed. However, when a Shudra marries a Brahmana woman, the children thus born have qualities which are much worse than their father's—they are truly the outcasts of society and are called *chandalas*.

This logic is self-contradictory. If the male seed determines the quality of the offspring then the children of *anuloma* marriages should merge with the father's varna while in reality they merge with the mother's varna.

On the other hand, the children of *pratiloma* marriages, instead of being considered inferior to the father's varna, actually merged into their father's varna. The reason is that the father's varna generally had no objection to such marriages. Such marriages were and are very rare. *Pratiloma* marriages attracted and still continue to attract strong community reaction and such couples are often forced to leave their native villages and go elsewhere. Nowadays, it is the city that welcomes them.

The *Manusmriti* recognizes 16 categories of marital relations between the four varnas. Four out 16 form the normal Brahmana, Kshatriya, Vaishya, and Shudra varnas; then we have six *anuloma varnas*, and finally another six *pratiloma varnas*. The latter are also known as *samkara varnas* and they are allowed to engage only in the worst type of occupations—as executioners for the king, the keepers of burial and cremation grounds, hunters and fishermen, etc.

In the case of *anuloma varnas*, there is enhancement in the quality of the offspring, although it would be assumed to belong to the mother's varna. If, for example, the daughter of a Shudra woman and a Brahmana is married to a Brahmana, and the process is repeated for six generations, then the later progenies may be equated with Kshatriyas (the varna next lower to Brahmana).

In Kerala, the Namboodiri Brahmanas, who practised an extreme form of patriarchy in which only the eldest son could marry within the varna, had such a relationship with the matriarchal Nair families for centuries. The system came to an end in the early 20th Century. By this time, the Nairs of Kerala have been elevated to the Kshatriya status, which they claim today. The main point to be remembered here is that this process did not generate a third group. We still have only two categories—Nairs and Namboodiris. The theory that mixed marriages will generate new varna (or *jati*) is not realistic.

Many of the mixed varnas were named by Manu after well-known regions of *Aryavarta*, such as, Magadha, Videha, Malla, etc. Andhra and Dravida are also mentioned, however, these regions were either within *Aryavarta* or close to it (they have no relationship with the present day connotations of those words).

Associating a person of a mixed marriage to a region reflects regional stereotypes and prejudices of that time. One offspring of a mixed marriage cannot form a new varna, or account for the population of an entire region.

Another interesting point made is that Kshatriyas can degenerate into Shudras by not respecting or following the advice of Brahmanas; in other words, by not following their *varna dharma*. Names of such Shudras given in the text include Yavanas (Greeks), Sakas (Scythians), Pahlavas (Iranians), China (Chinese), Khamboja, Dravida, and so on. Most of them are non-natives or recent immigrants to *Aryavarta*. Further, it is mentioned that some of them speak a different language—different from the ones in *Aryavarta*.

Occupational Confusion

The *Manusmriti* asserts that a Brahmana performing the functions of a Shudra does not automatically become a Shudra if he continues to study the *Vedas* and perform the prescribed karmas. It is the study of the *Vedas* and performance of rituals that count; however, non-performance of *varna karmas*, especially the study of the *Vedas*, to the extent possible, can lower one's varna status.

When the *Manusmriti* was written, major political and social changes were already taking place in *Aryavarta*. This chapter of the *Manusmriti* therefore relaxes and broadens rules regarding occupations for all varnas during the time when earning a living becomes difficult.

At this time, Shudra kings had taken over in many regions. The *Manusmriti* mentions the Yavanas (Greeks), Pahlavas (Iranians) and others who became the new but 'degraded' Kshatriyas. As a result, the Brahmanas and the original Kshatriyas had to seek new occupations to maintain their life. It is in this context that the *Manusmriti* mentions adoption of other occupations, other than the one prescribed, for the three varnas.

The upper three varnas were allowed to practice occupations prescribed for lower ones in times of difficulty; however, they were still required to study the *Vedas* and perform ritual karmas prescribed for them. The first preference for the Brahmanas was to take up arms and assume kingship. In Northern India, starting from Sungas and Kanvas, many kings were in fact Brahmanas. Later, Brahmanas migrated to the south and became kings and established dynasties, for example, Satvahanas, Rashtrakutas, Chalukyas, Pallavas.

The majority of Brahmanas had to seek other avenues such as trade or agriculture, and a large number of them became landlords and agriculturists by proxy. In this they were helped by Brahmana and Shudra kings especially in the south. Brahmanas survived in all parts of India in this way. Kshatriyas could perhaps obtain and maintain land by force, while Vaishyas had the least difficulty, since trade was necessary everywhere and they had developed special skills in this profession. In fact, Vaishyas prospered even under the Muslim rulers in medieval times. Somehow all three varnas survived the difficult times.

Those Brahmanas who refused to deviate from the prescribed occupations chose to live by collecting grains and food from forest and cultivated land and by accepting unsolicited gifts from all.

Shudras had no problem whatsoever; apart from service to other three varnas, they could engage in work as artisans—carpenters, smiths, weavers, etc., and above all as farmers and herders of cattle, sheep, or goats.

The Kshatriyas, Vaishyas and Shudras were under no circumstances permitted to practice the three Brahmana occupations, that is, teaching the *Vedas*, working as *purohits*, and accepting gifts from others. They had no real need to do the above, since these options were never really attractive. Further, these occupations require years of learning and training.

The chapter concludes by saying that it is the king's duty to see that all varnas could make a living by the occupations prescribed by Manu. Under normal conditions, there should no compelling need for the varnas to look to other occupations.

Prayaschita

There are three forms of punishment for wrongdoing: punishment by the king or the State, by God, and self punishment.

There are three types of wrongdoings: wrongs done unintentionally, wrongs done knowingly for extraneous reasons, and those done intentionally. The last should be punished by the king; if not, then God will punish. While the first and the second type may be fully compensated by self punishment (*prayaschita* or remorse and penance), the third may be partly offset by remorse.

There are many types of wrongdoings for which the right type of penance will undo the damage. Similarly, there are many types of penance. Some are easy to perform, others are extremely difficult while there are some (most from a modern perspective) which seem to be more in the nature of punishment rather than penance.

Chapter 11 of the *Manusmriti* lists the wrongdoings and mentions the type of penance required, with variations according to the varna of the offender and the offended. It is a rather tedious reading. I have simplified them without bringing them together, except in a few cases.

The objective is to give an overview; for details one must consult the text.

Types of Wrongdoings

There are three basic types of wrongdoings—non-performance of prescribed karmas, performance of proscribed karmas, and self-indulgence. In reality, the performances of proscribed karmas are by far the most important and serious, while for the other two, there are simple remedies through penance. The *Manusmriti* elaborates on a very long list of wrongdoings; these number well over a hundred items. It is not possible to list them all. They, however, fall into seven recognizable categories—violent acts, stealing, eating prohibited food, sexual offences, association with bad characters, non-observance of rituals, and secret offences.

Violence This category is indeed the longest and most serious of all. Above all, this involves killing of humans, animals, birds, insects and even worms; at a lesser level, violence may involve only body injury and bleeding. Killing a Brahmana is the cardinal sin and there is no escape from divine punishment even after penance. At the other extreme, killing an insect such as a fly requires only one *pranayama.*

Interestingly, violence against plants is also punishable. Cutting down trees of various kinds, destroying plants, and even weeds will entail penance and remorse. This possibly illustrates Jaina influence.

Stealing This is a very common crime. One can steal petty articles of common use, or even water. One can also steal valuables, cows and cattle or other domesticated animals; and surprisingly even women, children and also men for self-benefit or due to enmity or both.

Consumption of prohibited food This may be done deliberately or unknowingly. In most cases, the latter is common. Eating meat and drinking liquor are common vices of the first kind. The second consists of eating worms, hair, etc., in food without noticing it. The remedies differ according to severity of the offence.

Sexual offences These are rather serious. Mention is made of intercourse with sister, cousin sisters, friend's wife, teacher's wife, daughter-in-law, and young unmarried girls. More offensive is intercourse with men, women in menses, even cows and horses. These may fall into the secret category as well.

Association with bad characters Sitting, travelling, dining and begging together, teaching, and marrying a bad character are sinful. Guilt by association may result in excommunication from village or town. This was considered to be a very serious offence in those days.

Non-observance of rituals In those days, this occurred due to illness or other factors beyond one's control. Probably, deliberate non-observance also existed. Luckily, the penance is *pranayama* and reciting of Vedic mantras.

Secret offences These are not mentioned, but obviously, in this case only the offender knows and he would not want to reveal his secret. Again, the remedies are simple—more *pranayama* and reciting of Vedic mantras. Both of these must always be done without generating any sound, that is, silently.

Types of Penances

There are 10 types of penances:

Prajapatyam It is a *kricha* or *vrata* and it involves 12 days. During the first three days, one takes food only in the morning; in the next three days only in the evening; in the next three days one eats only what is offered; and finally in the last three days no food is consumed. The last is called *upavasa*.

Santapam In this *kricha*, one takes cow's urine, cow dung, milk, curd, ghee, and water as food for a whole day and the following day one abstains from taking any food (*upavasa*).

Mahasanthapam This is a modification of the previous one in which one takes only one item in a day and only after six days one abstains from food for a day.

Athikricham Here one takes one mouthful of food in the morning for three days, in the evening for another three days, yet another three days with unsolicited food, and the final three days without any food.

Taptakricham One should take hot water, milk, ghee, and air, in that order, for three days each, practice *dhyana*, bathe once a day for a total of 10 days. Water and other items should be as hot as possible; it is said that it should burn the stomach.

Paraka kricham This includes 12 days of *upavasa*—no food at all—with control of all *indriyas* and no misconduct towards anyone. It is a panacea for all sins.

Chandrayanam In this, one is supposed to bathe thrice a day. Starting with 15 mouthful of food on full moon day, reduce one mouthful every day, then fast on new moon day, and increase food by one mouthful daily till the next full moon. This completes one lunar cycle. The *prayaschita* may involve several such cycles.

Danam One is supposed to give gifts of various kinds to Brahmanas; the categories of Brahmanas eligible for such gifts is listed. The most meritorious gift is that of a cow—the number of cows is increased with the severity of the crime.

Pranayama The simplest of all *prayaschitas*, *pranayama* is for minor offences, particularly those of a secret nature. It involves reciting the *pranava*, *vyahrithi*, followed by the *gayatri mantra*. This has to be repeated 108 times or more.

Tapas *Tapas* means *atma jnanam* to Brahmanas, people's welfare to Kshatriyas, trade or agriculture to Vaishyas, and service to the three upper varnas to Shudras. Doing all these dutifully is *tapas*.

Reciting Vedic Mantras Reciting Vedic mantras throughout the day is another form of *prayaschita*. For this, around 20 mantras (*suktas*) taken from the *Rigveda* are suggested. This is obviously possible only for those who have studied the *Vedas*.

During the performance of all penances, one should stand during daytime and sit during nighttime; if this is too much, one can sleep on the floor. One should not entertain the company of women; he should worship his guru and the Gods. He should recite (silently) the *gayatri mantra* throughout the day.

Epilogue

The more severe forms of *prayaschita* are done under the supervision of elders. The offender may bring his offence before the elders himself. Hence, it is still in the nature of self-punishment. He should divulge his offence, but he need not divulge all the details. He can even say that he has committed such and such offence in general terms. He should express his remorse over his action and declare that he will never commit the same crime again. The sincerity of his statement is all important and this would be reflected in his conduct of the prescribed penance.

In the 20th Century, Hindus have all but given up this aspect of our religion. No one is willing to admit his or her crime and everyone pleads his or her innocence.

End Results of *Karma Yoga*

The final chapter consisting of 126 verses focusses on divine punishment for not following the *varna ashrama dharma* or *karma yoga* and for committing sinful acts. Punishment involves going to various types of hells and thereafter being born as a plant, insect, or animal, or as man, often as a lowly person. The mechanism of rebirth revolves around the concept of *jivatman* and the *gunas* that influence it. There is a great deal of Sankhya school of thought here. On the positive side, the possibility of going to heaven and attaining *moksha* are also mentioned.

Good and Bad Karmas

All acts performed according to the prescriptions of *varna ashrama dharma* are good and those that are proscribed are bad. People commit a great variety of acts, both good and bad. Hence, one's progress after death depends on the balance of good over bad or vice versa. If the balance is favourable, one goes to heaven for some time and then returns to earth as man at a slightly higher level. If it is equal, he would come back to earth immediately under similar circumstances. If the balance is in favour of bad, he will spend some time in one or more hells and return to earth either as a man of very lower status or as a plant, insect, or animal.

Good and bad acts are invariably instigated by the mind and by instinct. The latter is determined by the *gunas*. However, by using one's intellect one can control the mental tendencies and direct them in the right direction, that is, overcome the influence of *gunas*.

All acts good and bad relate to the mind, word, or body. Those relating to the mind are desires of various kinds such as for wealth, pleasures of the body, or for causing hurt to others. Verbal acts involve telling lies, telling unpleasant things, criticizing others, or pointless and irrelevant talk. Examples of bodily acts are violence against others, adultery, and stealing others' property.

One needs to control one's mind, speech, and body. Mind is controlled by *jnana*, speech is controlled by silence, and body is controlled by *pranayama* (breathing exercise).

Atman and *Gunas*

Rebirth involves the atman. There are two concepts of atman according to *Manusmriti*—the pure atman or *purusha* and the impure atman or *jiva*. The pure atman is one and the same as *Brahman*, the Absolute God. The *jiva* of all living things is created by Prajapati initially by including *gunas—satva*, *raja* and *tamas*—in varying proportions. The *jiva* enters a body, again created by Prajapati, and the body is made up of the five elements or *bhutas*.

Once the *jivas* with their respective bodies arrive on earth, their actions on earth are conditioned by the *gunas*. However, good and bad actions can modify the proportion of the *gunas* and in the next life, it is this modified *jiva* that enters the new body. Further, after death the human *jiva* may spend some time in heaven or hell in a make-shift body and then return to earth in a normal body.

The *Manusmriti* categorizes all living things, including man, into nine types, three for each *guna*. A person may be in the lower, middle, or upper category in each of the three *gunas*. It must be noted here that all living things have all the three *gunas*, but one *guna* dominates over the others in each individual and it is then classified by the dominant *guna*. A long list of animals, plants, different varnas of man and even *devas* are given for each one of the categories above.

Among animals, worms and insects represent the worst of the *tamas guna*, while Shudras represent the next step in the ladder. The middle of *rajas guna* is represented by Kshatriyas and priests. The highest among those with *satva guna* are *jnanis*. The actual list is indeed very elaborate.

Punishment by Rebirth

Those who have committed crimes or sins would go to one of the 21 hells and then return to earth and become an animal or plant according to the nature of the crime. The *Manusmriti* gives a large number of examples; only a selected few are mentioned here.

- Those who kill a Brahmana will be born as a dog, pig, ass, camel, goat, sheep, any wild animal, a bird, etc. The choice of the animal depends on the motivation to kill.
- A Brahmana who drinks (alcoholic beverages) will be born as an insect, butterfly, or a bird which eats worms.
- A thief of gems, pearls, etc., will be born as a goldsmith.
- Women who commit various crimes will be born as the females of the species mentioned for men.
- Those who fail to follow *varna dharma* will be born as servants of their enemies or if they have no enemies, they will becomes ghosts of various kinds.
- Others who are fortunate enough to be reborn as men for their sins will undergo suffering in their next life—loss of near and dear ones, a life in the company of bad people, loss of income and wealth, absence of friends, affliction with various diseases, old age afflictions, or untimely death.
- It is common among Hindus to explain away various issues and problems, concerning themselves or others, in terms of punishment for sins committed in their previous birth or births. This is in accordance with the *Manusmriti.*

Pathways to *Moksha*

On a broader canvas, there are two dharmas—*pravritti dharma* and *nirvriti dharma*. The first applies to the vast majority of people and living things which by nature have to earn their living. However, there are a select group of men to whom the above rule does not apply. They take *sanyasa* from *brahmacharya* itself and follow a life of seclusion. The *nirvriti dharma* applies to this class of born mystics or saints. Those who follow the rules of *nirvriti dharma* alone attain *moksha*; all others will be reborn into this world.

Ways to Clear Doubts

In conclusion, the *Manusmriti* outlines the procedure for clearing doubts about various prescriptions made in the text. Doubts may also occur because of variations from one region to another and with the passage of time.

A Brahmana who is learned in the three *Vedas* must be accepted as the absolute authority to clear all doubts.

If such a Brahmana is not available, then a committee of 10 partially learned people may be consulted. This is called a *parishad*. All members of this committee should be men of character.

Bhrigu's Advice

Everyone should try to know the *Brahman* in himself. He must see himself in all living things and he must also see all living things in himself.

Manusmriti in Retrospect

The *Manusmriti* is today a much-maligned text on Hindu social laws. Nevertheless, it was the law for over 2,000 years. Brahmanas all over India interpreted this law along with other *Smritis* and they were supported by kings, feudal chiefs and village *panchayats*. In the South, the Smartha Brahmanas (popularly known as Iyers) were well-versed in the *Smritis* and in particular the *Manusmriti*.

The Smartha Brahmanas specialized in the *Yajurveda*, which was compiled by Yajnavalkya. As a result, they were also experts in *Yajnavalkya Smriti*. However, Smartha Brahmanas have given up their traditions and no longer practice Vedic rituals. Also, they do not have any knowledge of the *Smritis* now.

The *Manusmriti* does not mention any Gods other than *Brahman* and *devas* of Vedic origin. While there were six schools of thought in Hinduism at that time, the main conflict was between Hinduism on the one hand and Jainism and Buddhism on the other. The Vedantins, Poorva Mimamsikas, and the Tantriks did quarrel among themselves; that is, when they were not arguing with the Buddhists.

The *Manusmriti* provides us a detailed account of life of ordinary people around 300 BC from the point of view of Hindus. It is basically rooted to the Poorva Mimamsa school, but it does take into account the Uttara Mimamsa school (Vedantic school) and the Sankhya school. It acknowledges the contribution of Jainism by accepting ahimsa and vegetarianism. The *Manusmriti* is an important historical document. It provides us with a true picture of society and religion as it prevailed around 300 BC; it enables us to judge the changes in later time periods.

However, its support of Kshatriyas is rather tenuous and feeble. The times have already changed; new classes of rulers have emerged who did not belong to the Kshatriya varna, although they were accepted as such later. The *Manusmriti* caustically names them as degenerate Kshatriyas. It feared the collapse of the varna society, with Brahmanas holding the top position. However, it could do very little to save the situation.

The religious prescription in the *Manusmriti* is indeed very rigid. Although it was practised until a few centuries ago with vigour, it has been abandoned completely in recent times. Again its religious prescriptions (performance of Vedic rituals) were followed only by small groups of Brahmanas; it had no popular following at any time.

When Buddhism and Jainism lost their shine in the north, the ordinary people needed a new religion with mass appeal. Thus the Puranic religion with the two epics emerged. Here, the Gods take human form and take part in human affairs. They are more approachable and people could emotionally identify with them. Furthermore, the stories and legends were already current in some form and were not entirely new. We now enter an age of fantasy. Legends and myths about the past are woven together with social values and religious principles; The *Puranas* and epics were very successful and they constitute the mainstream Hinduism today. The Puranic school has ever since overshadowed the earlier schools of Hindu philosophy. Nevertheless, the Vedantic school has survived thanks to the *Bhagavad Gita*. The *Manusmriti* has failed to survive, partly on account of its social value system and partly on account of its strict ritualistic prescriptions. Along with the *Manusmriti,* the Poorva Mimamsa school of Hinduism has also passed into history.

Seventeen

The Caste System

Western Views

Caste is defined as class in Indian social system. It originated from Portuguese and Latin where it connotes a breed or race which may be pure or mixed. In English, caste is an all embracing word related to Indian, and more specifically, Hindu society. Western social anthropologists, while dealing with castes at the village level, include the notion of degrees of pollution and purity; non-specialists stress that these characteristics are inherited. Commonly, the term caste includes names of ethnic and linguistic groups, the four varnas, various religious sects, and thousands of *jatis*. It may be comprehensive, but it lacks clarity. The varied connotations of the word 'caste' confuse all and yet it is popular.

Varna and *Jati*

In Sanskrit and other Indian languages, there is no equivalent word for caste. Our concepts are more specific. Principally, there are two concepts—varna and *jati*. These two are independent, although the term *jati* itself is of later origin. Varna is a religious concept and there are only four varnas as stated earlier. Those outside these varnas are known as *mlechas* and hence are considered untouchables. The four-fold varna system is specifically suited to a feudal order with a king at the top. According to Sanskrit scriptures, this order was created by God. However, all feudal societies the world over have the following four classes—the ruling class of nobles and warriors, the priestly class, the traders and farmers, and finally the service classes. In the Hindu society also the four varnas represent this social order.

Jati is a vernacular concept and it includes varna too. Varna has no equivalent in some languages, such as Tamil. According to a very strict sociological definition, *jati* means an endogamous group of people, meaning that all marriages are within the group only and none with members outside it. As a result, a *jati* is homogenous in terms of language, religion and cultural practices. There are over 6,000 *jatis* among Hindus. *Jati* is an important factor in social relations at the micro level—village level. The names of specific *jatis* are recognized only at the regional and local levels. These *jatis* are relevant regionally, whereas varna is understood by Hindus all over the country.

The *Manusmriti* mentions another social group—*gotra*. A *gotra* consists of persons who are agnates. Marriages between members of a *gotra* are not allowed according to *Manusmriti* and also in actual practice. In technical language, a *gotra* is an exogamous social group. The concept of *gotra* has a direct relationship with the lineages of Brahmanas and in fact, this term should be applied only to Brahmanas. However, centuries later, it has been adopted by the Kshatriyas too. Often it is used as a substitute for tribal clans, and in such a situation, the *gotra* may represent a *jati*. The origin of *gotras* among Brahmanas and their numbers is already well-known to us. The *pravara* or lineage of Brahmana *gotras* may have names of one to as many as five Rigvedic poets. As a result, the concept of *gotra* has a direct linkage to Rigvedic society, although it did not originate at that time. The Rigvedic society was tribal and egalitarian in nature and hence these concepts are alien to it. The concept of tribe did exist in Rigvedic times as *pancha jana*.

All four varnas in India have a lot of *jatis* included within their fold. Each linguistic region has it own Brahmana communities. In Tamil Nadu, the two principal Brahmana communities are Iyers and Iyyangars; besides, there are significant numbers of Brahmanas from other States, for example, Maharashtrian, Madhwa, Telugu Brahmanas and so on. In a similar way, every linguistic region has been subdivided into smaller groups having distinct names. I would estimate that there are several hundred Brahmana *jatis* in India. In a similar way, Kshatriya and Vaishya varnas are also subdivided into hundreds of *jatis*. The number of *jatis* among Shudras is around 4,000 in India.

The placement of *jatis* in the varna system is and has always been a matter of dispute and debate. Some *jatis* have claimed dual status in the varna scale. Numerous examples of such problems have been studied by social anthropologists in India.

To illustrate, let us see some. All relate to North India where the varna system originated. The first relates to the Kayastha community. We have Kayasthas in Punjab in the west to Bengal and Orissa in the east; in all these States, they are considered to be an educated class of professionals. Originally, they were supposed to be a writer class, meaning a literate class of people. It is also thought that the Kayasthas are a product of the Harappan civilization. Kayasthas are neither classified as Kshatriyas nor as Vaishyas. In fact, their position in the varna scale remains indeterminate. They are, however, highly respected by all. Many eminent personalities, including the first President of India, belong to this group.

The second example relates to the class known as Banias in Hindi-speaking areas. It is believed that the term Bania is derived from Panis, who were known as a trading class in Harappan and post-Harappan periods. Banias are well known as a trading class today and they are accepted as Vaishyas. They have played a prominent role in trade and business as well as professions. They were never farmers. Here, there is no problem as far as placement in the varna scale is concerned, but their origins go back to the pre-Rigvedic societies of India. The Banias are divided into two principal groups; each of these in turn is further divided into several groups or *jatis*.

The third and last example is that of Rajputs. They are the best known and commonly accepted Kshatriya group in northern India and yet the Rajput clans migrated to the middle Ganga Plains only in the 14th Century. It is notable that Rajputs are divided into distinct clans with names which are often used as surnames. They arrived in India from Central Asia probably in 8th Century AD. Rajputs still worship their clan Gods and some of their religious practices differ sharply from classic Hinduism as outlined in the *Manusmriti*. A host of communities migrated to

India after 300 BC and they were assimilated to the Hindu fold and assigned to the varna of their choice; the most popular choice was the Kshatriya varna. As a result, most Kshatriya groups have really nothing to do with the Rigvedic people.

It is interesting to note that the British were reluctant to recruit Rajputs into the Indian army, although they were known as a warrior class, while Jats and Yadavas (Ahirs) were recruited in large numbers; the latter are not considered as Kshatriyas.

As far as placement in the varna scale is concerned, there is a commonly accepted scheme in general terms at the local level. In some cases, the claims of certain communities to a higher varna status is not accepted by other communities. Thus there is mutual non-recognition of each other's status in the varna scale. The most negative aspects of the varna concept are the notions of inferiority or superiority. In course of time, these notions penetrated into the system of *jatis*, particularly at the local level. During the decennial censuses, from 1872 to 1930, people were classified according to their caste. This resulted in considerable acrimony, and enumeration based on caste was abandoned from the 1940 Census onwards. The 1930 Census data on castes, which is often cited, is at best a very unsatisfactory classification.

Sects and Cults

Besides *jati* and varna, the Indian society is also organized into religious sects and cults which have changed from time to time. The principal Hindu sects are Shivaites, Vaishnavas and Shaktas. These are subdivided into several sub-sects. There were and there are hundreds of cults at any point in time in India. The principal ones in South India today are the Ayyappa cult and the Saibaba cult. These cults have no basis in our scriptures. The acid test for recognition is reference in one of the 18 *Puranas*. Cults that have no foundation in the *Puranas* are not sacred. For example, the Radheshyam cult is founded in the *Brahmavaivarta Purana* of the 1400 AD, and therefore, it has scriptural sanction.

People who belong to any sect or cult generally adopt distinctive marks. From the Western viewpoint, sects and cults are also treated as castes. The so-called caste marks have nothing to do with *jati* or varna and they actually relate to a sect or cult.

A religious cult is a social group which may transcend both *jatis* and varnas. For example, people from different varnas and *jatis* participate in the practices of the Ayyappa cult. This is true of most religious cults. In a similar way, religious sects often encompass many *jatis* and even varnas. These cannot, therefore, be equated with the concepts of *jati* or varna. Religious sects and cults represent social grouping which is both transient and less rigid.

The Lingayats of Karnataka and Maharashtra, who belong to the Shivaite sect, do not recognize varna and *jati*. The founder of this sect, Basava, who lived in 1300 AD, denounced the division of Hindu society into varna and *jati*, though he belonged to the Brahmana varna. Nevertheless, *jati* persists even among Lingayats today.

Race and Ethnicity

The Indian population has a very varied racial composition. There are fair skinned and dark skinned people. There are also people with yellow complexion. Hair forms, stature and general appearances differ. There are people with distinct Negroid or Australoid, Mongoloid features and even Nordic features, though the latter are rare. Anthropologists have never accepted or used the terms Aryans or Dravidians in the sense of races. These words are used to designate linguistic groups.

Of the 6,000 odd *jatis*, very few can claim to have pure racial characteristics. All *jatis* in India are a mixture. The noted anthropologist Guha, in the early 20th Century, abandoned the concept of races of India and instead he talked about racial elements in Indian population. The Indian population has elements drawn from all the major races of mankind. The terms *jati* or varna have nothing to do with the concept of races of mankind. It may have something to do with ethnicity since *jatis* originated from tribes. However, in course of time, *jatis* got mixed up with other ethnic groups and their distinctiveness slowly eroded.

Caste and Occupations

In the scriptures, namely *Manusmriti* and *Bhagavad Gita*, varna is interpreted in terms of occupations. Brahmanas can engage in education, both teaching and learning and in priesthood; Kshatriyas in administration and the military or police forces; Vaishyas may be engaged in trade or cultivation; occupations of Shudras are not mentioned, which may mean that they can perform any of the occupations that are not prescribed for the other varnas. In general, they are duty bound to serve the other three varnas. However, it is doubtful if these prescriptions were ever followed. They are, in fact, theoretical in nature. For example, Brahmanas took up arms and became kings. There is a long list of Brahmana dynasties. Most of the post-Nanda dynasties were from the Shudra varna. Vaishya in India today may be a trader or a professional or a teacher but rarely a cultivator or farmer. The most prominent and well-recognized farmer communities are from the Shudra varna. The majority of Shudras are engaged in farming, while this is the prescribed occupation for Vaishyas. The 12 leading farming communities in India belong to the Shudra varna. Theory and practice do not correspond to each other. Today people in all *jatis* and varnas follow different occupations.

Nevertheless, caste in the sense of *jati* has still a lot to do with occupations in rural India. This is especially so in the case of agriculture, animal husbandry, and various other services, especially rural-based services. There are several well-known caste groups who specialize in agriculture. Mention may be made of Jats of Punjab and Uttar Pradesh, Kurmis of Bihar, Marattas of Maharashtra, Patidars of Gujarat, Khammas and Reddies of Andhra Pradesh, Vellalar of Tamil Nadu, Vokkaligas of Karnataka and many others. Ahirs of the Hindi region, who normally use the surname Yadav, are proud of their cattle herding tradition besides agriculture, while the Gujjars from Himachal Pradesh to Rajasthan and Uttar Pradesh have been traditionally herders of goats and sheep. Some are still nomadic or semi-nomadic communities. Recently, they have claimed the status of Scheduled Tribes.

There are *jatis* identified as potters, weavers, black smiths, carpenters, leather workers, goldsmiths, and a host of other traditional occupations. Two points should be kept in mind here. Firstly, many belonging to these *jatis* no longer practice their trade and some of them have entered the professions and the skilled workforce of an industrial society. Secondly, a number of people belonging to these *jatis* have converted to Islam or Christianity and still continue to practice their traditional occupations and even retain their old identities and customs. The last point assumes importance at the time of marriage.

Confusion over Caste Names

While the terms *jati* and varna are well defined, there are several levels or categories of social groups among them. The problem relates to the process by which new *jatis* originated. It is this aspect that accounts for the use of the terms caste groups and sub-castes. Every member of *jati* may have one or more levels of identification above his own *jati*. This means that his *jati* is derived from a larger social group. The process of *jati* differentiation occurs again and again at various points in time through history and hence multiple levels of identity of individuals. The social status of these subdivisions or even varna may have regional variation. This leads to a lot of confusion.

What is this confusion? Well, ask yourself what is your caste? In my case, I can think of many answers—I am Brahmana, a Smartha, an Iyer, a Palakkad Iyer, and a Vadama. These multiple identities reveal a lot about my background, but it hardly provides a clear answer to the basic question, What is my caste?

Now, if we use the criteria of endogamous group (most people do not understand this sociological concept), I belong to the Vadama *jati*. Among Iyers there are several *jatis*, such as, Vadama, Vathyama, Ashtasahasram, Mankudi, Brihacharanam and many others. They do not intermarry, at least in the past. In most Brahmana villages called *agraharams*, Brahmanas belonging to only one *jati* were found. This is not true anymore. In fact, most Brahmanas have abandoned their original or native villages and gone elsewhere.

The point is that most Indians when asked about their caste will come up with an appropriate answer. While answering a person from another State, one is likely to mention only his or her varna. A person would reveal his *jati* only in a regional or local context where he is sure it would be understood properly. The actual *jati* comes into play only at the time of marriage. Thus marriage is the crucial test for determining a *jati*.

It is because of the contextual answers and the confusion that it generated that the British gave up the use of caste in the decennial censuses. They simply could not cope with the confusion and the fury it generated when people claimed that they have been misclassified. Recently, politicians have demanded collection of information on castes in the population census. This is in the context of affirmative action by the government. One could expect considerable confusion and acrimony if ever such a census is carried out.

While most educated Indians do not care about *jati*, varna, and caste, there are many others, literate and illiterate, who do.

Caste System among Christians and Muslims

There is an outward pretension on the part of educated Christians and Muslims in India that they do not have a caste system. This is not true. Scholars from among these communities have written books on the caste system among Muslims and Christians in

India. Mother Teresa herself pleaded with the Prime Minister to give Scheduled Caste status to Christian converts from among the Scheduled Castes. The implication is that religion made no difference to the caste system. The fact is that we have Jat Hindus, Jat Muslims, Jat Sikhs, Rajput Hindus, Rajput Muslims and so on. I know quite a few Muslims and Christians who asserted with pride that they are converts from among Brahmanas. Among Muslims in Mughal period, Turks enjoyed the highest status, followed by Iranians, Afghans, and finally the Rajput converts to Islam. The Mughal emperor paid differential salaries for each of these and lower categories of employees.

The majority of Muslims and Christians in India are converts from the socially and economically-disadvantaged *jatis*. They practice their traditional occupations, just as they did before and their *jati* identities remain more or less the same. At the time of marriage, these caste identities come to the fore even among Muslims and Christians. This is the case among Hindus as well.

The so-called caste system is all pervasive in India. It is simply a part of our historical heritage. However, all this has nothing to do with the Hindu religion.

The fact is that all societies, including those in Europe and America, have a great variety of divisions called by different names. There are all kinds of Americans—Blacks, Latinos, Cubans, Irish, Italian, etc. Besides, there are Protestants and Catholics of various types. There are the church denominations which were by and large endogamous. Things are changing but so is society in India. In every society, marital alliances are governed by unwritten rules. However, no one wants to discuss these rules in public.

Caste and Constitution of India

The problem of the lowest rung of Indian society received a lot of attention from the makers of the Constitution of India. Dr Ambedker, who was born as a member of this category of India's population, was one of the principal makers of India's Constitution. Who are these people? They are in fact outside the varna system and were known by various derogatory names. Gandhi used the term Harijan for them. Today, people object to the term Harijan and prefer to use the term Dalit. They were considered to be untouchables by people of the four varnas. For that matter, Christians and Muslims were also considered as untouchables by some. The Constitution abolished untouchability or practice of it and the use of derogatory words to describe the Dalits. In fact, the Constitution went far ahead in terms of providing this category of India's population several privileges. This affirmative action is unique in the whole world. It came long before affirmative action was taken in the United States.

The Constitution of India created two categories of people—Scheduled Castes and Scheduled Tribes. The term Scheduled Castes includes all those *jatis* which were considered to be untouchables. The list of such *jatis* is to be made by a statutory body which will have authority to make changes in it from time to time. In a similar way, the Scheduled Tribes are also listed. Scheduled Castes constitute about 15 per cent of India's population while Scheduled Tribes form 7.5 per cent of India's population. A census of Scheduled Castes and Scheduled Tribes is made and published in each census. This gives information on the progress they have made since Independence. All these statutes have been in force for over 50 years now.

Scheduled Castes and Scheduled Tribes were given reservation in legislatures and government employment which equalled or exceeded their population ratio. However, the converts from Scheduled Castes among Muslims and Christians were not given any privileges, since their religious leaders, for the most part, denied the existence of such classes. Recently, Buddhists and Christians and some Muslims have demanded reservations for themselves as Scheduled Castes.

The Constitution of India does not mention caste in any other context. However, it has an article on socially and economically backward classes which provides legal sanction for affirmative action such as reservation in government employment and membership of legislatures. The laws in this regard have now been made. The term backward class is defined almost exclusively on the basis of varna scale. Those who do not claim to belong to the first three varnas are considered to be backward class. A list of *jatis* belonging to the backward classes now exists. Again Christians and Muslims are excluded, although both now are openly seeking such a privilege.

The constitutional recognition of caste has in fact assured the perpetuation of caste system for ever. This is unfortunate. We are now in an age where the problem is one of reverse discrimination. An upper caste individual would find it difficult to get jobs in government and to get into the legislatures through election.

The upper castes, namely Brahmana, Kshatriya and Vaishya varnas, put together constitute only 12.5 per cent of India's population, the backward classes constitute 52 per cent of the population, Scheduled Castes 15 per cent, Scheduled Tribes 7.5 per cent, Muslims 11 per cent, and Christians two per cent.

Besides we have Sikhs (two per cent) and Jainas and Buddhists, half per cent each. This arithmetic is of great importance in Indian electoral politics.

Caste and Politics in India

Caste used in a broader sense, that is a unit larger than *jati* but mostly smaller than a varna, plays an important role in Indian politics. At the national level, the Scheduled Castes and Scheduled Tribes are politically important as 20 per cent of the membership of legislatures is reserved for them. Muslims are another important community in national politics; they have an all India presence. The Hindu castes or really caste groups are relevant only at the regional level; there is no national alignment of Hindu castes.

The notable regional caste groups include the Jats in Haryana, Punjab, western UP and Rajasthan, the Ahirs of Bihar and eastern UP, the Marattas of Maharashtra, the Kolis, Kshatriyas (Solankies), and Patidars of Gujarat, the Lingayats and Vokkaligas of Karnataka, and the Reddies, Khammas, and Rajus of Andhra Pradesh, and the Vanniers, Thevars, and Nadars of Tamil Nadu. There are many others of lesser or equal importance at the regional and local levels.

Democracy has enabled the lower social classes to come to power in the States. The notable example is that of Tamil Nadu, in which the so-called Dravidian movement with its roots in the Justice Party of 1916, led to the first DMK government in 1967 and thereafter power has remained with them. Bihar and UP now lead the way for the empowerment of lower castes with Muslim support, who also predominantly belong to this group.

The upper castes (varnas) have lost power and privilege, although they are still dominant in the central government and in some major States as well. The most privileged status enjoyed by the three upper varnas has given way to a new system where the underprivileged now enjoy power and influence. This transition has taken place peacefully.

The upper castes are still very well off in all parts of India and they have the skills to prosper in an age of globalization. In South India, where Brahmanas had a commanding position in society in the past, are still very prosperous, although they have no voice in the legislatures or in government.

Caste and Social Change

Apart from political empowerment, there is a wave of social change noticeable at the level of individuals and small groups. This is a continuous process. MN Srinivas, the noted social anthropologist, has described four processes of social change in modern India. They are Sanskritization, Westernization, Secularization and Modernization. It is neither necessary nor possible to go into these processes of change here. However, a short clarification of the term Sanskritization may be in order. Sanskritization refers to the process by which lower caste Hindus imitate the behaviour and practices of upper caste Hindus, in particular Brahmanas. The Brahmanas still form the role models for most Indians and perhaps will continue to do so for some more time.

There are certain trends in terms of marriages among Brahmanas in the South. The old endogamous *jatis* have no relevance now and there is a clear trend of horizontal integration among Brahmana communities in the South as a whole. If this trend widens to all other varnas and to other parts of the country, the number of *jatis* would indeed decline in the future but one should not expect anything spectacular.

India is a plural society. The caste system does not constitute a hurdle to India's socio-economic progress. Peace, progressive social change, and social justice have made India a model democratic society.

Eighteen

Janma, Karma and *Bhaga*

This chapter focusses on the basic determinants of human life on earth. These were known for a long time; however, the interpretations of the determinants have changed. The pattern of human life has changed in unmistakable terms. Man's knowledge and understanding of this world has leaped manifold and in the past few decades we have truly become a world society—a society where family members have travelled widely and where people of all descriptions meet on an everyday basis. Yet, the fundamentals remain unaltered. Let us look at these in the light of contemporary societies.

Three Determinants

What determines an individual's life in all societies in the world? The answer is indeed very simple. It is more or less determined by three factors, namely, birth, action, and chance. In Sanskrit, these are known as *janma*, karma, and *bhaga*. We shall explore the meaning of these terms in some detail below:

Janma

Janma or birth has two basic aspects. The first has to do with a person's biological inheritance and the second with the societal environment. The latter also has two aspects—the economic and social status of parents and the type of society.

Biological Inheritance

At the time of birth, an individual inherits around 36,000 genes. Of this, 99 per cent are common to all human beings. Only around 300 to 400 genes vary from one individual to another, if we take all races of mankind from all parts of the world together. However, if we go down to the level of the family and look at siblings, the variation in the number of genes will be reduced to 10 or 20. However, this variation occurs in a random fashion; for example, 10 genes would be selected from 20 genes in a random fashion. The reason for reduction from 20 to 10 is because all of us carry a pair of genes of the same type, only one of which is effective while the other is dormant. As a result, siblings do not look alike or behave in a similar way, at least not always.

At birth a person's biological makeup is determined and he cannot change it.

The genes (and also chromosomes in which the genes are a constituent part) determine sex, physical appearance, quality of the brain, propensity for hereditary ailments, congenital deformities, and even one's mental make up. This will include aspects such as level of intelligence, aggressiveness, selfishness and many other character traits.

Psychologists believe that around 50 per cent of a person's mental attributes are inherited biologically through genes. Of the rest, a great part is shaped by family, educational, and social environment. The negative or positive effects of some genes may be modified or altered by human action. We can also enhance or reduce their effect by right or wrong action.

Social Inheritance

A person is born into a family, in a specific geographical location, in a specific country or State, and at some point in time. If we look at this more carefully, what really matters is the socio-economic status of the parents or family and the character of the State in which he is born. The first determines his immediate upbringing as a child, while the latter determines the socio-political environment in which his life will progress. Both are crucial.

In feudal and democratic societies of the world, it matters a great deal if one is born to rich or poor parents. The variations here are enormous; from royalty to serfdom and from a business magnate to a common daily wage earner. While the children born to rich parents have advantages for advancement in life, the children of poor parents inherit the parents' misery and stay at the same level. This amply illustrates the extreme relevance of status of the parents.

Parents also determine the child's religion. Theoretically, the child can change his religion, but it is done only rarely and most tend to follow the religion of parents. Whatever the religion, it has a strong bearing on one's life. In the modern world, it is easier to abandon one's religion and adopt a new one. A lot of people reject all traditional religions as being outmoded and anachronistic in the modern world.

The freedom to change one's religion and to enhance one's social status was very limited in a feudal society. In the modern world, life is highly controlled in theocratic States, such as Saudi Arabia, and in communist countries, such as China. Only in democratic countries does the individual have the freedom to pursue his vocation and beliefs. A person born in a theocratic State is handicapped to change his way of life, while in democratic societies this can be done rather easily.

Life in free societies is also conditioned by laws which are uniformly applied to all citizens. The laws do change for the better and society also undergoes change rather slowly but surely. Every individual participates in this change.

In the *Manusmriti,* Kshatriyas and Brahmanas are given the power to uphold and interpret the law. The law here is the law of the feudal State. The injunction to ordinary people is to follow the laws of the State enforced by the State through the Kshatriya varna and interpreted by the Brahmanas. The *Manusmriti* is no longer law in India, although it is one of the sources of our laws. Today, individuals in India enjoy freedom. However, this was not so in the recent past. Manu's laws had a stifling hold on Hindu society for centuries.

Karma

Karma means individual action. All living things are active in one way or another all the time. These activities are of various kinds:

- Basic activities such as bathing, eating, sleeping, etc.
- Learning activities
- Work—activities related to earning a living

- Play and leisure activities
- Service such as helping any living object without expectation of reward

While basic activities are common to all, there is a need for discipline in one's basic activities. Food habit needs to be controlled, so also all other activities essential to life maintenance. Lack of discipline in these matters can lead to health problems of various kinds while controlled habits can reduce them or even eliminate them. One pays for ones misdeeds is very true in this case and this punishment happens in one's lifetime.

Learning is a fundamental mental activity which distinguishes man from animals to large extent. Formal learning has become very important nowadays and this continues into early adulthood. Parents spend a lot of money and effort in educating their children. While inherited intellect is important, effort and chance pay their part in the outcome of the educational process. The more advanced the education that one receives the better are the prospects for employment and improved life. As a result, boys and girls study very hard and toil for 15 to 20 years. Learning continues throughout one's life. Those who do this are better off than others, though not necessarily in economic terms.

The most important activity in life has to do with working for earning a living. It provides a purpose and meaning to life. This activity continues throughout one's adult life There are people who do not work or neglect work or earn a living by doing harm to others. All these bring negative consequences to one's life. If work is done according to the laws of the land, there is no problem; breaking the laws may result in punishment. There is no divine rule here. The nature of work varies and in the modern world, work means everything that contributes to making life possible or better; this includes unpaid jobs done for the family and friends. A religious teacher is also doing work so also others.

Life, it is often said, is for enjoyment. While work can be enjoyed, in India it is often considered as pain in the neck. This is a very bad value system. However, after work one needs leisure and should enjoy it. This is legitimate. Again some leisure activities are termed as vices and these tend to ruin one's life. Some leisure activities may be enjoyable in the short term but harmful in the long run. One has to pick and choose. Good and bad outcomes result from one's own decisions.

Serving other human beings either in distress or even ordinarily is considered to be very good religiously. Leaving the religious merit apart, it is a good thing if one enjoys doing it. Service is not for reward in this or the next life. It is a way of life in itself.

The focus of human action or karma varies depending on the stage of life cycle. In childhood the focus is on learning and this goes on until 20 years of age; thereafter it focusses on work and earning a living which last about 60 years of age; and finally, in old age the focus is on service. Throughout all three stages, the basic and leisure activities continue to play. Only its relative importance of the activities change during one's life cycle but they do exist all the time.

In the modern world, there is a belief that 'karma' or human action determines everything. A person can achieve anything if only he applies himself, body and mind, to the objective in mind. The objective may be to get rich or become famous in any one area such as sports, arts, science, etc. This is only partially true, unless one is exceptionally talented. The very talented persons form a small minority of the population of any country.

In the Hindu tradition, 'karma' is often interpreted to mean ritual action which earns merit in the next life; a second view limits 'karma' to one's occupation and work related to it. The latter is fixed by birth and hence an individual has no scope for independent action based on his own judgment or free will. Thus karma is determined by birth. This traditional interpretation has few followers today. The overwhelming view of 'karma' is that it is action resulting from human judgment and free will and it has only two constraints:

- Ahimsa or non-violence or action that does not hurt anyone in any way, by way of words or physical action. Action is good if it helps one and even better if it helps others. Action is bad if hurts self or others in any way.
- The laws of the State in which one lives. Whatever be the nature of the State, one has to obey the laws. There is no choice. The laws are more or less good in democratic countries. In others, it varies.

Every human action generates a reaction. If the action is good, the reaction is also good and if the action is bad, the reaction is also bad. Human action, therefore, has a built in mechanism for reward and punishment. Both occur either in the present or in the near future. If we help others, they will help us. If we do harm to others, they will harm us in return. This rule does not work in an automatic fashion but it does in the long run.

Bhaga

Bhaga means luck or chance. It plays a major role in life. An accident in which one gets disabled or killed is one example of chance factor in life. Outcomes in an interview or an examination depend partly on chance. Chance plays a part in every aspect of life. Why is this so?

In nature, chance plays a key role. Gender is determined by chance during conception. The probability of having a male child is almost exactly fifty percent. New species are evolved by mutation of genes, which is also based on chance or probability. This is in fact a world of probabilities. There are literally infinite number of examples of natural events in which chance plays a part. Energy and matter, which are one and the same, follow laws that are based on probabilities; the entire cosmos is based on probabilities.

Cascading Effect of Luck

Chance or luck favors those who are better placed than those who are disadvantaged. The following Sanskrit verse highlights this:

आस्ते भग आसीनस्योर्ध्वस्तिष्टति तिष्टतः।
शेते निपद्यमानस्य चराति चरतो भगः।।

> For a sitting person dame luck sits, for the standing, it stands on top.
> For the person who has fallen down, it lies flat. That is the way of luck.

A very harsh insight, but for most who have gone through bad times it sounds familiar. There is a sound theoretical basis for this insight.

For a poor man it is extremely difficult to become rich. Why? An economist will say the poor man spends too much on food and has no savings. On the other hand a rich man spends little (as percentage of total income) on food and has high proportion of savings which he invests. Investments increase income and thus the rich get richer while, for lack of any investment, the poor remain at the same level. This is the essence of the Keynesian theory. The poor man's problems are compounded by lack of access to education and medical help, while the rich man has in abundance.

People contract infections and diseases of various kinds. Most depend on chance factor. For example cancer can occur in anyone; even if one does not smoke or chew betel nuts. Once contracted, the disease has the potential to enlarge its scope and make the patient even more vulnerable.

If a person has diabetes his woes multiply in course of time; his economic condition will weaken and he becomes highly vulnerable to diseases. A healthy person is able to withstand diseases and he remains in good health.

One setback in life leads to another and the problem multiply. Luck has a cascading effect. Good luck leads to further, while bad luck does not.

Bhaga or chance, therefore, brings good and bad things for man. However, he cannot create it or alter it. It is totally independent of man.

Time Factor

Birth, action, and chance are independent variables in life. Of these, man has control over action, but none at all over the other two. Further the three variables represent what are past, present, and future.

Birth and all the things inherited from birth are already partially or fully known. Only the secrets of our gene composition are not ordinarily known to us, but even this can be verified at great cost. In fact, the first thing anyone should do is to understand his inherited advantages and disadvantages. This is not an easy task. Most often people are not even prepared to think about the health problems that their parents or relations have faced and its implications for themselves. We often ignore or underestimate our inherited virtues and defects, particularly the latter.

Chance concerns the future. All of us are very much interested in the future and we try to shape it the way we want by present action. In this we succeed only partially. Our own effort, it is said, counts only for 50 per cent of the outcome, while the other 50 per cent is left to God or chance.

Human action has limitations, but man has to act to survive and act he must. This is *karma yoga*. Do what you must do, for your own good and the good of others.

In theory, the past and the present determine or at least influence the future. Let us see how this works in real life.

Three Part Rule

Janma, karma and *bhaga* together determine the future. The relative importance of these factors varies from one situation to another. It is not possible to go into the details here, but at this stage we may express the proposition in mathematical terms as follows:

$$aX + bY + cZ = F$$

Where F represents the future outcome, X, Y, and Z represent *janma*, karma, and *bhaga* factors. The parameters a, b, and c reflect the relative importance of these factors in a given situation and they add up to one:

$$a + b + c = 1$$

Another way of looking at this is to assume, *a priori*, that a, b, and c are equal or that life is influenced equally by all three factors. Is this true? Not always.

Example A

Let us take up a rather serious but basic question. How long could I expect to live?

In the aggregate, this question can be easily answered. Estimates of expectation of life at birth are available and we can add several criteria, such as age, sex, and other health factors and look at the altered statistics about the expectation of life. This will not answer an individual's question fully. One can make an educated guess.

At this stage, a person who believes in the right to die with dignity may say that this is irrelevant as one can in fact decide the time and venue of one's death in a peaceful manner. Assuming that the laws permit such a thing, a person may die before his date of appointment with death. There is obviously something more to it, namely, the chance factor which no one can control.

Alternatively, most people would like to ask how they can prolong their lives beyond the average expectation of life. One can prolong life with medical treatment or by changing food habits, exercise and so on. However, the effectiveness of all these methods, if anything, is rather minimal; they can prolong life for extra short distance. I would think that this is no more than 20 percent of years one is expected to live.

Chance, as we noted earlier, plays a crucial part. If we look at statistics on accidents and all other unnatural deaths, including murders, we get a slightly better view. Unnatural deaths are by no means common and the number of people who die through unnatural means is less than 5 percent, perhaps even lower.

If we take all this into consideration the equation for this example will be:

$$0.75\ X + 0.2\ Y + 0.05\ Z = F$$

Where F is expected years of life ahead of a person, X his State of health at that time, Y his level of discipline and medication, and Z the chance factor.

The conclusion in this example is that *janma* or birth factors are more important than others; human action in the form of disciplined life style and proper medication are of secondary importance, and chance, over which no one has control or influence, even less so. The last part is the most surprising insight, namely, that chance does not always play a major role in life. Life is after all pretty much predetermined by birth characteristics.

Example B

While expectation of life at any stage is of greater significance to the aged, marriage concerns the youth and in fact overwhelms them at some stage. This concern about the spouse lasts until late into middle age. The critical question in the initial stage, before marriage, is whether one would get a person of one's liking and choice—the ideal mate. After marriage, the view will be to find what went wrong and why? What is the prognosis?

The answer to the first question is a simple no and if people accept this the second question may not arise. The fact is that there are no ideal spouses except the one in our imagination. Why? The reason is that there are far too many attributes and qualities that one is aspiring for in a spouse and out of these hardly a few are actually met. In astrology, they look for 32 types of match but are often satisfied with less than half of them. In reality, the number of criteria is far more than 32 for a successful marriage.

We also have to look at the ability of men and women to make a correct choice. Most boys and girls simply do not have this ability. Self estimates are grossly exaggerated as also of the person who is liked for some reason. The problem is far too complex.

Apart from the ability to judge self and the potential spouse, one has to remember that the range of practical choice for selection of a spouse is invariably very limited. Given this paucity of choice, one has to accept the reality.

Even a rationalist will admit that making a decision on one's potential spouse is beyond the realm of rationality. One should be reminded about Arrow's Impossibility Theorem, where he proves that if we impose more than five conditions to a problem, there is no optimal solution to that problem. In marriage, we impose many more.

Almost everyone does indeed get married. In traditional societies, parents decide with or without the consent of the boy or girl. Only basic birth attributes are taken into account in this decision and rest is left to chance. What happens after marriage is fate or *vidhi*. Here chance becomes fate. In the model framework, this may be written as: $0.5\ X + 0.0\ Y + 0.5\ Z = F$. Karma is absent because the boy and the girl did not participate in the decision making.

In modern societies, boys and girls make their own choice. While physical appearance matters a lot besides economic and social considerations, the range of choice available to them is indeed very small. However, it must be emphasized that even here the birth attributes must match to some extent before the decision can be thought of. Decision making is time consuming and sometimes thoughtful. We have to give due weight to this process. But finally, there far too many loose ends and chance is allowed to take over. The marriage model of a modern boy or girl is: $0.4\,X + 0.2\,Y + 0.4\,Z = F$

Summary

Life begins with birth and birth determines life. Most, including myself, would like to believe otherwise. The empirical evidence, however, overwhelmingly supports the birth factor. Certainly, a few persons of outstanding or even mediocre merit have shaped their own lives in good and bad ways; the majority follows the path of their parents.

From early childhood, one is brought up in the cultural milieu of parents—language, religion, values and social linkages circumscribe the child's mental growth. It has no choice and choice, if at all, will come in early adulthood. Cultural shocks and values linger on during one's entire life span. Even if one transplants one self to another country and another culture, one's personality and life are still influenced by birth.

Science and technology have facilitated the globalization of culture which has started an invasion of the privacy of homes all over the world through television channels. Children are affected by this trend even if they watch only cartoons. What does this portend? Will local cultures vanish from the scene and will they be replaced by a global culture? Will individuals lose their roots and identities?

Hard to say, but things are bound to change.

Life is no longer the same as before. Even in India, life expectancy has doubled. It is increasing all over the world. Major threats to life in the form of small pox, malaria, tuberculosis, plague, etc., have been controlled or even eliminated.

Man has gained control over births and even death. Death, even if inevitable, can be painless and peaceful. No need to fear death. Births are now highly regulated. People all over the world are having fewer children and some no children at all by deliberate action. It is no longer in God's hands. People can even decide to have only a male child, however perverted the desire may be. The birth of children with congenital defects can be detected early and avoided altogether.

Has not the power of karma or human action increased manifold in various walks of life? This is to a large extent true. We are in greater control of our lives than ever before. Most of these powers have come to us without our making a personal contribution to it. Yet we can exercise the power to restrict the number of children or even decide to terminate life when it no longer is worth living. The power of karma has increased and will continue to increase.

In spite of everything, the future is uncertain. No one can foretell what will happen to an individual. From time immemorial, man has been intermittently obsessed with the desire to become immortal and with the craze to know the future. Both are unachievable. Uncertainty or chance is a basic ingredient of life. If future is known threadbare, man will definitely try to alter it. He will be very unhappy if cannot do that. The best thing is to accept that the future is not entirely in our hands. In this context religion, and in particular Hinduism, has a very positive role to play.

Nineteen

Society, Religion and Science

Introduction

Science and religion shape societies and societies in turn provide the environment in which religion and science either prosper or decline.

There is, however, a common perception that religion and science are in conflict with each other and that one is a threat to the other's very existence. This is not really true and indeed, religion and science coexisted (and still do) for a couple of centuries, with only minor problems.

The major religions of the world are about 2,000 years old, while science has made an impact only in the last two hundred years. Here, I have deliberately identified science with the industrial revolution since my concern is with the social impact of science. In India, the industrial revolution began in the latter half of the 19th Century and it has taken off during the past 50 years.

India today is an industrial nation. Agriculture contributes less than one-fourth of the gross national product, although agriculture itself has made tremendous progress with the introduction of scientific methods of farming. Advances in information technology, biotechnology, medicine, etc., has transformed life of even ordinary people in India. Science has definitely made an impact on Indian society.

What is the net result of all this on Hindu religion? To understand this we must go back to the past. A hundred years ago, life of all sections of the population in India was dominated by religion. Every aspect of our daily life was regulated by religious beliefs and practices. The daily religious rituals were an important part of everyone's life. Today, this is no longer true. On the other hand, one comes across ironical situations. Leading religious men use a variety of modern gadgets for communication and they often travel by luxury cars or private jet planes, while learned scientists seek the advice of religious leaders in matters of family and spiritual concerns. In spite of such seeming contradictions, religion no longer dominates life in India anymore and in fact its day-to-day importance is declining.

It has to be pointed out that apart from the progress of science, religion has a direct relationship with the quality of government and the level of poverty. Wherever we have good government and rule of law, people are becoming more and more secular and less religious in their outlook. This is particularly evident in northern and western Europe. On the other hand, religion flourishes where there is a weak government. Weak government is reflected in the high level of corruption and poor law and order situation. Science, on the other hand, flourishes where we have good governments, and it is neglected in countries that are badly governed. In such countries, religion is given a much higher priority. The poor in every country have immense faith in religion; they have nowhere else to go. Their governments while paying lip service to religion have let them down when it comes to poverty alleviation. The importance attached to religion in any country varies directly in proportion to the number of poor people residing there.

In India, we have a very complex society and it is hard to make any sweeping generalization. Nevertheless, science is here to stay and will definitely become more important in the future. On the other hand, religion, based on ancient scriptures and practices, has less than a rosy future. The foundation of Hindu law, *Manusmriti*, is no longer acceptable. Religious texts other than the *Bhagavad Gita* are rarely read. There are far too many contradictions in Hinduism. Besides, there are many sects, cults and new religious movements. There are conflicts of values between Hinduism and other religions with which it coexists. All religions contain much that is obsolete and irrelevant to the present society. Nevertheless, religions thrive in India due to a variety of reasons; the most important reasons being poverty, illiteracy and lack of faith in their political, administrative and legal systems.

Two Exclusive Domains

Religion and science are in fact are mutually exclusive. Science does not interfere with religion in any way. However, religion used to be all pervasive and it dealt with all aspects of human life. It still has its own theories of the origin the Earth, of man, social system, personal and individual problems, and so on. Religion was and is still considered to be a panacea for all problems.

Science, in most or all cases, negated these old religious theories. As a result, some religions (actually the fundamentalists in that religion) oppose science. Science, in general, ignores religions and religious beliefs. However, some scientists are very religious. Here one has to segregate the dual roles of a person—as a scientist and as a believer in a religion. This is so because a scientist is to begin with an ordinary human being and he becomes a scientist only when he functions as such.

Ordinary people often have to make decisions in which the choice is between science and religion. Let us take some examples. A married couple not having a child for years would nowadays consult a medical expert and try to correct the problems. If this approach does not yield results, they may go on a pilgrimage or seek the help of pundits. In the same way, for any health problem a person would go to a medical doctor; failing which he may go for other non-scientific solutions. In the past, the first preference was always for the religious method. The scientific method was chosen only as a last resort.

Over the past few decades, the faith in allopathic medicine and surgery has increased manifold while faith in religion-based cures has gradually gone down. While one finds allopathic drug stores in all parts of city, one will have considerable difficulty in locating an Ayurvedic or Unani medicine shop. The domain of religion is gradually declining and it is being taken over by science.

In the area of communication, travel, consumer goods, education, and entertainment, science plays a major role while religion has become irrelevant. On the other hand, religion plays a major role in marriage and in family affairs. Religion, however, plays an important role in providing relief from mental stress in work place and at home.

Statics and Dynamics

Religion is static while science is dynamic. Religion looks to the past and glorifies it, whereas science looks to a better future. Science has no difficulty in rejecting the past if it is found to be wanting. In religion, the past is sacrosanct and one cannot find fault with it. The ancient texts cannot be changed and in fact all changes are looked down upon. Religions cannot adapt themselves to social change, as they still harp on the glorious past. Like dinosaurs, they face the possibility of becoming extinct. This is particularly true of religions which are rigidly defined on the basis of a scriptural text. Hinduism is slightly better since there is no acceptable scriptural text that defines it. *Manusmriti* is the only text that comes close to defining Hinduism in clear terms. However, this text does not command much respect today. It is interesting to note that Hindus have all but rejected one of their basic religious texts, while no other religion has done such a thing. This speaks volumes for the flexibility of Hinduism and the rigidity of Middle Eastern religions.

In Hinduism, the *Vedas* are hardly read by anyone. Even Adi Shankaracharya did not comment or write on the *Rigveda* or any of the other *Vedas*. The *Atharvaveda* claims that it has solutions for various diseases and other problems. I have read the *Atharvaveda* and I do not find any credence to such claims. No one reads or follows it. The situation is very similar to that of the *Manusmriti*. However, in case of the *Atharvaveda*, it is ignored but not altogether rejected. The *Bhagavad Gita* is the only scripture that is still read and respected.

Science commands universal respect and it is dynamic and progressive. New theories and findings are welcomed.

Everything is duly scrutinized. Science and scientific knowledge are expanding rapidly and are keen to solve contemporary issues and problems and improve living conditions for all. On the other hand, in religion nothing is or can be added. No new religion has emerged to replace old ones. Nor has any religion shown signs of reforming itself to the reality, except perhaps Hinduism.

There are quite a few new cults in all religions and each looks bizarre. The established religions oppose them but none of the new cults have achieved mass appeal.

Universal and Regional Influence

The difference between science and religion is that while science has universal implications, religion (namely any specific religion) has restricted validity. Hence, at the global level, science is shaping society and contributing to the emergence of common world culture and social life. Television and entertainment industry are the portals of this globalization. Religion, with all its traditional values, is all but ignored. Television commercials in India often plagiarize and even ridicule it in their advertisements. On the other hand, science has emerged supreme.

Models of Man

Human beings are highly individualistic and have different mental make ups. According to a very well-known work, there are basically three models. They are the rational man, the irrational man, and the non-rational man.

The rational one makes decisions after getting full information. He then examines alternatives available to him and their expected outcomes and he chooses that particular alternative that gives him maximum benefit. In other words, his reasoning is thorough and the validity of every statement is rigorously examined.

The irrational man looks at the available information and decides on the basis of tradition or past practices or the advice of elders and so on. He generally ignores the validity of the arguments. The fact that it is recommended by someone is good enough for him. His reasoning for his decisions tends to go haywire but he would still stick to them.

There is a grey area between rational and irrational. In theory, perfect rationality is nearly impossible in this world of uncertainties. Hence, we have a category of bounded rationality. This person is rational only within the restricted sense.

The non-rational man is commonly known as a lunatic since he is devoid of reasons.

All of us, save lunatics, can be ranked on a scale of rational to irrational. Some are more rational and others are less or vice versa. Often the same person is rational in a given situation and irrational in another.

Faith and Rationality

Religion in general and faith in God in particular is considered to be irrational. Why? The proof is beyond man. One has to trust the scriptures or have faith in it. In India, the *Vedas* are the foundation and they are unquestionable. In the discussion on Vedanta, Adi Shankaracharya often uses the term *aprameyam,* meaning something that cannot be proved or something that does not require proof. People profess faith in the *Vedas*, even when they have not read them. The *Bhagavad Gita*, it is asserted, has to be believed in totality because it comes from God's mouth. Such a situation exists in all religions. Further, faith in any religion often involves intolerance of differing points of view, which in itself, is irrational.

Rationalists reject religion and they are by definition atheists for there is no proof to sustain the existence of God. However, rationalism is indeed a very difficult proposition. Rationalists, in general, are wedded to science where proof is a must. Further, proof must be continual.

Faith in Science

In today's world, people believe in science. Often, what goes for science is actually pseudo-science. Those who have total faith in science and no faith in religion are rationalists. Most however, have partial faith in science and religion. They want to be on the safe sides of both.

As in the case of religion, there are many people and businesses that exploit people. This is particularly so in the case of some allopathic medicines and a great variety of food and other consumable. There are many who exploit religion as well. People are gullible and exploitation will continue to exist either using religion or science.

Science and technology have made spectacular advances all over the world in the last 50 years. Both have reached almost all corners of the world. The world has shrunk as a result of improved transportation and communication. Science is now in a strong position.

Faith in Religion

People all over the world have faith in some God or the other. Most have faith in religions of the world. The degree of faith may vary. The number of atheists in the world is indeed very small. However, they include some well-known scientists and intellectuals.

Most countries in the world today profess secularism and allow religious freedom. Democracy and secularism go together and India is a secular democratic State where people enjoy full freedom.

Christianity and Islam are other two major religions of the world. While secularism is by and large is an accepted principle in countries where the people are predominantly Christian, it is not so where Muslims are in majority barring exceptions to this rule.

Faith in religion has declined in most Christian and democratic countries where science and technology have advanced. Interestingly, Western Europe is less religious compared to United States. Only around 10 per cent of Western Europe go to church as against 50 per cent in the United States.

India and Nepal are the only countries where the majority is Hindus. In India, there is a general trend of shying away from Sanskrit-based religions. Except for a few, most temples of the Hindus have an abandoned and are in neglected ambience. Quite a large number are in ruins. The Rigvedic and other connected religions are now part of history. The *Puranas* are hardly ever read, so is the case with epics.

As in most countries, the educated in India are moving away; they have for the most part given up the traditional religious practices followed by their *jati* or varna. And the interest is mostly in non-spiritual aspects. Religion plays hardly any role in their daily life.

Science and Concept of God

What have eminent scientists to say about God? A few believe in God and others are atheists. Einstein, who believed in God, has said that God does not play the game of dice and that everything is predictable and he worked for a unified theory of everything; in this theory, the forces of gravity and electromagnetism are put together. He, however, did not succeed. At the same time, he was at odds with his fellow scientists. While Einstein spent all his time working on the theory of everything, other scientists made progress in quantum mechanics which lead them to further advancements. The point is that the emission and absorption of energy is now believed to be unpredictable. The laws of particle physics are now based on probabilities rather than certainty. Does God indeed play the game of dice?

What does the word 'God' mean? God is energy in various forms. Gravity and electromagnetism are the main forms of energy. All activities in the universe are based on energy.

All living things derive energy by combining carbohydrates with oxygen. The brain works on the basis of electrical currents. When the supply of oxygen stops brain also stops and a person is declared dead. The human mind is simply electrical energy in action within the space of the brain.

In Hinduism, the concept of energy as God is acceptable. *Agni* and Sun are both very important Vedic Gods and both represent energy. Human life on earth depends on the energy given out by the Sun.

As in particle science, life is unpredictable and chance plays an important role in life. We may, therefore, think of God as chance. The two concepts of energy and chance are in fact interrelated. This is now accepted as a scientific paradigm.

Whether God is understood as the behaviour of particles or chance factor or something else is not very relevant to the common man. What are relevant are the aspects of uncertainty, unpredictability, and probabilistic nature of life on earth. All these generate mental stress and disturb man's peace of mind. Religion can deal with this problem of mental peace in ways that science cannot.

Twenty

Common Beliefs Among Hindus

Introduction

The Hindu society is perhaps the most diversified. It is often said and cited that there is very little in common among Hindus. The very word Hindu, that is continued to be used by Hindus and others, presupposes some commonalities which this chapter attempts to explore.

At the grassroots level, there is a very high degree of uniformity in religious beliefs and practices among Hindus. The reference here is not to the village but to the *jati*. A *jati* is bound by marriage and kinship and there is a very high degree of commonness of values, beliefs and practices among the members of a *jati*. On the other hand, even in one village, there may be as many as 20 *jatis*. Each *jati* may have its own God or even a small temple. In Indian villages, spatial segregation of different *jatis* is very common and each *jati* may have its own temple. Nevertheless, the religion at the village level is shaped by the dominant *jati*, numerically and economically superior. Village studies by social anthropologists have highlighted this concept of a dominant caste. Another important factor is the presence or absence of Brahmana families in a village. This definitely has a bearing on the practice of religion in the village. If there is a common temple and associated festivals, this fact also has significance. Often such temples are managed by the dominant *jati* who deny access to some of the lower *jatis*.

The common beliefs of Hindus, however, can be dealt with only at the level of educated urban or rural elites. I have assembled here a set of common beliefs under eight headings.

About the Past

- In ancient times, people lived much longer than at present.
- People were healthier and stronger in the past.
- People were good at heart, honest, and sincere in the past while at present they are not.
- Life was a lot happier compared to the present.
- People of the Rigvedic times knew a lot more than what we know today.
- The Rigvedic people could foretell the future in exact terms.
- All major scientific discoveries were already known to Vedic scholars.
- The four *Vedas* contain all the knowledge and wisdom that is known to humanity today.

About Religion

- The Hindu religion is more advanced than either Christianity or Islam.

- All of us will be born again after death.
- God, described as atman, resides in our heart.
- All our actions on earth involve *paapa* or *punya*. Cumulatively, they add up and one spends a shorter or longer time in hell or heaven.
- One must do everything that is right and prescribed by tradition so that the next life is better than the present.
- The sole objective of life on earth is to attain *moksha* or the lotus feet of the Lord.
- *Sanyasa*, which is giving up one's family and worldly life, is a must for spiritual enlightenment.
- "I have done nothing wrong in this life knowingly and hence all my present suffering is due to sins committed in the last birth. Consequently, life in the next birth will be better for me."
- People suffer for the sins committed in this life. There is no escape from punishment for wrong acts in this life.
- One must perform all actions (karma) without expecting any reward.
- The term yoga means the practice of *asanas* and/or meditation.

About Gods

- Birth and death are in God's hands.
- If a prayer to a God does not result in a desired outcome one should blame oneself for it and not find fault with the God.
- All sins will be forgiven by God if one surrenders to him.

- *Bhakti* to a chosen God will bring lasting happiness.
- God may test his devotees but steadfast devotion will be rewarded.
- Lord Rama was an ideal human being and God at the same time.
- Sincere prayers to one's *ishta devta* can solve all problems.
- A guru is next only to God. He must be trusted and obeyed at all times.
- All Gods are one and the same; but one may prefer one to another.
- Lord Ganapathy (Vinayaka) is mentioned in the *Rigveda*.

About Scriptures

- The message of the *Bhagavad Gita* has more to do with bhakti to Lord Krishna than about *karma yoga* or *jnana yoga*.
- Despite criticism, the *Manusmriti* is still the main foundation of Hindu social laws.
- *Ramayana* and *Mahabharata* describe historical events which actually happened a long time ago.
- Lord Shri Rama was born in the exact spot where the Babri Masjid stood some years ago.
- Valmiki *Muni* (the author of *Ramayana*) comes from the Balmiki *jati* (now recognized as a scheduled caste).
- Adi Shankaracharya died at the age of 32 years. All the events mentioned in the *Shankara Vijayam* are factually true.

- The *Sthala Puranas* describe the true history of a temple and its associated town or city.

About Rituals

- In *Kali Yuga* (the present time), it may not be possible to follow all traditional rules for rituals.
- Before doing anything important, one must check "*thithi, kalam, nakshatram, yogam,* etc." Otherwise the effort is likely to go waste.
- By reciting the words '*Hare Rama Hare Krishna*' one can attain mental peace and happiness.
- A bath in the Ganga River will purify the atman.
- A solemn promise to perform a puja, sacrifice, or give a gift to a chosen temple God will ensure a desirable end to a problem.
- A house warming ceremony (*griha pravesa*) will ensure family happiness.
- The Vedic mantras are very pleasing to hear and have a positive and beneficial effect on the listeners.

About Society

- Marriages are made in heaven.
- Matching of horoscopes before marriage is a must. It will ensure a happy married life.
- A son, like Lord Shri Rama, should obey his father's orders.
- *Jati* and varna are still important to marriage and family. Marriages should be from the same *jati*, if not from the same varna, and never from outside.

- The people of North India belong to the Aryan race while the people of South India belong to the Dravidian race.
- The Aryans invaded India around 1500 BC and pushed the Dravidians to the south of the Vindhyan Mountains.
- Girl's parents must bear all the expenses of her marriage and also provide jewellery, clothing, furniture and appliances for setting up a new home.

About Personal Conduct

- A woman should always wear *mangal sutra*, *sindhur* on forehead, rings on toes, and *pottu* on the forehead.
- Sari is the best dress for Indian women at all times.
- A *panja gachham* (dhoti) is the ideal dress for a man.
- Men of the first three varnas should always wear the sacred thread (*yajnopavitham*). Others, namely, Shudras should not wear it.

About Medicine and Science

- Ayurveda is far superior to allopathy as a system of medicine.
- Most diseases of the present time, like cancer and heart problems, did not exist in the past.
- Numerology, palmistry, homeopathy, *vastu shastra*, and astrology are scientific in nature and origin.
- Astrology originated in India and is truly an Indian system for predicting one's future based on the positions of sun, moon and planets.
- One's *nakshatram* holds the key to one's future.

- *Vastu shastra* must be kept in mind while constructing a house or flat.

Conclusion

Hindus believe in many things and the list given above is only a small sample. One can question the way the statements are phrased. One is at liberty to characterize each statement as true or false. It is not necessary for anyone to believe in everything. He can pick and choose or even ignore. My intention here is to give a collective image of ourselves for our own understanding.

Twenty One

Hindu Defined

It would appear to be very naïve to attempt a definition of a Hindu in the light of what has been discussed in the previous chapters. The question about one's religion has been always a voluntary one among Hindus and anyone who claims to be a Hindu is accepted as such. There are sometimes problems arising from one's name but a name can be changed at will. The term Hindu is defined in law in India only in the context of marriages and property rights. The legal definition broadens the outlook rather than narrows it down. Thus even those who claim to be Jains or Sikhs are defined as Hindus as far as marriage and succession are concerned.

The *Bhagavad Gita* does provide us enough ground for defining a Hindu and what is written here is based on the *Bhagavad Gita*. The definitions occur when Lord Krishna categorizes *bhaktas*. In short, a Hindu is a *bhakta*—one who has faith in a God. This God need not be Lord Krishna; this possibility is granted by Lord Krishna himself. One can have faith in any God. The only rider to this broad interpretation is that those who seek other Gods go to that God, and that they would not attain *moksha*. This is not an issue for *bhaktas* of Shiva or other Gods, since they consider them all to be supreme. Finally, all Gods are one and the same.

There are, however, differences among *bhaktas* in terms of the level of *jnana* or awareness of the nature of the Absolute God. Thus there are four classes of Hindus—*jnani* (*jnana yogi*), *yogi* (*karma yogi*), *bhakta*, and *tamo-bhakta*.

Jnani

God is in the cosmos (*om kham brahma*)
God is in the Sun (*asavaditye brahma*)
God is in me (*savasavaham*)
One who understands this knows (*jnana*)
One who knows (jnani) is a Hindu
(Source: *Yajurveda*, Chapter 40, Verse 17)

Only one among a million Hindus is a *jnani*.

Yogi

Only one in a thousand makes an attempt to practice karma, *bhakti*, or *dhyana yoga* as prescribed in the *Bhagavad Gita* (Chapter 7, *shloka* 3). They are all *karma yogi* by definition. Further, they are considered to be *ajnani*, since they have an imperfect understanding of *jnana*. *Jnani* and *karma yogi* together form less than one per cent of the Hindus as stated in the *Bhagavad Gita* itself.

Bhakta

Bhaktas worship *devas* for their own welfare and that of their family. The *Bhagavad Gita* justifies this form of worship in Chapter 3, *shlokas* 10–13. The *bhaktas* form about 20 per cent of all Hindus. The *bhaktas* are of two types—those who worship out of pain, distress or fear, and those who worship for money or welfare (Chapter 7–13). Nevertheless, the *Bhagavad Gita* looks down upon them since they wish to enjoy the fruits of their actions (Chapter 2, *shloka* 49). All those who worship or pray to any God for whatever reason are Hindus. The *Bhagavad Gita* in the context mentioned above restricts the term 'Gods' to Vedic Gods, but this may be enlarged to include Gods mentioned in the *Puranas* as well.

Tamo-Bhakta

In Chapter 7, the *Bhagavad Gita* mentions *bhaktas* of a lower order. The main characteristic of these *bhaktas* is that they are ignorant. The word *tamas* in Sanskrit means ignorance. Another frequently used term is *moodha*, which also means the same thing. However, this term is less technical and it is frequently used to mean foolishness. In the context of Hinduism, the term *tamas* may be interpreted as ignorance of Hindu scriptures. Further, these *bhaktas* generally worship ghosts, demons or Gods of recent origin and Gods not mentioned in the scriptures or follow blind beliefs and rituals. The Gods, beliefs, and rituals of *tamo-bhaktas* may be based on an oral tradition. In the *Bhagavad Gita,* these *bhaktas* are in *tamas* category (Chapter 7, *shlokas* 2–6). *Tamas* means ignorance based on the dominance of *tamo-guna*. Unfortunately, the *tamo-bhaktas* constitute a majority of about

80 per cent of the Hindus. They have, as a rule, never seen or read any scripture in any language.

Knowledge of scriptures by which we mean any text, in Sanskrit or any of the Indian languages, on religion such as the *Bhagavad Gita*, the two epics, any of the *Puranas*, or any of the *Upanishads*. Even one who has read but not fully understood would also qualify as a true *bhakta*.

The fact is that the majority of the followers of major religions of the world have never read their scripture; this happens due to illiteracy, lack of knowledge of the language, as in the case of the holy *Qur'an* and various other reasons. Hindus need not be ashamed for not having read any of the scriptures. They are in good company at the global level. Hindus have the problem of illiteracy, inability to read and understand Sanskrit, and even more significantly non-availability of scriptures; unlike the holy *Bible* and the holy *Qur'an,* our scriptures are not printed in large volumes and given free of cost. On the other hand, even the *Bible* which is given as free is hardly read. According to one study, majority of Christians have never read the *Bible.* Religion is by and large a matter of faith and belief; knowledge obtained by word of mouth is sufficient. Nevertheless, those who depend on word of mouth are vulnerable to propaganda and even dangerous misconceptions about their own religion. They are often exploited by vested interests, leading to serious social chaos. On the contrary, welfare of mankind is the true objective of all religions of the world. In the 21st Century, religious leaders and others should focus on educating the public about the true nature and objective of their religions and apply the brake to exploitation by unscrupulous elements.

Twenty Two

Conclusion: The Message

People have always sought help from supernatural powers. Every community in the world, past and present, had a set of beliefs concerning the supernatural, and this, along with customs and rituals, constitute religion. As civilizations advanced, religions became more elaborate; some of the major religions explored the metaphysical aspects in great depth while others concentrated chiefly on the social aspects. There are many major religions, innumerable smaller ones, and bouquet of cults within major religions coexisting in the modern world. Hinduism is perhaps the most ancient and complex of the major religions. The *Rigveda* is the oldest religious work of humanity. It survives to this day in its original form, although at the time of its origin, writing was not known. It has survived because of sheer human ingenuity.

The scientific industrial revolution of the 19th Century has changed people's attitude towards religion, particularly among the elite and the educated, and overshadowed the relevance of religion. Many of its fundamental tenets are no longer believed to be true. Religious leaders find it difficult to cope with reality.

Excepting the fundamentalists, no one is prepared to accept any religion in its totality. Each one has ready interpretation and practices the religion differently. This is true of Hinduism as much as other religions.

Hindus no longer adhere to age-old religious practices. Hindu dharma, as defined by the *Manusmriti*, is no longer relevant or acceptable. The *Bhagavad Gita* has been criticized for its excessive stress on *varna dharma*. The various *yogas* outlined in the *Bhagavad Gita* are impractical. People cannot even think of giving up all desires, not desiring the fruits of one's actions, giving up all worldly possessions and their enjoyment, and abandoning one's family and friends. People want their desires to be fulfilled; this is the reason why Poorva Mimamsa has mass appeal than the intellectual and theoretical *Vedanta* of the elite, and hence Hinduism practised today is altogether different from *Manusmriti's* espousal.

Actually most people do not understand the *Bhagavad Gita* but they do have full faith in Lord Krishna. It is faith that matters. People perform pujas and *homas*, worship a great many Gods, celebrate festivals and visit holy places. While faith in Lord Krishna is acceptable to the Vaishnavite sect, it is not accepted by other sects, particularly the Shivaites and Shaktas. The Shivaites consider Lord Shiva as *ishwara* in the same way as Lord Krishna is considered as *ishwara* by the Vaishnavites. Nevertheless, *bhakti* in various forms is the main stem of Hinduism.

People admire science and are keen to acquire more and more gadgets. Thanks to all the new gadgets, life is no longer the same. In spite of this, it is not as though people understand science. On the contrary, they do not. This resulted in a stalemate between the two. People want both and see no conflict.

Why do people seek God's help in the 21st Century of science and technology? It is the primordial fear of death and suffering. Fear is intrinsic to all forms of life and it is essential for survival. In man, fear extends to future happenings and thus his fear is partly rational and partly irrational; the irrational dominates and has given rise to many religious beliefs and practices. An equally important reason for the survival of religion is the inherent unpredictability of nature and of life on earth and that will continue to afflict mental stress on humans. There is no reason to believe that these perplexities will altogether disappear and hence it is most unlikely that religion would vanish from the face of the earth.

However, not all old religious beliefs would survive; those concerning social life will drastically change. Since people today love freedom, they are unwilling to be cocooned by accepting everything without question Days of unquestioned loyalty are gone. Only those religious leaders who can provide services that people want would survive and prosper.

The Rigvedic religion was appropriate to a tribal society; *Manusmriti* was written with an emerging feudal society in mind, where social inequality is sanctified through religious means; the *Bhagavad Gita* was written to promote Vedantic values in a mature feudal order mixed with fiction and reality. The Puranic religion was well-suited to the feudal social order. It ended in the last century after Independence when India has emerged as a plural democratic society. Kings and queens are now irrelevant.

Hence the adaptability of Hinduism in times of necessity is thus well-demonstrated. However, it is too early to speculate on the nature of the changes that are bound to occur.

Whenever changes took place in Hinduism, the past religious ideas were never totally discarded. The new religions that emerged in the past were always a mix of the old and new. In this process, certain values were discarded and new values added. We need not enter into an exhaustive discussion on these aspects but can uncover selected facets.

Perhaps the caste system inherited by us is the most contentious. Both *Manusmriti* and the *Bhagavad Gita* assert the sanctity of the four-fold varna system. It is enshrined in the *Purusha Sukta* of the *Rigveda* (this section is considered to be a later insertion). The term *jati* does not occur anywhere in the Sanskrit texts; its origins are traced to pre-Rigvedic times. It is a sum of our social ethos, from times immemorial, wherein we allow communities to retain their identity and traditions without any hindrance. In my view, the process by which communities retained their identities through endogamous marriages is to be commended rather than condemned. It is true that this has resulted in over 6,000 *jatis*.

The problem is not with *jatis* as such but its claim to superiority or rank. There are stark inequalities here, besides discrimination based on concepts of purity and pollution (*Manusmriti* concepts); the new democratic process, which is a game of numbers, is gradually and peacefully ending the special privileges enjoyed by the three upper varnas, who do not muster that much (barely 15 per cent). In my view, the upper varnas possess enough intellectual resources to face any eventualities of life.

The varna system has already lost its efficacy in modern India. There is some evidence of horizontal consolidation or merging of *jatis* among upper varnas and the process is likely to filter down; as a result, there is every reason to hope that the divisive caste system will disappear in the long run.

Even more important to all religions, including Hinduism, is the progress made by science and technology. This has visibly impacted the social life in all parts of the country. The modern medicine has considerably increased the life expectancy. Communication and transportation have shown vast improvement. Other spheres are also not too far behind. The inevitable march of science and technology will not harm Hinduism and it will continue to live. The *Vedas* recognize the Sun as the most important Objective God, a proposition that appears to be very rational. The concepts of God in Hinduism are consistent with the notion of energy as the basis of all life on earth. Matter and energy are one and the same. At another level, the methodology of *asanas* (yoga) and *dhyana* (meditation) is a significant contribution; the aim is to attain mental peace. This is something that people all over the world want. The *Rigveda* and the *Upanishads* have much to offer to all Hindus and in fact to one and all in the world.

The message of Hinduism, in the ultimate analysis, is best summarized in the closing verses of the *Rigveda*. First, the worship of all Gods is for the welfare of mankind. Secondly, equality among one and all is the highest principle of life. Prayers and the study of religious scriptures are for common understanding and harmony among all. Fourthly, everything—pain, pleasure or food—should be shared equally among all. Unfortunately, these sublime Vedic values have been neglected for long. We should revive them, if religion is to have any meaning at all in the 21st Century.

This book has explored the nature of Hinduism and its transformations through historical times. Perhaps the most important lesson learnt is that Hinduism has successfully adapted itself when social conditions changed in the past. It more dynamic than all other major religions of mankind. Other major religions of the world are rigidly defined in terms of one or more scriptures and they focus on social values and dogmas that are centuries behind. The central values of Hinduism have universal applicability and are valid for all times. It is only the peripherals that require change according to the modern needs. It has happened several times in the past and it is capable of doing so in the future.

Glossary

Aapa	Goddesses of water
Aarsha	One among the eight types of marriages in the *Manusmriti*
Aartha	Troubled, distressed or afraid
Aasura	One among the eight types of marriages in the *Manusmriti*
Acharya	Teacher
Adhyatmam	Self-purification
Adi Sankaracharya	A religious savant of 8th Century AD.
Aditi	Guest
Aditi poojanam	Worship of a guest
Adwaryu	One among 16 categories of Vedic priests
Agamas	Texts on temple management and rituals
Agni	Fire God or just fire

Agraharam	A land grant village of Brahamanas in South India
Ahimsa	Non-violence
Ahirs	A numerically important caste group in North India
Aithreya	One of the *Upanishads*
Ajnani	Lacking in *jnana* or knowledge of the atman
Akam	Literally meaning inside in Tamil
Akarma	Not considered as karma
Akshara	Non-decaying or permanent
Amman	A Goddess in Tamil Nadu
Angiras	The first of several Rigvedic poets
Anityam	Transient, not lasting
Anna prasam	Initiation of an infant to eating rice
Anuloma	Marriage of a man to a woman of a lower varna
Anushtup	A meter used in Vedic prosody
Apara	The phenomenal world including man
Aprameyam	Not provable or not requiring proof
Arjuna	One of the five Pandavas and a cousin of Lord Krishna
Artha	Wealth
Arthartha	Desiring wealth or prosperity
Arthasastra	The science of wealth or material things
Arudah	Fully committed
Arurukshuh	Desiring to practice yoga

Arya Samaj	A Hindu reformist organization (19th Century)
Aryan	A respectable person
Aryavarta	The land where respected people live
Asana	Sitting posture
Asaucham	Unclean
Ashoka	A Mauryan King of 3rd Century BC.
Ashrama	Stage in life
Ashrams	Hermitages
Ashtadhyayi	A Sanskrit text on grammar
Ashtaka System	A system used in compiling *Rigveda*
Ashtanga Raja Yoga	A Sanskrit text on *dhyana yoga* by Patanjali
Asura	Ungodly
Asura	An asteric class of demons of the under world (Patala Loka)
Aswalayana	A Rigvedic Brahmana — explanatory text
Atharvaveda	The fourth *Veda* relating to cure for problems of health and life
Atma hatya	Suicide
Atma sudhi	Self-purification
Atman	Soul
Atri	A Rigvedic poet
Aurangzeb	A Mughal King of the 17th Century
Avatars	Incarnations
Ayurveda	The science of life or medicine
Ayyanars	Gods in Tamil

Ayyappan	The God of the Ayyappa cult
Azhwars	Bards of the Srivaishnavite sect in South India
Balabhadra	The elder brother of Lord Krishna
Baniyas	A caste group classified as Vaishyas in the Hindi-speaking areas
Bhaga	Luck or chance
Bhagavad Gita	An exposition of Vedanta philosophy in *Mahabharata* epic
Bhagavata Purana	The oldest and the most important of all *Puranas*
Bhagavatas	An ancient religious sect who worshipped the God Vishnu
Bhagavati	The Goddess Parvati
Bhaja Govindam	A collection of 33 verses composed by Adi Shankaracharya
Bhajan	Devotional song
Bhakta or Bhaktas	Those having faith in a God
Bhakti	Devotion or simply faith
Bhakti yoga	A combination of *bhakti* and *jnana*
Bhandarkar R. G.	A Sanskrit scholar of the 19th Century
Bharadwaja	A Brahmana *gotra*; name of a Rigvedic poet
Bhashyam	Commentary
Bhokta	One who enjoys the results of one's actions
Bhumihar Brahmanas	Brahmanas who adopted farming for a living

Bhur Bhuah Swah	The worlds of the Gods, man, and ancestors
Bhutas or bhutagana	A class of demons associated with Shiva
Biksha	A gift or an offering
Brahma	God of creation
Brahma yajnam	The study of the *Vedas*
Brahmacharin	A bachelor
Brahmacharya	Observance of bachelorhood
Brahman	The Absolute God
Brahman	A chief priest in charge of a *yaga*
Brahmana	A person belonging to the Brahmana varna
Brahmanas	A Sanskrit text accompanying any one of the four *Vedas*
Brahmanaspathi	Lord of the chief priests
Brahmasutra	A important Sanskrit text on cosmogony and karma theory
Brahmi	The mother of all Indian scripts
Brahmin	A Brahmana
Brahmo Samaj	A reformist forum of the 19th Century
Brahmyam	A form of marriage recommended only for Brahmanas
Brighu	A Rigvedic poet as well as a legendary figure in *Smritis*
Brihaspathi	The title given to Angiras, a Rigvedic poet

Chalcolithic culture	Copper-stone age culture of 5,000 to 2,000 years ago
Chalukyas	A dynasty of kings who ruled South India
Chanakya	The author of *Arthashastra*
Chandala	A person born to a Shudra man and a Brahmana woman
Chandas	The term in Sanskrit for any metre used in prosody
Charana	The Veda or Vedas in which a Brahmana is proficient
Cholas	A dynasty of kings in Tamil Nadu
Daivayajnam	The daily worship of Vedic Gods
Daivikam	A bride offered in marriage to a priest as a gift to God
Dalit	The preferred name for Scheduled castes
Dandam	The stick used by *brahmacharins* about shoulder high
Darba grass	A type of long grass used in performing *homas*
Dayananda Saraswati	The founder of Arya Samaj
Deepavali	The festival of lights
Deva	Any God; originally a Rigvedic God
Devanagari	A script used for writing Hindi and other Indian languages
Devta	Goddess

Dharana	The sixth stage in *dhyana yoga*
Dharma	The moral code of the Hindus
Dhoti	A loin cloth worn by men
Dhyana	Meditation; also the seventh stage in *dhyana yoga*
Dhyana yoga	The path of meditation involving *jnana*
Dravidian/Dravida	A group of South Indian languages; or simply the South
Durga	A Goddess equated with Shakti
Ganasangha	A lineage
Gandarva	An asteric class of people
Gandhara	A region of North Western India
Gayatri	The first metre used in Sanskrit prosody
Gayatri mantra	The most sacred of all mantras in the *Rigveda*
Gita Govindam	Lyrics in praise of Lord Krishna by Jayadev 12 Century AD
Gotra	Brahmana lineage traceable to a Rigvedic poet or poets
Govinda	Another name of Lord Krishna
Griha pravesam	Formal entry into a new residence and associated rituals
Grihastha	A householder
Grihasthashrama	The householder stage of the life cycle
Grihyasutras	A Sanskrit text on family laws
Gunas	Mental tendencies
Guptas	A 4th Century dynasty of Magadh

Guru	A teacher or precept
Gurukula system	A system where students live with the teacher's family
Harappan civilization	The oldest civilization of the Indian Subcontinent around 2500 BC
Harijan	The name used by Mahatma Gandhi for untouchable castes
Havis	Meat or cooked rice offered to *Agni* in a *homa*
Hiranyagarba	The golden egg
Holocene	The current geological period dating from 10,000 years ago.
Homa	A Vedic ritual performed in front of burning fire
Hotri	A priest who specializes in reciting Vedic mantras
Hunas	A Central Asian tribe who came to India in about 9th Century AD
Illams	Joint family households of Namboodiri Brahmanas
Indra	A Rigvedic God of rain, lightening, and thunder
Indriyas	Includes limbs as well as sensory organs
Isavasyopanishad	An important *Upanishad*
Ishta	Liked
Ishta devta	Favourite God
Ishwara	Supreme God
Iyers	Smartha Brahmanas; derived from Arya+r showing respect

Iyyengars	Srivaishnava Brahmanas; derived from Aryan to Ayyan, etc.
Jagadi	A metre used in Rigvedic verses
Jagannath	The presiding deity of Puri temple
Jaimini	The author of the Poorva Mimamsa school
Jamadagni	A poet of Rigvedic times; appears in the *Puranas* as a legend
Janapadas	Originally tribal territories; later used in the sense of kingdoms
Janma	Birth
Japa	Recitation of the name of a God, mantras, or *shlokas*
Jati	A endogamous community or a larger group (of *jatis*)
Jats	An ethnic population of NW India
Jijnasu	A person desirous of knowing
Jiva	The impure soul or the outer crust of the impure soul
Jivatman	The impure soul or the atman enslaved in it
Jnana	Knowing atman and *Brahman* to be the same
Jnana yoga	The State of self realization attained by a few born mystics
Jnanendriyas	Sensory organs, such as eyes, ears, skin, etc.
Jnani	One who knows atman and *Brahman* to be the same

Kaalam	Time
Kali	A Goddess equated with Parvati
Kali yuga	The present time phase
Kalidasa	A well known Sanskrit poet of 8th Century AD
Kama	Love or lust
Kamba Ramayanam	Tamil version of Valmiki Ramayana belonging to 9th Century AD
Kamya	Liked or desired
Kanchi Acharya	The late Chandrasekhara Saraswati who was a noted scholar
Kannada	The spoken language of Karnataka
Kanvas	A dynasty of rulers succeeding the Mauryas
Kanyadan	The gifting of a virgin
Kapila	The originator of Sankhya school of philosophy
Karma	Includes all types of human actions including ritual actions
Karma Sanyasa	Giving up of occupational and ritual karmas
Karma theory	Theory about the consequences of good or bad actions
Karmedriyas	The limbs of the body used in physical action
Kartha	Doer
Kartikeya	Sanskritized name for Lord Murugan
Kasi	Name of a kingdom; also applied to its capital

Kathopanishad	A very famous *Upanishad*
Kautilya	Another name of Chanakya
Kayastha	A caste group of Northern India from Punjab to Bengal
Kedarnath	A Shiva temple consecrated by Adi Shankaracharya
Kham	The cosmos or the sky
Kricham	Undergoing body pain and discomfort
Krishna	An incarnation of Vishnu born in the Yadava clan
Krishna paksha	The period following full moon and before new moon
Krodha	Anger
Kshatriya	A warrior class
Kshetra	The phenomenal world including the human body
Kshetrajna	The atman residing in the body
Kurrukkal	Temple priests of Tamil Nadu in earlier times
Kuticharan	A person living in a hut
Lingayats	Name of Veerashaiva sect who wear a *linga* on their body
Lobha	Desire for things that belong to other people
Lord Ganesh	A son of Lord Shiva and head of the Bhutaganas
Lord Sri Ram	An incarnation of Vishnu in *Ramayana* epic

Madhuchanda	A Rigvedic poet
Magadh	One of the early kingdoms now in Bihar
Magha	A month of the Hindu calendar
Mahabharata	The second and very lengthy epic that includes *Bhagavad Gita*
Mahaprasthanam	The great departure meaning leaving this world
Maharishi	The Puranic recreations (legends) of Rigvedic poets
Mahaveera	The founder of the Jaina religion
Manasara	A Buddhist text in Pali language
Mandala System	A system of compilation of *Rigveda*
Mangala sutra	A chain or thread worn by a married woman
Mantra	A Rigvedic verse
Manu	The legendary author of *Manusmriti*
Manusmriti	A classic Sanskrit text on Hindu moral code of conduct
Marana	Death
Marga	Path
Mariamman	A Tamil Goddess equated with Parvati
Mauryan	A ruling dynasty of Pataliputra in 3rd Century BC
Max Muller	A German Indologist who compiled *Rigveda*
Mimamsa	Enquiry or a system of philosophy
Mitra	A Rigvedic God

Mlecha	Anyone who does not belong to the four varnas
Moha	Unrealistic and excessive desire
Moksha	Release of the atman from the cycle of births and deaths
Moodha	Ignorant or foolish
Mudgara	A hammer blow
Muni	A saint
Murugan	The Tamil God who is later identified as a son of Shiva
Mutt	The house of a Brahmana or a religious monastery
Nairs	A prominent Hindu community of Kerala
Nakshatram	One of the 27 stars on or near the celestial ecliptic
Namboodiri	A Brahmana community of Kerala
Nayanmars	Shaivite bards of Tamil Nadu
Neolithic culture	New Stone Age culture of 5,000 to 10,000 years ago
Nirvritti dharma	The dharma appropriate to mystics
Nishta	Firmly established in yoga
Nitya karma	The daily ritual of *sandhya vandana* performed three times a day
Nityam	Everlasting with no beginning and no end
Niyama	The five observances: not getting angry, cleanliness, etc.

Nriyajna	Worshipping the king - actually a guest
Ohm	Brahman—the Absolute God
Paisacha	Ghostly
Palakkad	An urban place in Kerala
Palaolithic culture	Old stone age culture relating to one million to 10,000 years ago
Pali	The language of the common people of Magadh in 4th Century BC
Pallavas	A dynasty of kings of Tamil Nadu
Pancha Bhutas	The five elements: earth, water, air, fire, and sky
Pancha jana	The five tribes of Rigvedic times
Pancha yajnas	Five daily observances or worships
Panchagacham	A loin cloth worn in a traditional way
Pandyas	A dynasty of kings of Tamil Nadu
Panigrahanam	Literally holding of hands; an important marriage rite
Panini	Sanskrit grammarian of 6th Century BC
Pankti	A meter used in prosody
Pantanjali Sutra	Another name for his text on *dhyana yoga*
Papa	Sin
Para and apara	Brahman and the phenomenal world
Parishad	A committee
Parvati	A Goddess; consort of Lord Shiva
Pasupatas	A Shivaite sect and followers of the philosopher Pasupatha

Patanjali	Author of *Ashtanga Raja Yoga* and other books in 150 BC
Phala	Fruit
Pitr	Ancestor
Pitr Karma/ Pitr yajna	Worship of ancestors
Plaistocene	Geological period from one million years to 10,000 years ago
Plate Tectonics	The recent theory about movements of the earth's crust
Poorva Mimamsa	The first of the six schools of Hindu philosophy
Pottu	The dot on the forehead of a woman
Prabhava	Origin of the universe, earth and men
Prajapati	The creator of the phenomenal world and men
Prajapatya	A form of marriage
Prakriti	The phenomenal world
Pralaya	The deluge—signifying the end of the world
Pranayama	A breathing exercise; formal recitation of *gayatri mantra*
Prasada	The offering from a deity to the *bhaktas*
Pratiloma	Marriage of a man of lower varna to a woman of higher varna
Pratyahara	The fourth stage in *dhyana yoga*
Pravara	Rigvedic Rishis from whom a Brahmana claims decent

Pravritti dharma	The moral code for common people
Prayaschita	Penance
Prayopavesa	Entering or approaching death
Puja or Pooja	Form of worship with offering of flowers to an idol or image
Punya	Merit for good act
Puranas	A series of 18 Sanskrit texts from 2nd Century AD
Purohit	A common priest
Purram	The outside in Tamil
Purusha	Brahman; also the cosmic man or creator
Purusha sukta	A cluster of verses in *Rigveda* on the creation of man
Purushartha	The four goals of life
Purushottama	The most perfect person
Raghuvamsam	A Sanskrit text by Kalidasa on Lord Rama's grandfather
Raja Dharma	The moral code for kings and the State
Raja Ram Mohan Roy	The founder of the Brahmo Samaj
Rajagriha	The capital city of Magadh at the time of Buddha
Rajaji	He was a highly respected statesman of Tamil Nadu
Rajas or rajoguna	One of the three *gunas* of *tatva jnana*
Rajasic	Pertaining to *rajoguna*

Rajputs	One of the Kshatriya groups of North India
Rakshasa	A class of demons, for the most part but not wholly evil
Ramayana	The earlier of the two epics, held to be sacred
Ras Leela	The story of Lord Krishna and the Gopis or damsels
Rashtrakutas	A dynasty of kings of Central India
Rigveda	The oldest religious text of the Hindus
Rishi	A Rigvedic poet mentioned in the *Rigveda*
Rishikesh	A holy city on the banks of the Ganga in the foothills
Ritwik	A priest
Rudra	A Rigvedic God equated with Shiva later
Saibabha cult	The current head of this cult lives in Puttaparthi in Andhra Pradesh
Saktas/Shaktas	Followers of the female Goddess Shakti
Samạdi	A state of bliss attained by *dhyana yoga*
Samatwam	Equality
Samaveda	The third *Veda*
Samgraha	Maintenance of order
Samkara	Unification through marriage of varnas
Samsara	Life
Sanatana Dharma	The universal moral code

Sandhya vandana	The daily ritual prescribed in the *Shastras/ Smritis*
Sangam literature	Tamil literature belonging to the Sangam period
Sangam Period	2nd Century BC to 2nd Century AD
Sankara	A name of Shiva
Sankara Vijayam	The legendary accounts of the life of Adi Shankaracharya
Sankhyas	Followers of the Sankhya school of philosophy
Sanyasa/Sanyas	Withdrawal from worldly life
Sanyasi/sanyasin	A person who has taken *sanyasa*
Sapindies	People having same agnates for several generations
Saptapadi	Seven steps taken in front of *Agni* during marriage
Sari	A long fabric worn by women in India
Shastra	Any Sanskrit text considered to be sacred
Sati	A woman who enters the funeral fire of her husband
Satva guna	The first of the three *gunas*
Satvasudhi	*Atma shudhi*—purity of soul
Saucham	Cleanliness
Savita	The Sun God
Scythians	Also known as Sakas who came to India in the 2nd Century AD
Shaivas/Shivaites	Worshippers of Shiva, the God of destruction

Shardha	The formal worship of ancestors
Shravan	A month of the Hindu calendar
Shruti	That which is heard
Siddas	Shivaite mystics
Sikhism	A religion established by Guru Nanak in the 16th Century
Sindhur	Mark on the forehead of a woman indicating marital status
Shloka	A verse in classical or later Sanskrit
Smarthas	A group of Brahmanas of the South
Smartha karmas	Ritual and non ritual karmas prescribed in *Smritis*
Smriti	That which is remembered or renowned
Soma	The Moon God
Soma ras	An intoxicating drink extracted from the Soma plant
Srivaishnavaites	A sect of Hindus who worship Vishnu and his incarnations
Srautha karmas	Vedic rituals; rituals prescribed in the Brahmanas
Stapathis	Temple architects of South India
Sthala Purana	Local legends focussing on temple Gods
Stree dhanam	The property of a woman usually given by her father
Subbalakshmi, MS	A well-known Carnatic musician
Subhadra	Sister of Lord Krishna

Subham	A greeting expressing good tidings
Sufism	A Muslim religious sect or movement
Sukla paksha	The time after New moon and before Full moon
Sukracharya	The teacher or Guru of the demons or *Asuras*
Sungas	A Brahmana dynasty of kings of the Ganga Plains
Sura	God
Surya	Sun
Sutras	Aphorisms in Sanskrit and also texts based on these
Swadhyayam	Self-learning
Tamas/ Tamoguna	One of the three *gunas*
Tamasic	Relating to *tamas*
Tamil	The spoken language of Tamil Nadu having ancient roots
Tamizhakam	The territory where Tamil was spoken in the Sangam period
Tamo-bhakta	Ignorant devotee of a God
Tantriks	A religious sect practising black magic
Tarpanam	A ritual offering to the ancestors
Thithi	A day of the lunar calendar
Thriam	Three fold
Tirukkural	A text containing 1,300 aphorisms in Tamil of 2nd Century AD
Trishtup	A meter of Sanskrit prosody

Tulsi Ramayan	16th Century rendering of *Ramayana* by Tulsi Das in Hindi
Tyaga	Giving up ownership
Tyagaraja	A saint and musician of Tamil Nadu
Tyagi	Brahmanas who gave up *varna dharma*
Uccha vritti	The mid-day procession of *bhaktas* seeking grains or food
Udgadha	A form of marriage
Unani medicine	An Indian medical system with West Asian roots
Upakarma	The ceremony initiating Vedic studies during a year
Upanayana	The initiation into *brahmacharya*
Upanishad(s)	Philosophical texts of the later Vedic period
Upavas	Abstaining from food
Uttara Mimamsa	Another name for Vedanta school
Vadama	A *jati* among Smarta Brahmanas (suggests Northern origins)
Vairagya	Giving up all possessions and their enjoyment
Vaishnavas	A religious sect who worship Vishnu and his incarnations
Vaishnodevi	A new Goddess or cult of Northern India
Vajra	The weapon of the God Indra
Valmiki	A poet who wrote the *Ramayana* in Sanskrit

Vanaprastha	The third stage in the life cycle
Varga	A cluster of verses in *Rigveda*; another term for *sukta*
Varna	A category or class of men; there are only four *varnas*
Varuna	A Rigvedic God
Vasisht	The teacher of Lord Shri Ram
Vasisht	A Rigvedic poet; or a descendant of that poet
Vatsu sastra	The science of settlements and homes
Vayu	Wind or the God of winds
Vedanta	One of the six schools of Hindu philosophy
Vedas	The first three *Vedas*; there are other definitions
Vibhuti	God's exemplary attributes and gifts
Vidhi	Fate
Vijnana	Empirical experience or sensory experience
Visarjana	Giving up or throwing away of something
Vishayas	The object of sensory perceptions or experiences
Vishnu	One among the three principal Gods; also Brahman
Vishwa-dharshan	A visual spectacle of events—past, present, and future
Viswamitra	A Rigvedic poet or his descendents

Viswedevas	A group of 10 Gods of Rigvedic origin
Vivaswata	The name of Manu of *Kali yuga*
Vrata	A vow
Vriksha	Tree
Vrishan	Bull
Vyasa	The title given to the legendary compiler of the *Vedas*
Webber, Max	A noted sociologist who wrote a classic on Hindu religion
Yaga	A Vedic sacrificial ceremony
Yajna	Worship of Vedic Gods through the medium of *Agni*
Yajnopavitham	The sacred thread worn by men of upper varnas
Yajnvalkya	A scholar who compiled *Yajurveda*
Yajurveda	The second *Veda*
Yaksha Prashna	A Sanskrit text containing definitions of major concepts
Yama	God of Death; also self-control or discipline
Yavanas	A frequently occurring word in Sanskrit texts meaning Greeks
Yoga	Literally joining together; the joining of karma and *jnana*
Yogam	A predicted outcome for a given time
Yogi	One who practises *yoga*

References

1. *Rigveda Samhita*, Nag Publishers, College Road, Kamla Nagar, Delhi (This volume contains 10,552 mantras in Devanagari script)
2. *Yajurveda Samhita*, Nag Publishers, College Road, Kamla Nagar, Delhi (This volume contains 1,800 mantras in Devanagari script)
3. *Samaveda Samhita*, Nag Publishers, College Road, Kamla Nagar, Delhi (This volume contains 1,500 mantras in Devanagari script)
4. *Adharvaveda Samhita*, Nag Publishers, College Road, Kamla Nagar, Delhi (This volume contains 4,000 mantras, organized into clusters according to the purposes for which they are to be used)
5. *Shreemadbhagavadgita*, Govidbhavan Karyalay, Gita Press, Gorakhpur (Sanskrit text in Devanagari script with Sankara's commentary in original and a translation of the same in Hindi by Harikrishnadas Goyendka)
6. *Manusmriti*, Sri Ramakrishna Math, Puranattukara, Thrissur, Kerala State (This book presents 2,700 verses of *Manusmriti* in the Malayalam script with a commentary in Malayalam by Siddinadanandaswamy)

7. Rajagopalachari, C, *Bhaja Govindam*, Bhavan's Book University, Bharatiya Vidhya Bhavan, Mumbai (original Sanskrit text in Devanagari script with commentary in English)
8. *Kathopanishad*, Sri Ramakrishna Math, Puranattukara, Thrissur, Kerala State (Sanskrit text in Malayalam script with commentary in Malayalam by Mridanandaswamy)
9. Sarma DS, *The Upanishads: An Anthology*, Bhavan's Book University, Bharatiya Vidya Bhavan, Mumbai (Contains selected mantra's in Devanagari script from the major *Upanishads* with explanations in English by the author)
10. Balasubramania Iyer K, *Yaksha Prashna*, Bharatiya Vidya Bhavan, Mumbai (The entire Sanskrit text in Devanagari script with English translation and commentary)
11. *Sandhyavandanam*, Sanskrit text in Devanagari script with meaning and instructions in Tamil by R Subbaratnam Iyer and published by the author from Rockfort, Teppakulam, Tiruchirapally, Tamil Nadu.
12. Bhandarkar RG, *First Book of Sanskrit*, Keshav Bhikaji Dhawale, Shree Samarth Sadan, First Bhat Wadi, Girgaon, Mumbai (A classic book on Sanskrit grammar for beginners by a great Sanskrit scholar)
13. Bhandarkar RG, *Second Book of Sanskrit*, Keshav Bhikaji Dhawale, Shree Samarth Sadan, First Bhat Wadi, Girgaon, Mumbai (A classic book on Sanskrit grammar for advanced students)
14. Sastry KLV, and Anantharama Sastry L, *Sabda Manjari*, RS Vadhyar and Sons, Kalpathi, Palghat, Kerala State (A very useful text on declinable words—nouns and adjectives—in Sanskrit in Malayalam script)
15. Sastry KLV, and Anantharama Sastry L, *Dhaturupa Manjari*, RS Vadhyar and Sons, Kalpathi, Palghat, Kerala State (A text on Sanskrit verbs in Malayalam script)

16. Apte, VS, *The Practical Sanskrit English Dictionary*, Motilal Banarasidass Publishers, Delhi
17. Weber, Max, *The Religion of India*, Oxford University Press, New Delhi
18. Subramanian N, *Sangam Polity*, Asia Publishing House, Mumbai, 1966
19. Srinivas, MN, *Social Change in Modern India*, Allied Publishers, Mumbai, 1966
20. Thapar, Romila, *From Lineage to State: The Middle Ganga Plains in the First Half of the First Millanium BC*, Oxford University Press, New Delhi

Index

G

H

I

J

K

L

M

S

T

U